STORIES OF MINJUNG THEOLOGY

INTERNATIONAL VOICES IN BIBLICAL STUDIES

Jione Havea, General Editor

Editorial Board:
Jin Young Choi
Musa W. Dube
David Joy
Aliou C. Niang
Nasili Vaka'uta
Gerald O. West

Number 11

STORIES OF MINJUNG THEOLOGY

The Theological Journey of Ahn Byung-Mu in His Own Words

Translated by Hanna In. Edited by Wongi Park

Atlanta

Copyright © 2019 by Society of Biblical Literature

All rights reserved. No part of this work may be reproduced or transmitted in any form or by any means, electronic or mechanical, including photocopying and recording, or by means of any information storage or retrieval system, except as may be expressly permitted by the 1976 Copyright Act or in writing from the publisher. Requests for permission should be addressed in writing to the Rights and Permissions Office, SBL Press, 825 Houston Mill Road, Atlanta, GA 30329 USA.

Library of Congress Cataloging-in-Publication Data

Names: An, Pyŏng-mu, author. | Hanna, In, translator. | Wongi, Park, translator.
Title: Stories of Minjung theology : the theological journey of Ahn Byung-Mu in his own words / Byung-Mu Ahn; translated by In Hanna, Park Wongi.
Description: Atlanta : SBL Press, 2019. | Series: International voices in biblical studies; 11 | Includes bibliographical references and index.
Identifiers: LCCN 2019025818 (print) | LCCN 2019025819 (ebook) | ISBN 9781628372571 (paperback) | ISBN 9780884144090 (hardback) | ISBN 9780884144106 (ebook)
Subjects: LCSH: An, Pyŏng-mu. | Minjung theology—History. | Korea—History—1945–.
Classification: LCC BX4827.A34 A3 1990 (print) | LCC BX4827.A34 (ebook) | DDC 230.092 [B]—dc23
LC record available at https://lccn.loc.gov/2019025818
LC ebook record available at https://lccn.loc.gov/2019025819

Printed on acid-free paper.

Contents

Note from the Translator vii

A Profile of Ahn Byung-Mu
   Rev. Jin-ho Kim ix

Introduction
   R. S. Sugirtharajah xi

Preface: An Apology xix

Part 1

1. Until I Discovered Minjung 3

Part 2

2. The Bible as the Book of Minjung 35

3. The Minjung Jesus 65

4. The God of Minjung 101

5. The Church as Community of the Minjung 123

6. Sin and the System 145

7. Minjung Liberation and the Event of the Holy Spirit 163

8. The Kingdom of God Is the Kingdom of Minjung 177

Part 3

9. The Transmission of the Jesus Event by the Minjung 199

10. The Minjung Biography of Jesus 223

11. The Realization of the Table Community 245

12. The Event of Minjung's Resurrection 257

Ancient Sources Index 271

Subject Index 275

Note from the Translator

The main text of this volume is a translation of the second edition of *Minjung Shinhak Iyagi*, by Ahn Byung-Mu (Seoul: Korea Theological Study Institute, 1988). The profile written by Rev. Jin-ho Kim, the introduction written by R. S. Sugirtharajah, and the footnotes supplied by the translators are not part of the original Korean text.

With the names of the translator and editor, "Hanna" and "Wongi" are first (given) names, and "In" and "Park" are last (family) names. This differs from the way names in the translation are represented. For example, with "Ahn Byung-Mu," "Ahn" is the last (family) name, and "Byung-Mu" is the first (given) name.

A Profile of Ahn Byung-Mu

Rev. Jin-ho Kim

Ahn Byung-Mu (1922–1996) was a person of faith and an intellectual who fought against injustice.

He started three churches, established four journals, and successfully ran one of the most prominent institutes of theological study in Korea. These churches, journals, and institutes made a significant contribution in the advancement of Korean democracy and human rights.

Since 1975, Ahn led the minjung theology movement together with Suh Nam-dong and others. Minjung theology was at the forefront of the progressive movement of liberal intellectuals. In 1980, after being expelled from his university post for the second time, he organized a minjung studies workshop with other professors who were also dismissed from their position. This workshop invigorated minjung studies in economics, history, sociology, literature, and education.

Ahn started teaching at Hanshin University in 1970 and retired in 1987. Due to his resistance, however, he was expelled from his university position two times for a total of nine years, which included a period of imprisonment. While in prison between 1976 and 1977, he developed a heart condition. In 1985 his health deteriorated and became life-threatening. This made him unable to write. Out of approximately one thousand of his writings, several hundred were dictated orally to his students. The texts produced by his pupils were reviewed by Ahn before publication.

Stories of Minjung Theology is a book based on Ahn's conversations with his students when his health was very poor. However, in this book, more than any other writing before or after, his original and provocative minjung theological insights shine. In this respect, despite its humble origins, this book represents one of Ahn's most important writings on minjung theology.

Introduction

R. S. Sugirtharajah

Stories of Minjung Theology is an unusual volume. It is a rare autobiography that combines the personal story of Ahn Byung-Mu (one of the leading biblical scholars of his time), his hermeneutical awakening, the Korean nation's history as it went through political upheavals in the 1980s, and the birth of the minjung movement that Ahn helped to shape as it struggled to define its theological purpose and political vision. Such autobiographical reminiscences suffused with profound theological and exegetical reflections are rare in Asian Christian discourse. Readers might find anger, pain, and disappointment in Ahn's recollections, but his message was ultimately rooted in love for the minjung.

Stories of Minjung Theology narrates how a Western-trained academic scholar was forced to rethink his hermeneutical presuppositions in the light of the dramatic social, political, and cultural upheavals that Korea went through in the 1970s. What is clear from reading this volume is that Ahn loved his Bible, Bultmann, Jesus, and minjung—but not necessarily in that order.

I see this book not only as a valuable record of minjung theology, one of the vigorous theologies to emerge in Asia, but also as an excellent testimony and introduction for twenty-first-century readers about the life and theological legacy of Ahn and the resistance movement he helped to shape and develop.

This fascinating story is not told through the conventional method of straight-forward narrative but through several conversations that Ahn had with his students. As he says in the introduction, it was a "product of the collaboration" between him and his young colleagues. The process took nearly two years to complete, and the book came out in 1987. The volume was published at a time when minjung theology was at its peak, and there was a serious lack of a substantial book on its basic theological orientation.

It provided for the first time, in an orderly way, the key elements of minjung theology and a reinterpretation of stock Christian doctrines such as God, creation, the fall, redemption, and salvation from a minjung perspective. One could call it a minjung dogmatics based on a traditional Christian framework.

A number of Korean theologians have considered *Stories of Minjung Theology* to be one of the best works in minjung theological thinking. The Korean version of the book sold more than ten thousand copies. Granted, these figures are not in *The Da Vinci Code* league, but considering the Christian population of that country, it is an enormous achievement. This was one of the rare Christian books that had a wider appeal outside the church, especially among Korean intellectuals. Now, for the first time, the book is available to the English-speaking world, thanks largely to the efforts of the Ahn Byung-Mu Foundation who financed the translation project.

This book devotedly conveys the spirit and the core of minjung theology as a witness to the minjung way of doing theology. It manifestly shows the critical perspectives of Ahn and his students who were living through the exciting and at the same time frustrating years of the minjung movement. It provides answers to questions that Ahn himself, his junior colleagues, and Korean Christians were struggling with and looking for. It adopts an animated form of storytelling, the very method adopted by the minjung to convey the truth and reality of both their wretchedness and their hopes.

This Korean version came out at the height of contextual theologies. This was the golden age of liberation theologies and emancipatory movements. The Americas had the Latin American liberation theologies in the South and the Black theology of liberation in the North. The Caribbean created the theology of emancipation. The Filipinos worked out their theology of struggle, and the Taiwanese, yearning for a homeland, came up with their homeland theology. South Africa produced the Kairos Document, which offered a stringent theological critique of the Apartheid regime. This was the time when identity hermeneutics burst upon the scene. Feminists, Indian Dalits, the Japanese burakumins, and indigenous peoples were engaged in articulating their identities, which were denied and debased. This was also the time when doing theology was seen as a dangerous business, and theologians were jailed, tortured, and even killed. Liberation theologians like Camilo Torres of Columbia and Michael Rodrigo of Sri Lanka were murdered by government forces.

Then there was the brutal killing of six Jesuit scholars and nuns in El Salvador. Their crime was helping the Salvadorian peasants. Ahn himself was imprisoned and psychologically tortured.

These resistance theologies questioned the hegemonic and universalistic tendencies of Western discourse and power politics of the time. Some of them were thinly disguised Marxist influenced discourses. In almost all these writings, Karl Marx's famous words were quoted as a kind of rousing hermeneutical exhortation: "The philosophers have only interpreted the world in various ways; the point, however, is to change it." But minjung theology was different in that it was not only political but also an intensely cultural discourse. Minjung are not the proletariat in the Marxian sense but much more than this socioeconomic description allows. They are cultural bearers. Korean minjung theologians, especially Ahn, who were consistently adamant in refusing to define who the minjung were, have come up with hazy descriptions, such as minjung as "politically oppressed," "economically exploited," "socially alienated," "culturally and intellectually uneducated," but crucially as agents who change society and history. They are, essentially, subjects of history—a phrase that minjung theology made famous. Minjung theology had another noble cause—the unification of Korea. The minjung was the rallying power for those who were manipulated by the small elite in the name of proletariat dictatorship and for those who were deprived by the capitalist system in both North and South Korea. As Ahn told his interviewees, his concern was how to "overcome the reality of the minjung groaning in a divided country? This question has brought minjung theology into being." For Ahn, the minjung was the rallying power to unite the Korean peninsula.

This volume has three parts. In the first, Ahn narrates how his passion for the historical Jesus led him to Germany to study under Rudolf Bultmann, how on his return he quickly realized that Western learning was totally inappropriate for Korea, which was suffocating under military rule, and how he discovered the minjung. The pivotal event that changed Ahn was the self-immolation of Jeon Tae-Il, who died for the cause of workers' rights. The second part consists of the conversations between Ahn and his students, in which they discuss wide ranging issues from the birth of the minjung movement to how Ahn's readings of the Bible were shaped by the minjung experience. The third part contains lectures Ahn gave in Japan, which further explicate Ahn's understanding of the minjung and the refinement of his theological thinking.

There are three things that are fascinating about this volume. First, the level of theological literacy of the Korean readership. The fact that the names of dead Western philosophers like Immanuel Kant, Georg Wilhelm Friedrich Hegel, and Friedrich Schleiermacher and theologians like Bultmann and Ernst Käsemann, who reigned supreme at the time when Ahn was pursuing his studies, were introduced without patronizing readers shows a high standard of theological proficiency among Korean Christians. I cannot think of any comparable Asian vernacular theological writings that have references to Karl Barth and Bultmann in one paragraph, at least not in Tamil, my mother tongue. Reading about these theologians gives a retro feel for a generation like mine who were raised on their writings and are now considered and condemned as "male," "pale," and "stale."

Second, we come to know the human side of these very Western masters whom we normally encounter largely through their often dense writings. We see Bultmann, the initiator of demythologization, who spurned anything supernatural, joining in prayers, and how he took it unflappably when he was rebuffed by a pastor who took issue with the German's view on resurrection. We see how Käsemann and Günther Bornkamm urged their colleague Herbert Braun to answer seminar questions that he tried to avoid.

Third, the sensitive side of Ahn, who in his courteous and gracious way, points out where he both aligns with and distances himself from his fellow minjung theologians and from Western theologians, especially his mentor, Bultmann, and those who espoused kerygmatic theology.

The nature of this volume does not permit a lengthy evaluation of Ahn's theological contribution. Moreover, it should be undertaken by a person who is more competent than me, who has access to all his Korean writings. It suffices to say that Ahn will be remembered for two hermeneutical achievements: his exegetical work on the *ochlos* and his search for the historical Jesus. For Ahn, the gospels were about people. While biblical scholars at that time were strenuously arguing about the apocalyptic components of the gospels or about the imminent arrival of or postponement of the kingdom, or were engaged in prophetical predictions fulfilled in Jesus, Ahn reminded them that the gospels were about the people—the minjung. For him, reading the New Testament is to read the lives of the ordinary people. Ultimately, you have to care about the people you encounter daily. He took ordinary, everyday people as the center of the gospels and to the life of Jesus.

The second contribution is his relentless search for the historical Jesus.[1] He undertook this pursuit at a time when the quest for the historical Jesus came to a dead end, especially in Germany where he went to do his research. As he said, the search for the historical Jesus for him was a lifelong ambition and task. His search was distinguished in three ways. First, he retrieved Jesus from the kerygmatic language in which he was couched. Ahn's constant mantra had been that "in the beginning there was the event, not the kerygma."[2] This event was, of course, the actual suffering and resurrection of Jesus. Ahn even blamed the neoliberal theologians for putting blocks to such a search and for making historical events related to Jesus into an abstract idea. Second, Ahn's distinction lay in his rescuing of Jesus from the single savior narrative and making him a collective *persona* whose identity was inseparable from and entwined with that of the minjung. While Bultmann argued for an "existential solidarity with Jesus," Ahn insisted on experiencing Jesus "socially" and "collectively."[3] Ahn asserted firmly that such a collective concept or what he called the "sociability" of Jesus, was found in christological titles such as the "Son of Man" and "Son of God." The search for the historical Jesus is part of the social biography of the minjung. His repeated refrain had been: "Where there is Jesus, there is the minjung. And where there is the minjung, there is Jesus."[4] In other words, Jesus needed the minjung as much as minjung needed him. Third, for Ahn one encountered Jesus only in and through minjung events and not through preaching as the existentialist and individualistic theology of the Word of the time insisted. What was encountered was not the Word demanding existential decision, as the German theologians advocated, but the historical and material life experience of the minjung. He disputed Bultmann's claim that one experienced Jesus through the proclamation in the pulpit.

---

1. For a detailed analysis of how Ahn's quest for the historical Jesus differed from those of the Western endeavors, see R. S. Sugirtharajah, *Jesus in Asia* (Cambridge: Harvard University Press, 2018), 198–223.

2. Ahn Byung-Mu, "Minjung Theology from the Perspective of the Gospel of Mark," in *Reading Minjung Theology in the Twenty-First Century: Selected Writings by Ahn Byung-Mu and Modern Critical Responses*, ed. Yung Suk Kim and Jin-ho Kim (Eugene, OR: Pickwick, 2013), 85.

3. Ahn Byung-Mu, "Jesus and People (Minjung)" [Korean], *CTC Bulletin* 7.3 (1987): 10.

4. Yong-Yeon Hwang, "'The Person Attacked by the Robbers Is Christ': An Exploration of Subjectivity from the Perspective of Minjung Theology," in Kim and Kim, *Reading Minjung Theology in the Twenty-First Century*, 224.

The context out of which Ahn's exegesis emerged does not exist any longer. Current Korean theologians do not have the experiential advantage of living through harsh political and economic realities. The agitated, confrontational, and campaigning environment that enabled Ahn to work out his hermeneutics is sadly no more. The present Korean exegetes suddenly find themselves in the wealthier, prosperous, and neoliberal phase of Korea. They fail to grasp or relate to what it feels like on the underside of history. After the democratization of Korea, the new crop of theologians talk not about minjung but about "national people" or "citizens" who compliantly incorporate national aspiration for the realization of their own ambitions. This postminjung, postapartheid, and postliberation-struggle exegesis looks tame and stale by comparison. Suffering and wretchedness do not inherently yield better exegesis, but the political force and vigor that marked these earlier expositions are woefully missing in the current expositions.

Some of the exegetical insights that sounded stimulating and gripping and made Ahn an inspiring and an important biblical scholar may not have the same invigorating purchase now. His views on Galilee and the *ochlos* will come under heavy scrutiny. His blatantly one-dimensional reading of Galilee as the land of poverty and protest may not have the same fascinating appeal. Current scholarship views the region with far more skepticism and in complex terms. Similarly, the *ochlos* would be seen as a wide-ranging collection of people composed of both oppressed and oppressors liable to be lured by the enticements of the empire and not as a single group consisting of victims and the poor, as Ahn would have liked to portray. Recently, showing solidarity with Ahn's work, a new generation of Korean interpreters have offered internal criticism with a view to strengthening his ideas. Jin-Ho Kim has remarked that the sufferings and powerlessness of the minjung have to be better nuanced than Ahn conceived and envisaged.[5] Approaching from a feminist perspective, Keun-Joo Christine Pae has shown how gender analysis would further elevate and enhance Ahn's understanding of the *ochlos*.[6] Postcolonial critics would find that the kingdom of God that Ahn comes

---

5. Jin-ho Kim, "The Hermeneutics of Ahn Byung-Mu: Focusing on the Concepts of 'Discovery of Internality' and 'Otherness of Minjung,'" in Kim and Kim, *Reading Minjung Theology in the Twenty-First Century*, 13–26.

6. Keun-joo Christine Pae, "Minjung Theology and Global Peace Making: From Galilee to the U.S. Military Camp town (Kijich'on) in South Korea," in Kim and Kim, *Reading Minjung Theology in the Twenty-First Century*, 164–83.

up with ignores numerous biblical passages that reinscribe the colonial impulses of the kingdom. They point to clear signs of power and dominance associated with and exercised by the kingdom (Matt 19:28; Luke 22:29–30). What Ahn fails to notice is that buried behind the anticolonial oratory of Jesus there lurks an imperial thinking which speaks the language of control, supremacy, and judgment. Ahn's insistence that any recurrence of a liberating movement is a minjung event and in these emancipatory occurrences one finds the presence of Jesus is condescending and insulting to people who are not within the paradigm of the Christian faith.

Postcolonial criticism was at its infancy when Ahn was engaged in his theological activities. David Sánchez, in his study of Ahn, has shown that Ahn's deliberate liberation hermeneutic was couched in postcolonial impulses and tendencies.[7] In the first part of the book, Ahn describes vividly the horrors of Japanese colonialism and its impact on the nation and on his own family. Had he had the postcolonial tools at that time, he would have used it profitably. Ahn himself gives examples of how the Bible was used to read against the Japanese occupation. Another clue is found in the way he articulated who the minjung were. Ahn, who was reluctant to define who a minjung was, came up with the following description, which bears potential hallmarks of postcolonial tendencies: "Indeed, the phrase 'minjung-like people' refers to the minjung and people who were grief-stricken under the colonial rule, are exploited by the foreign powers, and are oppressed and deprived by the ruling class of their own country; and in this regard, the word *minjung* comprehends all three ideas."[8]

At least one of Ahn's hermeneutical aspirations has come true. He was tireless in his attempt to reunite both Koreas. As he remarked in this volume, "Minjung theology was born for the unification of the people, and the ultimate purpose of this theology must be nothing but the unification of the people." Although the meeting of the two heads of Korea would have delighted him, he would have preferred that this unification be led by the minjung.

Ahn would be the first one to admit the changing nature of the situation, and, as he says in the volume, the minjung could not "ever be stagnant within a certain form." He would be as keen as ever to find out

---

7. David Arthur Sánchez, "Ambivalence, Mimicry, and the *Ochlos* in the Gospel of Mark: Assessing the Minjung Theology of Ahn Byung-Mu," in Kim and Kim, *Reading Minjung Theology in the Twenty-First Century*, 134–47.
8. See further p. 28, below.

the latest progressive developments in biblical scholarship and if it could be harnessed to repurpose the cause of the minjung. He would be more than happy to rectify some of his exegetical conclusions. More importantly, he would be searching for the new minjung who were made outcast and powerless by the new liberal economy and newer forms of colonialism. Ahn was not helping to find the voices of the minjung. He was aware that it would be arrogant on his part to say that he was in the business of raising the consciousness of the minjung. His conviction was that the minjung already had a voice, which was purposely unheard or intentionally silenced. They need to feel empowered to use it, and others around them need to be encouraged to listen. Reading his story confirms my view that Ahn has a lot to say. I hope this volume will introduce him to a new generation of readers and allow them to hear his voice again, and more pertinently, as Ahn would have wished, to look out and hear again the voices of the minjung in their midst.

Ideally, this introduction should have been written by a Korean scholar. I undertook to do this after persistent requests from Ahn Byung-Mu Memorial Foundation.

Preface: An Apology

By now, minjung theology has gained an international stature. Many European universities, especially in Germany, are offering seminars in minjung theology. Korean students studying there frequently ask minjung theologians back home for assistance. Also, some professors and students from the United States are studying minjung theology in Korea, and some of them frequently visit Korea Theological Study Institute. Already several PhD dissertations have been written on minjung theology, and a fair number of theses are in progress at the moment. The authors of these dissertations include both Koreans and foreigners. The demand of minjung theology is increasing. But regretfully, Korean minjung theologians do not seem to be meeting the need properly.

In this context, some of my younger colleagues, who have been working hard for the progress of minjung theology, came up with a plan to interview me with a number of questions raised in the process. They set out on, in their language, "the squeezing-out information operation." They forced me to answer questions they jointly prepared based on a critical and clearly defined agenda.

The questions were scrupulously prepared, but the answers were given off the cuff. The dialogues were recorded and transcribed, and I reluctantly revised the text. Additionally, there are the four lectures I gave on minjung theology in Japan in a storytelling format last year. The Japanese organizers recorded the lectures and sent me a booklet of their transcriptions. After translating it into Korean and revising the translation, I have included the lectures in this book. This accounts for the format of the book.

Minjung theology is the work of theologically examining the minjung event. For this reason, it marches together with the minjung event but cannot ever be stagnant within a certain form. Therefore, imposing a system or frame turns it into a stuffed animal or an antique, namely, another golden tiara on the head of Jesus. So I had no intention at all to publish anything like a textbook in the first place. Could this be an apology from a person who puts out a *story theology* like this?

The main participants in this project were Park Seong-jun, Yi Jeong-hee, and Kang Won-don; and other participants include Park Jae-sun, Kang Mak-sil, Park Gyeong-mi, Yi Jae-won, Yi Gang-sil, Kim Seung-hwan, and Choi Hyeong-muk. We originally intended to identify the person asking each question but decided against it for editorial reasons.

Therefore, the texts in this book are not my sole authorship but a product of the collaboration between me and my younger colleagues and former students. I offer my sincere appreciation to them.

May 5, 1987
Ahn Byung-Mu

Part 1

1
Until I Discovered Minjung

1.1. Childhood in Jiandao: Discovering the Nation[1] and Christ

Q: I am aware that you pioneered an original approach to biblical interpretation, and especially that you proposed minjung theology in the 1970s, attracting a great amount of attention from Third World and Western theologians. If, as is often said, a person's thought is connected with his or her[2] life, I am curious how your life bears on your unique theological thought. I am aware that you spent your childhood in Jiandao. Would you please begin by sharing a few stories from those early years?

A: I was born in Shinanjoo, Pyeongannam Province. But even before my first year was up, my family moved to Jiandao, which became my real home. My family had no associations with Christianity, but I was deeply immersed in an atmosphere heavily influenced by Confucianism. My father was a scholar in Chinese classics and a doctor in Eastern medicine. Since age four, I was forced to study Chinese classics. While studying the Four Books and the Three Classics,[3] I thought Confucius and Mencius were both Korean.

The footnotes (written by the translator) are not part of the original Korean text.

1. The English word *nation* can refer to both a country and a particular type of people. The latter is meant by *minjok*, the Korean word Ahn uses here. The same applies to other uses of nation in this book.

2. Personal pronouns do not have gender in the Korean language. Therefore, the issue of inclusive language does not arise in Korean. For the purposes of this English translation, inclusive language is used throughout where possible.

3. The Four Books consist of *Great Learning, Analects, Mencius,* and *Doctrine of the Mean*. The Three Classics are comprised of *Classic of Poetry, Book of Documents,* and *I Ching* (Book of Changes).

Looking back now, Jiandao was my true home. As my physical body grew in stature, the fundamentals of my sensibilities and thoughts were formed there. In the days before I entered elementary school, the Japanese army ruled us by day and the Korean Independence Army by night. Perhaps since I was five, I grew up hearing the legends of General Kim Il-seong—stories of using magic art to shorten distances, fleeing from one tree branch to another when under attack from the Japanese army, and so on. When I was five or six, he was already a mythical figure, and the name "Kim Il-seong" was deeply engraved in my young mind. I doubt that Kim Il-seong of North Korea today is the real Kim Il-seong because he is only about ten years senior to me.[4] Also, I grew up hearing songs about General Nokdu[5] all the time.

My father became a doctor in Eastern medicine and moved up to Jiandao with his family.[6] But it wasn't because he had a particularly strong national consciousness, but rather he found it difficult to eke out a living in Korea. About five miles away from the famous Myeongdong of Jiandao, there was a town called Dalaze. About a mile and a quarter further in from there, there was a village called Deulmidong. It was here that my family settled down. There was an elementary school in this village, and my father took a position similar to chair of the board of the school.

---

4. The name Kim Il-seong is associated with two different persons: General Kim Il-seong, a legendary fighter for Korean independence whose true identity has yet to be established; the other is the first leader of North Korea (1912–1994). The real name of the North Korean Kim Il-seong was Kim Seong-ju. He appropriated the name of the highly respected independence fighter in order to steal his fame. General Kim Il-seong is considered to have been much older than the first North Korean leader. This is consistent with what Ahn says about Kim Il-seong here.

5. General Nokdu is the nickname of Jeon Bong-jun (1855–1895), the Supreme General of the peasant army that fought in the Donghak Peasant Revolution of 1894. The Korean word *nokdu* means "mung bean," and it is said that it was associated with Jeon due to his small body size. The Donghak Peasant Revolution was a peasant movement of enormous scale that took place in Jeolla Province (the southwestern region of Korea) against the extreme exploitation of peasants by government officials. Designated as a revolution to honor its great significance in Korean history, the movement was subdued by the allied military forces of Joseon and Japan and so failed to attain to its aim. General Jeon Bong-jun was arrested and executed along with other leaders.

6. Jiandao refers to the southeastern part of Jilin-sheng in Manchuria. Beginning in the late nineteenth century, many Koreans crossed the northern border to Jiandao in order to find a better economic situation or fight against Japanese imperialism.

In those days, the Korean communists and Independence Army were fighting concertedly against the Japanese army, and I often saw the corpses of Japanese soldiers killed in a battle with Korean guerillas coming into the village. At that time, there were a whole lot of leftists. They wore a red armband, and I found it truly admirable for the ignorant, uneducated sons of farmers to be working hard for the country and the nation. I learned songs from them and still remember one that goes, "Our nation under the claws of the eagle-like Japanese army." I sang along without understanding what it meant. From time to time, while sleeping at night, I heard people murmuring in the room across from mine. I once opened my eyes and saw my mother treating strangers very courteously and giving them something she had obtained for them. Later I asked her what it was, and she said it was long underwear. My uneducated mother was doing remarkable things. I also remember a night when two young men were visiting wearing shabby uniforms and carrying rifles. They placed me on their laps and said, "Oh, what a good-looking boy you are! Grow up to join the Independent Army." My mother treated them to a meal, and they ate with such relish. They looked so admirable. I spent my childhood in such a climate. I grew up always hearing such words as *imperialism, capitalism, bourgeois, proletariat, individualism*, and words with the suffix *-jeok* in them.[7] I didn't know what they meant but had a vague inkling of the atmosphere they created.

As Japanese police surveillance and persecution worsened, Independence soldiers disappeared from the village. Printed *pira* (leaflets)[8] started appearing at every home of the village. Mimeographed copies were rolled up tightly into a cone and poked in the *changhoji*[9] door. At dawn, adults saw and carefully opened them to read. When I tried to have a look, they wouldn't let me, saying it's not for me. But sometimes, out of curiosity, I secretly pulled them out and read them. I still remember vividly the sight of the black ink smudges on the edges most likely due to the poor quality of the mimeograph.

---

7. *Jeok* is a Sino-Korean suffix meaning "of," "-like," and "in terms of." Words including this suffix do not occur often in an everyday colloquial speech and therefore sound rather formal and intellectual.

8. *Pira* is a Japanese word originating apparently from the English word "bill."

9. *Changhoji* is traditional Korean paper made from mulberry bark for doors and windows.

Q: They were socialists, weren't they?

A: Yes, they were. It was the socialists who did it. They were a step ahead in the ideological warfare. And in those days, as for the leaders of the nation, I only heard of Kim Il-seong. At the time, socialism was the strongest ideology, I believe.

One of the things I remember with particular clarity is organizing a strike against the principal of my school when I was in the fourth grade. The Korean principal was given to drinking and neglected teaching; during vacation we devised a plan to oust him. Three representatives were elected, and I was one of them and the youngest. I was most likely chosen because my father was chair of the board. As soon as the new semester started, the principal obtained the intelligence before we acted and called me in first and beat me. I was scared but resisted him yelling, "What's bad is bad!" Finally, the parents of the students were called together, the principal became the defendant, and we denounced him for his twenty-one misdeeds. The three of us never buckled, standing our ground to the end. A week later, when the notice came for the conference between the police chief and the three of us, I could not help but think I was finished. In the end, I got kicked out of the school as a fourth grader.

Around that time, I had a negative experience. As I wrote somewhere before, the communists came to the village and held the people's court. A bushy-bearded old man was beaten to death for the charge of criticizing the communists. I liked him, and the way they killed him was so cruel, so I began to feel bad about the communists.

Q: I heard you became a Christian as a young boy. When did you start going to church?

A: About three months after being expelled from school, I happened to be staying at a relative's home in a small town with the population of about three thousand. And it was there that I became a Christian. Previously, I saw a cross and felt shock after hearing the story behind it. A little further up from Myeongdong, there was a Catholic village. There I saw a cross on a hill and asked a boy from the neighborhood what that was. He answered, "Someone died for us." The story that someone died for us struck me in a strange way. And in the small town of my relative's, I saw a cross again. "Oh, in this place, too, a person died for others!" So I visited the place voluntarily. That's when I started going to church.

Church was truly a formidable place, for it was there that my national consciousness killed by the Japanese education at the elementary school was revived. The dawn prayer meetings always included prayers for Korean independence, and interpretations of the Bible were guided by a yearning for the independence of our country and the awakening of a national consciousness. For example, the passage in Acts 1:6, "Lord, is this the time when you will restore the kingdom to Israel?,"[10] was interpreted as "Lord, will you at this time restore again the kingdom to Joseon?" Diligent church attendance revived my national consciousness and brought home the reality that our nation was robbed by the Japanese.

My father adamantly disapproved of me going to church. But my father had a mistress at home and drank heavily. My disapproval of these behaviors motivated me to attend church more diligently. As a child, I was confronted with the problems of drinking and having a mistress, and the first reason for my going to church was perhaps that churchgoers stayed away from this kind of behavior. Nevertheless, some of the things my father said were reasonable. I still remember these words: "You believe in Jesus? Learning Jesus and becoming like him makes sense, but believing in him? We have many great figures in the East, but why should it be Jesus? What is believing in someone?" Also, "You reject our own things handed down for generations from our own ancestors and believe in a Western religion!" As I reflect on these remarks later on, I have to give him credit for rational thinking. At that time, however, I turned a deaf ear to him. Since I began to go to church, the question of how it was acceptable for two women to live in the same house became even stronger. And when a conflict arose at home toward the end of my sixth year in school, I said, "Mother, we must no longer live in such a squalid way. I will not go on to middle school. I will make money and take care of you. Let's move out of this house right away." This was how my mother, my younger sibling, and I left my father and began to live in a separate home. But for the church's influences, this would not have happened.

After graduating from elementary school, I didn't go to middle school. Instead, I worked as a clerk, helping my mother and getting more involved in church. My mother was not formally educated, but she was an extraordinary person. She saved every penny I gave her out of my earnings and

---

10. Biblical citations come from the New Revised Standard Version unless indicated otherwise.

used it to send me to middle school. In those days, there were six schools in Longjing of Jiandao, and only three of them were private schools: one associated with the Independence Army, one leftist school, and one mission school. With no hesitation at all, I chose Eunjin Middle School, the mission school. Daeseong Middle School and Donghun Middle School turned out many figures who were very active in North Korea up to the Korean War. Eunjin Middle School produced many Christian leaders. Some graduates from Gwangmyeong Middle School were pro-Japan. They joined the Manchurian Army, went on to the Japanese military academy, and went into politics. Included in this group are Jung Il-gwon and Kang Mun-bong.

Q: Which school did the poet Yun Dong-ju go to?[11]

A: He went to Eunjin. When I chose Eunjin, my teacher and many other people around me advised me against it, saying the school offered no good future prospects, but I stuck to my decision. Kang Won-ryong and Mun Dong-hwan were my schoolmates. Rev. Kim Jae-jun taught at the school at that time.[12]

Officially, Japanese was the only language of instruction, but there was a teacher who secretly taught the history of Korea. The school had a Religion Department. Its members went out to five preselected neighborhoods on Sundays to evangelize, educate, and promote literacy. Sometimes they

---

11. Yun Dong-ju (1917–1945) is a beloved Korean poet. He was born and grew up in Jiandao, and this is why the interviewer asks Ahn the given question. Yun was studying English literature at Doshisha University in Kyoto, Japan, when he was arrested in 1943 on the charge of being involved in activities for the independence of Korea and promoting Korean culture. He died in prison in February 1945, six months before the liberation of Korea. It is suspected that he died from an illegitimate medical experiment. For a fictionalized version of his life, see Lee Jung-myung, *The Investigation* (London: Pan Books, 2014). The novel was originally published in Korean in 2012 and has numerous references to the Bible, which Ahn would have approved and appreciated.

12. Kang Won-ryong (1917–2006) was a Presbyterian minister who played an important role in democratic movements, peace movements, and interfaith dialogue in Korea. Mun Dong-hwan (b. 1921) is a Presbyterian minister, theologian, and political activist. He suffered imprisonment for fighting against the dictatorship of Park Jeong-hui. Kim Jae-jun (1901–1987) was a Presbyterian minister, biblical scholar, and political activist who engaged in democratic movements during the military dictatorship in Korea.

took up residence in villages to teach evening classes, among other things. In Jiandao during those days, such activities were all the rage. In my second year in the school, I taught a women's evening class at my church. In my third year, I worked for a church about two and a half miles away. Working as the junior pastor and teacher for the evening school, I was able to influence the neighborhood. Come to think of it now, I was part of a church-based national movement. One day during my second year, I handed out a piece of paper to each of my classmates. The note asked them to come to school an hour earlier so I could teach them a song for the independence movement and how to draw the Korean national flag. Almost everyone in the class came. I wrote the Korean national anthem on the blackboard: "Until the East Sea dries up and the Baekdu Mountain wears down." I taught them how to sing the song and how to draw the national flag. Even though the teacher and the students were young, it was a very touching moment when we were of one spirit in the fervor of teaching and learning. I don't clearly remember where I had learned the song myself, but it must have been an influence from church.

Q: You might not have been aware of it at the time, but perhaps we can say that your experiences in Jiandao as a young person played a decisive role in shaping your Christian faith and thought with a strong national character.

A: Both the church and my father were my influences. Jiandao was decisively important for the formation of my national emotions and thoughts. Every Christmas we performed a play about Moses at church. Crying out in an anguished voice, "Oh, the son of the people of Israel!," we exalted Moses as the leader of his people. We also dramatized the story of Esther, who fought to win her country back. Every Christmas we staged a play with the theme of national liberation drawn from the Old Testament. The hope for our nation was dramatized through a play about Moses, the leader of his people in their struggles for liberation. Here, I want to emphasize that nationalism and Christianity can never be considered separate from each other. Since its inception, the Korean church has maintained a national and patriotic form of Christianity. Apart from this perspective, we would never have an accurate understanding of Korean Christianity.

1.2. The Roots of Minjung Theology

Q: Now, let's move forward to the present day. It is generally said that your theology took a significant turn to what is now referred to as minjung theology during the course of the 1970s. How should we make sense of this turn? Was it in continuity with your earlier thinking or an exploration into new territory?

A: Certainly, minjung theology was born under the *Yushin* (Revitalizing Reform) system,[13] and it is not possible to speak of minjung theology without mentioning how the Korean minjung found themselves under that system. However, my heartfelt thoughts about minjung trace back to my experiences in Jiandao under Japanese colonial rule. The life of Koreans there during the colonial years was typical minjung life. The experience has stuck painfully in my heart as a reminder of my mother's life. Ever since then, minjung has been a deep-seated and fundamental concern for me. Why do the minjung have to live so miserably? Why do they have to be oppressed and deprived like this? I experienced a bitter *han*[14] in my heart for my nation living in Jiandao in exile, unprotected, completely abandoned, extremely poor, and powerless. At the time Jiandao, like Galilee during Jesus's time, was a site of minjung's life, a land of gentiles. This is the root of my interest in minjung, and I believe this interest theologically blossomed under the Yushin system in the 1970s.

Q: Was it right after the liberation of Korea that you returned to Korea from Jiandao?[15] Would you please tell me about that period of time?

---

13. The *Yushin* system is a name for the Fourth Republic, the republic after the third constitutional amendment. It started in October 1972, about two months before the constitution was officially changed. In this system, the three powers of administration, legislation, and judicature were all at the president's discretion. The new constitution did not respect the basic rights of citizens and allowed the president to serve unlimited consecutive terms. Therefore, it was criticized for being the instrument of president Park Jeong-hui's permanent dictatorship. The *Yushin* system came to a practical end when Park was assassinated on October 26, 1979.

14. *Han* is a deep feeling caused by sustained experience of injustice and is considered one of the characteristic emotions of the Korean people.

15. The liberation of Korea from the Japanese colonial rule took place on August 15, 1945.

A: It was in 1946 that I returned to Korea, escaping a conflict with the leftists in Jiandao. Right before the liberation, I sought refuge from the Japanese police in a countryside village in Jiandao. Privately, I exerted influences on the village. After the liberation, I began to work openly as chair of the village self-government committee and chair of the board of the elementary school despite my young age. It was inevitable because it was a time of limited resources. When the Soviet army arrived, the whole village went out with placards to welcome them. But seeing the soldiers raping women at random, I fell into despair at the tragic reality that, even after the liberation, a weak nation could not escape exploitation. So I left Jiandao and crossed the Duman River in tears.[16] I had no set itinerary, only a desire to study, and so I came to Seoul. Coming down through the regions north of the thirty-eighth parallel, I experienced difficulties. But something worse was waiting for me in Seoul, where I finally felt free of life-threatening dangers: the unbearable humiliation from the fact that the American soldiers were treating Koreans like pigs—not as human beings. That rekindled my anger from childhood: "To the bitter end we are a nation that is trampled down!"

Q: You studied sociology in college, didn't you? What made you turn from sociology to theology?

A: Though I was a Christian, I had no intention of studying theology. I felt deeply troubled about the poverty of my nation and considered studying economics. But in order to study in a more comprehensive discipline, I chose sociology. Another reason for choosing sociology was that I thought, "Christianity is not enough. I have to engage in some kind of social movement." But I wasn't thinking in political terms but dreaming of building a new community. In pursuit of this dream during my Seoul National University years, some Christian friends and I formed a social group called One Faith Society. We pronounced, "We are neither left nor right," and met often. We continued to meet even after graduation until the Korean War broke out. While taking refuge from the war outside of Seoul, I had a sobering realization: "The present church doesn't work. I have to start a community that can give birth to a new movement." So I looked up the members of the

---

16. The Duman River starts on the southeastern slope of the Baekdu Mountain and flows downward into the East Sea. It currently forms part of the border between North Korea and China and the border between North Korea and Russia.

society scattered around by the war one by one and persuaded them to come together. We designated Jeonju[17] as our base and met as often as possible.

Q: I remember hearing that you published a magazine.

A: Yes, it was a magazine called *Yaseong*. It means "the voice from the wilderness." I was the publisher, and the eleven members of One Faith Society were the writing staff. None of us had studied theology. I wrote an essay entitled "The Meaning of Suffering" for the first issue, and it was my first published writing—a baby's first cry at birth, I'd say.[18] There was no printing house in Jeonju because it was during wartime. So the printing of the magazine had to be done in Busan,[19] but after publishing twelve issues we quit for lack of funding.

Q: What were the main points of the essays you wrote for the magazine?

A: I argued for simple points. It's not right to sell Jesus for a living. Let's do a church for the people and by the people with no professional ministers. Partial relationships don't work. A multidimensional community is the answer. This is a summary of my claims.

Q: I understand a church made up only of lay people with no professional ministers. But what is a multidimensional community?

A: The members of our society at the time were all in different lines of work and had diverse jobs. What I meant by "multidimensional community" was a monastery-like community formed by these people, whose activities would include studying and offering to people counseling in various areas from various angles.[20] At that time, there was a house named *Hyangrin-*

---

17. Jeonju is located approximately 210 kilometers (130 miles) south of Seoul and belongs in the Jeollabuk Province.

18. Ahn Byung-Mu, "The Meaning of Suffering" [Korean], *Yaseong*.

19. Busan, the second largest city in Korea, is located about 400 kilometers (250 miles) southeast of Seoul. During the Korean War, it belonged to a small area that was never occupied by the North Korean army and served as the temporary capital of South Korea.

20. The Korean word that renders the word "multidimensional" is *ipchejeok*. A literal translation is "three-dimensional." The nature of the community Ahn wanted to build was supposed to be a church that consisted solely of lay people who had their

won at the foot of the Nam Mountain, which was an upscale restaurant under Japanese ownership during Japanese colonial years. Someone gave it to me telling me to turn it to good use. I repaired it with my own hands, hammering nails and all, to prepare it as a residence for the community. I was the only unmarried person. Family is such a strong unit of egoism that it hampers community. At first, ours was a worship community for members only. But one by one the members got married and started families. As our community grew, we started attracting people from outside and eventually developed into a church. That was the precursor of Hyangrin Church. I struggled and struggled in order to maintain a strong sense of community to no avail. I felt deeply sad and despaired, so I decided to escape from church and the very idea of society itself. I declared myself to be an existentialist. As I wrote in *Yaseong*, I said, "I will go my own way alone," and left for Germany to study there.

1.3. German Theology and the Historical Jesus

Q: You went to Germany to study theology at Heidelberg University. At first, you worked for a laity's community, but what made you decide to study theology?

A: Before I left for Germany, some comrades and I reopened Jungang Theological Seminary. At first I taught sociology, then Greek, and not long after, theology. In those days, my most important theological interest was the historical Jesus. This after all has been the theme of my life, and back then I was already in its firm grip. At the time, I was a mere amateur in theology but really enthusiastic for a better understanding of Jesus. I had no intention of studying theology, but my interest in the historical Jesus was so strong as to eclipse all the other interests and fill me up with the determination to "know the historical Jesus himself by all means." The life Jesus lived appealed to me and was very compelling. I said to myself, "I will search for who he is even at the expense of my life!" That's why I went to Germany to study theology.

---

own jobs and contributed to the community according to their capacities. Members were expected to play multiple roles. There was supposed to be no distinction between the church life and everyday life. For Ahn, this was the ideal of a laity's church.

Q: In Germany you were deeply influenced by Rudolf Bultmann, weren't you? But your theology appears to lean towards sociological hermeneutics or political theology rather than Bultmann's existential hermeneutics. How did the transition happen? Would you please also comment on the kind of atmosphere you studied in in Germany?

A: As I said earlier, before going to Germany I developed a keen interest in the historical Jesus and already differed from Bultmann. He didn't quest after the historical Jesus. As for this difference, I never once conceded to him. However, his hermeneutics (*Hermeneutik*) for the Synoptic Gospels was very important for me as a scientific method of analysis. And his existentialistic thinking was significant for me because I had long been immersed in Søren Kierkegaard whose negation of the world was influential to me. The same can be said of Karl Barth. So I thought to myself, "Just stop everything. There's something wrong with your way so far." In this respect, the idea of an immediate refusal of everything was a seminal insight I learned from crisis theologians. In terms of scholarship, indeed Bultmann's influences were definitive as I had to study the Synoptic Gospels. However, I wouldn't give him an inch when it came to the historical Jesus.

In spite of having enrolled myself in the university—enrollment was a kind of social security in Germany—I took few classes and never even dreamt of getting a degree. By then Bultmann had already retired and was no longer at the university, but his former student Günther Bornkamm had just published a book, *Jesus of Nazareth*.[21] That's why I went to that particular school. I learned Bultmann's ideas, methodologies, and their backgrounds—including, existentialism. I became an avid reader on everything about the historical Jesus—whether it was a thesis or book. But the further I went, I reached the conclusion that Western methodologies would not lead you to a knowledge of the historical Jesus. When I came back to Korea from Germany, I declared, "I have come back only with the conclusion that I can't know the historical Jesus." However, it was impossible for me to give up the quest. Without taking the historical Jesus seriously, how could Christianity possibly overcome docetism?[22]

---

21. Günther Bornkamm, *Jesus of Nazareth*, trans. Irene and Fraser McLuskey with James M. Robinson (Minneapolis: Fortress, 1995). Translation of *Jesus von Nazareth* (Stuttgart: Kohlhammer, 1965).

22. Here the original Korean text gives a in-text note that says: "Docetism claims

Doesn't discarding the historical Jesus leave us only with ideas? This was my conviction.

Speaking of my interest in political theology, while I was in Germany, the problem of my nation never left my mind. I always worried about my nation and the situation of Korea and made an occasional contribution to the journal *Sasanggye*.[23] In the meantime, I couldn't get out of my mind the question, "Why do I have to ask Westerners' questions and give Westerners' answers?" So I renewed my interest in the East and began in Germany to study the Four Books and the Three Classics, which I had learned from my father in childhood. As for Confucius, I reached the point of forming my own understanding of him. The problem of my nation was still a concern deep in my bones. All of the introductory materials for Korea available in Europe was penned by Japanese writers during the years of Japanese colonialism and depicted Koreans as barbarous. Koreans were said to belong to neither Buddhist nor Confucian culture. They were portrayed as an uncivilized nation devoid of culture. Many of the books in the West were of this nature. Whenever I ran into such a book, I felt so ashamed that I bought and destroyed it in secret. Perhaps such an interest in my nation formed a strong undercurrent for my theological thinking. In this respect, I also differed from Bultmann. He was not political. He could not see Jesus politically. The event of Jesus's cross was clearly a political event to my eyes, and this point of view has consistently informed my quest for the historical Jesus. Yet, Bultmann's scholarship was so vast and profound that I could not challenge his scholarship. And even though I was unable to overcome his theology and stayed with it even after coming back to Korea, my questions remained unanswered.

---

that, since matter and the body are inherently evil, Jesus Christ as the son of God did not become a person with a body. Instead, he came to the world temporarily in a bodily disguise. When he was crucified on the cross, he shed his body and his spirit went up to heaven. Christianity considers this view a heresy."

23. *Sasanggye*, which means "the world of thoughts," was a monthly periodical started by Jang Jun-ha (1918–1975) in 1953. The journal dealt with philosophy, literature, and social and political critique. It received contributions from first-rate intellectuals of Korea and was influential on Korean society. The journal was discontinued in 1970 due to political oppression by the Park Jeong-hui government.

1.4. A Theology Based on the Reality of Minjung

Q: To sum up, while in search of the historical Jesus, you were greatly influenced by Bultmann in the hermeneutics for the Synoptic Gospels, but you maintained a political view of Jesus out of your interest in the Korean nation. Seen in this way, your proposal of minjung theology in the 1970s was not an accidental occurrence or an abrupt shift in direction, but fundamentally in continuity with your national interests and political concerns.

A: Right. It was not the case that my theology made a sudden change of direction in the 1970s. Going over my old writings, I see myself beginning to use the word *minjung* often already in the early 1960s. In those days, although minjung was not my main focus, topics such as the sorrow of minjung, the nation-like minjung, and the minjung-like nation held my attention as inseparable entanglements with one another. Indeed, our nation and minjung are inseparable from each other, for our nation is simultaneously minjung. We are a nation who has always been trampled down and exploited by powerful countries. Therefore, the sorrows of this nation are precisely the sorrows of minjung and vice versa. The *han*-filled sorrows of the minjung, oppressed and robbed by the ruling class, overlap with the sorrows of the nation. The two are inextricably tied together.

Q: If you took part in or criticized the political realities in a concrete way, would you please share that experience with us?

A: Yes. In 1962, when Mr. Ham Seok-heon[24] came to Germany, I placed a newspaper about the situation in Korea before him and said, "Sir, is this a time for you to be travelling like this? You have to return quickly!" Mr. Ham, in the middle of having lunch, cried tears, packed up immediately, and returned to Korea. As soon as he arrived in Seoul, he gave lectures

---

24. Ham Seok-heon (1901–1989) was a renowned and influential Christian thinker and social critic in twentieth-century Korea. Ham upheld the values of nonviolence and resistance against authority. He participated in the anti-Japanese movement under the Japanese occupation and engaged in the antidictatorship movement in postliberation Korea. He followed the nonchurch movement, the northeast Asian understanding of Quakerism, and his book, *The History of Korea Seen in Terms of Its Meaning*, has become a modern classic.

jointly with Mr. Jang Jun-ha[25] on topical issues at Daegwang High School in Seoul. He also lectured in many locations outside Seoul. That was his debut as a political critic. He jokes that I ruined his life and recalls with laughter that I made him start drinking beer. I have always been interested in politics. But the decisive moment was the constitutional change in 1969 for Park Jeong-hui's election for the third successive term.[26] I was the eleventh person to join the campaign for a million signatures for preventing the change, and it happened at the encouragement by Mr. Jang Jun-ha. He insisted that I dive into politics. He pulled out all of the stops to involve me in political movements. I still don't think he really knew the kind of person I was.

A little before that, I was arrested for the East Berlin Affair[27] and suffered a crushingly inhumane treatment. It was my first experience of such savagery and made me think that this should not ever happen to any human being. But after giving my signature to the campaign for blocking the constitutional change, I got arrested and underwent exactly the same

---

25. Jang Jun-ha (1918–1975) served in the Independence Army before the liberation of Korea in 1945. He subsequently worked as a journalist, social activist, and politician for the democracy of Korea. He started the journal *Sasanggye* in 1953 (see fn. 3). He was engaged in the movement against the *Yushin* system when he died from an accident. He was severely persecuted by the Park Jeong-hui government. It is suspected that his sudden death was an assassination by the government.

26. Park Jeong-hui (1917–1979) came to power through a military coup on May 16, 1961. He became president of Korea in 1963 and went to great lengths to stay in power as long as possible. His dictatorship came to an abrupt end when he was assassinated by one of his trusted subordinates on October 26, 1979. Park is praised for his contribution to the rapid economic growth of Korea but is criticized for his brutal suppression of democracy.

27. The East Berlin Affair refers to the incident that began some time before July 1967 and ended on August 15, 1970. The Korean Central Intelligence Agency announced that some Korean students and residents in East Berlin had interactions with the North Korean embassy in the city and that some of these people worked back in Korea as spies for North Korea. Two hundred and three individuals were investigated, and twenty-three were accused of espionage or attempted espionage. In this process, the suspects were illegally hauled to the police station and were subject to torture. The truth of the matter was that the Park Jeong-hui government imposed false charges on the interactions between South Koreans and the North Korean embassy in East Berlin. Of all who were convicted, two were sentenced to death. The others were released thanks to the protests in West Germany and France based on the principles of territorial sovereignty and human rights.

kind of humiliation again. These incidents turned out to be the beginning of my history with the intelligence agency.

Q: In the 1970s, you suffered your first imprisonment, and this experience gave your theology a clear definition as minjung theology. I wonder what were the theological connections in which your quest for the historical Jesus came to fruition as minjung theology?

A: My first writing with minjung as a theological theme dates back to 1972, when I wrote a short piece titled "Jesus and the Minjung (*Ochlos*)."[28] It was three years before I went to prison. I viewed the suffering of the minjung not as an individual but as a collective suffering. Even when a single person is suffering, she or he is suffering on behalf of the collective, that is, serving as the sacrificial offering for the collective. Since the institution of the military dictatorship, there were political outbreaks and incidents that caused many people to be arrested, jailed, and tortured. When this was happening, I thought of everyone under the dictatorship as minjung. Their suffering pierced me in the heart; and thinking that maybe this was the *han* of the nation, the *han* of the minjung, I looked for the solution to this problem in the Bible. There I discovered the *ochlos*. In the Bible, there are two Greek words for minjung: *laos* and *ochlos*. The former, equivalent to the national citizenry of today, designates the people who have the right to protection within a certain group boundary. The latter refers to those who are outside the boundaries and are therefore denied this right. The Gospel of Mark, the earliest written gospel, calls those who unconditionally followed Jesus and put their hope in him not as *laos* but as *ochlos*.

Westerners have failed to take interest in *ochlos* because they comprehend everything, including God, Jesus, and the Holy Spirit, as a *personality* (*persona*). They only ask, "Who is Jesus?"—inquiring only about personal and individual identity. And they get the answer that Jesus is a "such and such personality" and are satisfied. But I thought differently: "Jesus is an event! God is an event, too!" I realized, "You are wrong to see Jesus as a persona—a wrong view!" This realization was the turning point in my theology. Why should Jesus be a persona? Why not an event? What does Jesus as an individual who lived in Galilee two thousand years ago matter? It's

---

28. This essay was officially published in the December 1979 issue of *Hyeonjon* (the present existence).

the event that matters! Belatedly but blessedly, this realization came to me. *Jesus as an event*—this served as the link between my quest for the historical Jesus and minjung theology.

Previously, I was on the quest for the historical Jesus as an individual from my fascination with his personality. However, once I reimagined Jesus as an event—namely, the *Jesus event*—I felt like a new avenue opened up leading to the historical Jesus. Western theologians do what they call the "theology of the Word" and so see Jesus as the event of the *word*. However, it was not Jesus's word but the event of the cross that brought Christianity into being. Paul proclaimed Jesus as Christ in numerous sermons, but his evangelism made significant progress after the event of his suffering in prison. Based on this understanding, I came to propose the "theology of event."

I view Jesus as a minjung event and a collective event. This event (Jesus event) was never completed in a single occurrence two thousand years ago but has been recurring both within the church and in history in general. In this way, the theology of event connects itself very naturally to the theology of minjung. The German theologian Jürgen Moltmann challenged me to a debate because he disagreed with my claim that "Jesus is precisely minjung." He disagreed because he took Jesus for a persona, not an event. Jesus is an event. The Jesus event is still taking place in history again and again as the minjung event. It is just like the volcanic lava that repeatedly erupts, while streaming below the surface of the earth. That is, Jesus is the great volcanic lava of the minjung event!

Q: Why is minjung theology strongly opposed to conceptualizing minjung?

A: When asked "What is minjung?," I refuse to give a short and simple definition. Western sciences understand everything through conceptualization. I don't do that. Once born, a concept becomes estranged from its substance. Then we are left with not a living substance but an empty concept. This is why I was disillusioned with Western scholars. So I insist on not conceptualizing minjung no matter what. In addition, minjung theologians are criticized for glorifying minjung, but that is not true. We just see minjung as they are. One aspect of minjung I pay particular attention to is the fact that they have the ability of self-transcendence. I have seen many instances of minjung self-transcendence in our history, especially in the 1970s and 1980s. Look at laborers, students, and their mothers. They didn't have to bear the suffering themselves but dove into it, right? Those were the events of self-transcendence. Take, for example, the Donghak

Peasant Revolution. In terms of the intellectual history, it was far from possible, but the event took place. Such a power could not be born of individual farmers in Korea. But they rose up with such an immense power. I think that is exactly minjung's ability of self-transcendence. I cannot say anything else of minjung nor do I want to say anything more about them.

Q: Minjung as a collective can transcend themselves; the event caused by minjung who have transcended themselves is the Jesus event. This is your view. Can you tell us about the distinct feature in your method of doing theology? For instance, you always discuss the Bible in connection with our own current situation, don't you? Don't you think this is one of the characteristics of your method of biblical interpretation?

A: Well, I wouldn't call it so much as a distinct feature. But I can say one thing: when I discuss biblical texts, it is always in the context of our life setting.[29] I read the Bible from this perspective without fail. And naturally, the interpretation goes in that direction, too.

Recently, I was reminded again that, for Western and Japanese theologians, theology itself is the context. For example, Barth said this, Bultmann said that, then Bornkamm said this, and then Tillich said that. This has become the context in which they do theology. Words and opinions oppose other words and opinions—this is their theology. And this opposition, in turn, becomes the context for their scholarly work. When real-life circumstances are excluded, the science itself has become its own context. While visiting Japan this year, I saw it again and felt at once really amused and surprised. I sensed it while talking with Professor Arai Sasaku of Tokyo University, a New Testament scholar. I told him that the difference between him and me was that, while I did theology with the reality of the Korean minjung, he didn't have that kind of context. He admitted it. He is a fairly liberal theologian and holds similar views to mine. In the conclusions of some of his writings, he mentions the Korean minjung theology,

---

29. The Korean word used for "life setting" here is *hyeonjang*, which literally means "present site" and refers to a specific place where a particular action takes place. This is one of the most frequently used words in this book and also an important concept in minjung theology. In this translation, *hyeongjang* is variously translated as "site," "field," "reality," "life setting," "actual location," and "real life context," among others. The expression *minjung hyeongjang* is rendered as "the site of the minjung's life."

occasionally quoting my words in particular. This is because he doesn't have a real-life context for his theology.

1.5. Theology of Event and Theology for Theology

Q: Then we could say that Western and Japanese theology, in stark terms, comes out of its own theology and not from a lived context. Their theology works deductively, drawing logic from logic, instead of working inductively from specific life experiences, facts, and events.

A: After observing them, I felt very happy with doing theology in Korea. I realized, "I am doing theology at the site of real life!" This feeling grew stronger when I was in conversation with them. So here is my advice: Always identify questions from the sites of real life, the sites of current history, and the sites of present events and put them to the Bible. And when you draw the answers from the Bible, again, do it always in a way that offers fresh insight on the Bible from the sites of real life and therefore reveals the truth of the Bible anew. That's it. No big deal.

Q: You like quoting Bultmann concerning the Bible that the question determines the answer. That applies to what you just said, that the question from the site of real life determines an answer from the Bible, right?

A: Right. To put it straightforwardly, Western scholars still locate their theology and thought in the context of what Plato said, what Kant said, what Hegel said, and so on. Day and night, they go around and around in the world of concepts, never going out to reality.

We don't have that kind of habit. In the past, I thought it was our weakness. So I even thought that Eastern thinking could not engender science. But now I don't think so. There is no wall between the site of real life and science. I realized this is the best condition you could possibly ask for, something truly fortunate.

Western scholars tend to monopolize the truth in the name of science, build a thick wall between the site of the reality and the world of science, and ban the entrance of ordinary people into their exclusive realm. They have to break this wall down. Mr. Suh Nam-dong[30] deliv-

---

30. Seo Nam-dong (1918–1984) was a Presbyterian minister and theologian who

ered a critical remark that theology should become anti-theology. But in actuality it has to become anti-science. Science in the Western sense of the word (*Wissenschaft*) has to be broken up. Isn't it the case that scholars have turned trivial and everyday things—things that are so common in ordinary people's lives—into their own scholarly language unfamiliar to minjung? And in so doing haven't they constructed a strange castle inside which they enjoy fame and privileged status? Isn't that what scholars do? I think the same is true of theology. They think it is only they who can do science or theology.

Q: It seems to me that it is right there that your minjung theology, namely, your *theology of event*, your theology of the site of real life, departs pronouncedly from the Western ivory-tower theology. Now, in order to understand this difference better, I would like to ask you for a concrete illustration with a particular Bible passage in which your hermeneutic differs from that of Western theology.

A: Let me give you an example then. In the Gospel of Mark, there is the story that, while Jesus and his disciples were going through a wheat field, the hungry disciples pluck and rub ears of wheat to eat the grains, right? At that moment, the Pharisees attack Jesus, "Why are your disciples doing what is not lawful on the Sabbath?" Jesus answers, "The Sabbath was made for humankind, and not humankind for the Sabbath" (Mark 2:23–28).

Western theologians classify this passage as an instance of *apophthegma*. This is originally a Greek literary genre that centers an anecdote of a philosopher or saint around their words. Bultmann used this term for New Testament studies. This approach considers the words of Jesus as the kernel and the setting as a story-format addition made during the transmission of the words. It therefore relativizes the historical setting in which Jesus's words were originally spoken. With the story of the disciples eating wheat on the Sabbath, Western theologians, especially form critics, focus only on the words of Jesus rather than on the event itself. They think that Jesus's words "The Sabbath was made for humankind, and not humankind for the Sabbath" existed first, attributing primary importance to them. In the process of transmission, a circumstantial explanation for

---

introduced Western progressive theologies to Korea and worked as one of the early founders of minjung theology. In 1975, he was expelled from his university post and was imprisoned the following year due to his antidictatorship activities.

these words was added, and the story as we now see it came into being. Form critics view the gospels as a mere frame that contains the meaning of Jesus's words or the kerygma that Jesus is Christ. Bultmann even claimed the gospels were an expanded kerygma.

However, I flatly reject this view. It's the other way around. What counts is not the words but the event. It was not the words but the event that existed first. That is, in my view, prior to Jesus's words, there was the event of the hungry minjung of Jesus eating ears of wheat. I pay attention to the actual site of the hungry minjung and place it at the center of the story. The hungry minjung could not restrain themselves from plucking and eating the wheat, despite knowing it was the Sabbath. The Pharisees saw through the eye of the law of the existing system and accused them of violating the Sabbath laws. Jesus defended the hungry minjung in response, saying, "The Sabbath was made for humankind." This is the understanding that properly reveals the meaning of Jesus's words. These words can be seen as a declaration of the human rights of the minjung. So, in a more generalized expression, I used the term "the first declaration of human rights." Anyway, it is only when the story comes under the light of event that the great declaration in the passage reveals itself. Any system, institution, or law, must exist for minjung—not the other way around. There is a world of difference between the focus of Western theologians on Jesus's words in total disregard of the reality of the hungry minjung and my method of placing the event first and giving it central importance.

1.6. Jesus Is Minjung, and Minjung Is Jesus

Q: Listening again to your hermeneutic of the theology of event, I again find it original and impressive. Your hermeneutic can be said to constitute a hermeneutical revolution that launches a direct challenge to form criticism, a challenge powerful enough to shake the foundations of Western theology.

Western theology fails to understand the story of the minjung eating ears of wheat as an event at the actual site of the hungry minjung, since they have never been hungry. Instead, you construe it as the locus of the Jesus event, where Jesus and the hungry minjung become one. There you see the total unity between the two: Jesus is precisely the minjung, and the minjung is precisely Jesus.

When you discuss the equation of "Jesus = minjung," you often mention the words of John the Baptist in the Gospel of John 1:29, "the Lamb of God who takes away the sin of the world." And I am of the opinion that this passage makes your theory of minjung known in a profound way.

A: I offered my interpretation of the verse during a debate with the German theologian Jürgen Moltmann, and we still have not reached an agreement. I said, "This Jesus is precisely minjung!" and Moltmann gave a feverish "No!" Since minjung is an object of salvation by Jesus Christ, he protested arguing that identifying him with them made no sense at all. Concerning this disagreement, Moltmann wrote to me twice insisting that I clarify the point by means of a thesis or a letter. Someday when I get a chance, I will discuss this question with him.

What is crucial to my debate with Moltmann is that he accepts that "Jesus is minjung" but rejects that "minjung is Jesus." So I would like to ask him, "Then is it right to say 'Jesus is the messiah'"? It is wrong to identify Jesus with anything else, whatever it may be. Does it make sense to say, "Jesus is the son of God"? Is it right to define the living Jesus by analogy (*analogie*) with anything else? Moltmann contended, "Minjung is not Jesus," and this conveyed his assumption that he already knew who minjung were. But the knowledge of minjung is exactly the same as assuming the knowledge of Jesus. In fact, I believe that not knowing minjung is not knowing Jesus and that not knowing Jesus is not knowing minjung. That's where I stand. It is the same as Bultmann's logic when he said, "Not knowing God means not knowing humankind, and not knowing humankind means not knowing God." I'd like to apply this reasoning to minjung.

"Behold! The lamb of God who takes away the sin of the world!" Why is it not acceptable to say these words concerning those who are suffering in our land of Korea today? Who are those people who refuse to? I don't understand. Taking away the sin of the world does not carry a religious meaning. "The sin of the world" means just what it says literally, "the sin of the world." It is not just the sin of the dictator but the sin of those who cannot stop the dictator—not only those who commit corruption and injustice, but also those who allow them are sinful. For me sin is nothing peculiar. Political and economic contradictions, I believe, are also sin. We all need to bear sufferings due to structural contradictions of this world, but it is the minjung of today in this country who sustain the injuries, isn't it? Going to prison, getting fired, getting beaten, going hungry—do they deserve all of these? Aren't these sufferings caused by the flaws of Korean society? Aren't the minjung who bear them the victim? Aren't they "the Lamb of God who takes away the sin of the world"? Why on earth could we not use this description for these victims? Why do we refuse to see such a plain truth but grant Jesus a special and exceptional status by using trivial theological concepts? This stems from the stereotype of interpreting sin and the lamb of God within the sole confines of the religious realm.

I brought a painting with me when I returned to Korea after finishing my studies in Germany. It was a piece by a Polish or Romanian painter: a laborer is carrying a big cross, his back hunched over by a heavy load with a dark silhouette of the city in the background. On the cross a priest was sitting dozing off, a pot-bellied entrepreneur was sitting, a scholar was reading, a young man and woman were making love. All of these people were on the heavy cross carried by the laborer. This picture depicts a young Jesus who is walking towards Golgotha, and in this case, he is depicted as a laborer. He is carrying the sins of this world on his shoulder. He labors as the agent of production, and everyone else fares along sitting on his back. That picture was so impressive that, while in Germany, I had it hanging on the wall of my room and brought it back home with me. But Reverend Suh Nam-dong snatched it out of my hands. I came by that picture in 1961, and so it seems like I already had the minjung consciousness back then.

Q: I have already heard of that picture from you many times. And every time I hear of it, it never fails to touch me. It seems to me that the image of the young man in the painting is the very image of today's minjung. It is consistent with the biblical image of Jesus as the Lamb of God who takes away the sin of the world.

A: That's right. What's the matter with such a view? Isn't the young man taking away the sin of the world? What else could agree more with the words of the Bible than that?

1.7. Jesus Who Is Present outside the City Gate

Q: Illuminating specific Bible verses based on minjung theology helps me understand your unique theological methodology. Can you give another example that you frequently discuss?

A: In my reading of the Bible, I don't see Jesus, Christ, messiah, and the like merely as a religious figure. The Jesus event and the messiah event are not the exclusive property of Christianity. It is only because I am a biblical scholar, not a scholar of political science or economics, that I understand the event with reference to the Bible.

I compare the minjung event to a single great stream of volcanic lava that flows through many ages and erupts in different historical situations. It is my view that this lava erupted with colossal volcanic activity in the Jesus event and that this same lava is flowing ceaselessly below the crust of history in this age as well. Therefore, the minjung events in today's Korea, I believe, are not isolated and independent but are in continuity with the Jesus event two thousand years ago. This is important—I pursue the Jesus of present existence, namely, how he manifests himself in this very age. He is manifesting himself in the minjung event here today! Therefore, it is nonsense to pursue the Jesus of two thousand years ago or the doctrinal Christ. What matters is where and how the Christ of today—the Jesus event of today—is taking place. It is happening neither within the existing system nor within the existing church. Rather, it is taking place where you find yourselves after being alienated, deserted, and expelled from these places, that is, "outside the city gate" where Jesus was executed. This is how I see it.

The author of Hebrews said, "Jesus suffered outside the city gate.... Let us then go to him outside the camp and bear the abuse he endured" (13:12–13), and these are truly profound and beautiful words. A laborer's church took its name from this passage and calls itself The Church Outside the City Gate. I am not sure if I influenced the church's name, but I spoke about this passage early on. "Outside the city gate" is a residential area for the alienated, and there the Christ event is taking place. Even now, here in Korea, whether or not they confess the name of Jesus, the fight for building a minjung-owned society or the Jesus event is ceaselessly taking place. As a biblical scholar, unlike a political scientist or an economist, I see it clearly.

Q: In the name "The Church outside the City Gate," I sense a possible conflict between "outside the city gate" and "church." If "outside the city gate" refers to an alienated space, or the so-called periphery, then its location differs from the church. Aren't most churches actually located inside the city gate? Whether in an urban or rural area, regardless of its address, the church in essence appears to be within the existing system, that is, inside the city gate. In this sense, the designation "The Church Outside the City Gate" does not sound harmonious. In actuality, of course, churches exist outside of the city gate, and small communities endure many struggles in order to go *outside the city gate*. But isn't it obvious that the church is an enormous city now?

A: If I happen to be in Germany again someday, the first question I would ask theologians is, "What is your reason for doing theology?" I would add, "Do you have any other reason than preserving the status quo?" The existing church has property, and this—and nothing else—maintains its Christianity. There is no other reason for its maintenance. The church system has ossified, and the more people who cannot enter it (= minjung), the more the church tries to protect its vested interests. Therefore, the movement is from "outside the city gate" to "inside the city gate." Similarly, regarding Korean churches, are prostitutes welcome to enter? What about beggars? Isn't it the case that these churches are structured in such a way that none of the followers of Jesus, namely, the *ochlos*, are welcome or fit to enter? Isn't it true that this structure has become hardened resulting in a new system and hierarchy? Hasn't the church become a selfish group and a social gathering of this age? It has become a place for self-preservation and self-expansion rather than a place for others.

However, the word *ekklēsia* (church) originally had a simple meaning. This Greek word simply means the gathering of believers—a different image than the church as a sacred realm. In present day Korea, minjung churches (or "basic communities"[31])—are forming in residential areas of laborers and the urban poor. An *ekklēsia* that is established outside the city gate, at the site of the minjung's life where the principle, "Everyone is welcome here!," is alive and well. These are churches that have no form at all, no precondition at all, despite borrowing the word *church* for its name. They are communities that share in the anguish of the minjung. They live, fight, pray, and worship together with the minjung. This is the true church of Jesus Christ. And this is the church of the minjung. Existing churches must aim to be like this church, and, even if unable to fully conform to this radical ideal, they should begin by supporting minjung churches.

---

31. The Korean word Ahn uses for "basic" is *badak*, which means "bottom."

1.8. The Yearnings of Minjung and the Path to the Unification of the Nation

Q: Now let's turn to some issues concerning current affairs. Recently, young Christian activists suggest that Korean theology should focus on the *sammin* (three *min*'s) ideology. Here, *sammin* means "nation (*minjok*), minjung, and democracy (*minju*)."[32] We can say that *sammin* ideology aims at the realization of a democracy in which the independence of the nation and the subjecthood of the minjung are guaranteed. As a person who has often discussed nation-like minjung and minjung-like nation, what do you think of this suggestion?

A: I haven't given it much thought, but it seems to me that proposing these three ideas together under the name of *sammin* has been motivated by the realization from struggles on the field. Using less than these three ideas, whichever word or words they tried, does not adequately convey the full meaning intended. But I think that a proper usage of minjung includes the other two ideas. The word *minjung* represents all of the sorrows in the bosom of our nation. And it is only natural that the word *minjung-like* means a democracy with the minjung as the sovereign. Democracy is authentic only when the minjung are sovereign. The word *sammin* might be necessary as a temporary strategy, but I believe that the single word minjung comprehends all three ideas. Therefore, I feel no need to revise my theology with reference to *sammin*.

Minjung is a concept unique to Koreans. Westerners cannot say, "We are also minjung." Indeed, the phrase minjung-like nation refers to the minjung and nation who were grief-stricken under colonial rule, exploited by foreign powers, and oppressed by the ruling class in their own country. For these reasons, the word minjung comprehends all three ideas.

Q: The notion of *sammin* has the weakness of listing three separate ideas. I understand you saying that the meaning of minjung, when fully understood, naturally includes the other ideas. I agree with you here. However, when we try to grasp the Korean minjung as a concrete historical reality, doesn't this require the category of nation for those who have been ruled and exploited by foreign powers?

---

32. The three words have in common the syllable *min*, which means "people."

A: Well, I first addressed this issue in my 1975 lecture, "Minjung, Nation, and Church." The gist of the lecture was that "Minjung is a more significant category than nation in defining the history of Korea. What has true reality is the minjung, whereas nation is nothing more than a relative concept formed with respect to international relations. But while the idea of nation has always been lifted up, the minjung as the substance of the nation has been neglected in a state of oppression and exploitation for the apparently beautiful cause of serving the nation or the country. This is an on-going situation. It is time now to listen to the groans of the minjung that are drowned out by slogans for the nation." That was the basic point of the lecture. Our term minjung does not refer to the proletariat. The proletariat exists in all industrial societies all over the world. But that is not the case with minjung. Our concept minjung does not refer to any world-wide entity. We are talking about the minjung of Korea now. Therefore, I don't think that we have to begin to use the word *nation* in order to grasp the meaning behind minjung.

Q: I agree that the rhetoric of nationalism has often served as means of preserving the regime and that the designation nation has made invisible the minjung who are the immediate victims of oppression and exploitation. Recently, however, unlike in the 1970s, true nationalism, which seeks independence from foreign powers, is gaining more traction. Other ideas that are gaining currency include independence from foreign powers as a prerequisite for the minjung's liberation and the inseparability of minjung and nation as sharing the same concerns.

A: It means the same. It is the minjung, not the upper class, that are subject to exploitation by foreign powers. Once the minjung come to power, such a problem resolves itself naturally. I stand my ground on this.

Q: Recently, some Christian university students are wrestling with the question of whether or not to accept social science as a tool of understanding this reality and whether or not to accept violence as a means of transforming this reality. Please tell me what you think of the question of violence.

A: If I am allowed to use the qualifier "in principle," I think nonviolence is the right course to take. But the boundary between the Christian and non-Christian view on violence could turn out meaningless in real-life situations. The difference in principle might sometimes lose its meaning when it comes to acting in a concrete situation. Violence and nonviolence are neither metaphysical universals nor are they subjectively made choices. They are, I suppose, contextual ideas that presuppose a relationship and are defined in response to a given situation involving other parties in the relationship. For example, when we are working out strategies for a certain goal, I don't think there are different strategies for Christians and non-Christians. The unity of ends and means, as a principle, is right. But I don't think being locked up in either violence or nonviolence is biblical. It is evident that nonviolence is not a biblical concept. The Old Testament depicts Yahweh as a God who goes to war for the Israelite people. In church history, countless holy wars were waged in the name of faith. Nonviolence is often advocated based on Jesus's Sermon on the Mount in the New Testament, but even here we need to consider how violence is defined. The peace Jesus mentioned in the Sermon on the Mount is *shalom* in the Hebrew language. It is not a concept that signifies an absence of fighting, but a very dynamic one that aggressively creates peace by confronting the forces that hinder or destroy it. Originally, the language of violence belongs to the strong. The weak do not know it. Historically, the strong wield violence and make the weak not use violence. As for the weak, the expression *self-defense* does not apply to them. When the weak act with violence, it is a conditioned reflex; it is a response after countless afflictions when they are at the end of the rope. But in this case, the designation *violence* is not befitting.

When it comes to the question of violence, I think, we have to consider both strategic and moral aspects. Concerning the former, one has to be level-headed and consider whether a violent means would be effective, that is, whether it would bring the end result you want. To determine whether this is a good strategy, you have to make a scientific assessment. For example, Heinz Eduard Tödt, who is a theologian friend of mine at Heidelberg University, wrote a thesis that evaluated the student power movement in Europe in the 1960s. In this much-acclaimed work, he concluded that a peaceful means would have yielded more fruitful results because the use of violence strengthened the bureaucracy even further. Therefore, when the end is moral, I think, we have to weigh in strategic terms which means are more conducive to success. Yet, I don't think there exists the problem of violence in Korea yet.

Q: What tasks can theology pursue towards reunification of the two Koreas? If you have any thoughts about this question, please share them with us.

A: Of course, I have thoughts about the question! I think about it day and night. Minjung theology itself would not have come into being if it were not for the division of the two Koreas. The central question that motivated me to found Korea Theological Study Institute was how to construct a theology for Korean reunification. Back in those days, Korean theology was not interested in the question of ideology, and so the institute's first attention was confined to this question.

Some time ago I went to a meeting held by the Presbyterian Church in the Republic of Korea[33] and listened to a presentation on the status of North Korea given by an official from the National Unification Ministry. It was his assumption that North Korea would never give up their ideology and that the same was true of South Korea. So I asked him what would have to be done. He said that the two Koreas would have to acknowledge each other's ideology, write a unification constitution, and then take a gradual approach. Isn't it ironic to say "make no compromise at all" and "write a unification constitution" in the same breath? How can unification be achieved when North Korea remains committed to communism and South Korea to capitalism? For unification to occur, both sides must make concessions and compromise.

The word minjung expresses the yearnings of the nation living in an age when the two Koreas are divided. How can we overcome the reality of the minjung groaning in our divided country? This question has brought minjung theology into being. Frankly, we neither advocate the proletariat dictatorship nor acknowledge the capitalist system. The word minjung came to us while we were searching for a way for both Koreas to flourish. The goal is to empower the minjung who are oppressed by the capitalist system and manipulated by the elite in the proletariat dictatorship. In other words, the goal is to rally the power of the minjung in South Korea and North Korea in order to unify the nation—a minjung-led reunification. The word minjung signals all of these yearnings. Without this, I think, we would have no path towards unification or liberation of

---

33. The Presbyterian church in the Republic of Korean is a liberal Protestant denomination founded by Kim Jae-jun in 1953. Hanshin University, where Ahn taught, is affiliated with the denomination.

the Korean nation. The minjung occupy a place precisely in between the two systems of communism and capitalism. From the old days to now, one stratum of the Korean people has refused to change their thoughts whatever foreign influences came their way. Immune to the influences of foreign cultures, they have maintained purity. But educated people have been subject to foreign influences—the more a person was educated, the more they were influenced. This is true of both Koreas. I am working for the minjung under the assumption that, beside the communist and capitalist force, there is a genuine self-reliant force of our nation. In other words, I propose that we explain the already-existing minjung. The word minjung was not discovered by minjung theologians nor did it come into being by accident. It came into being with a special meaning in the division of Korea. In this regard, minjung theology was born for the unification of the nation; therefore, the ultimate aim of this theology must be nothing but the unification of the nation.

1.9. The Tasks of Korean Christians

Q: What do you hope to accomplish in the future?

A: I firmly believe that Korean people have to turn back to being Korean. They have to be Korean before being Christians. They need to overcome Western influences. Korea is likely to continue to become a Western civilization. Patterns of thinking and ways of asking and answering questions are all becoming westernized. How do we fight against this? Christianity has been highly influential in the westernization of Korea, and it is Christian theology itself that is changing Korean tradition and ways of thinking. How do we confront this problem? How can we renew Korean Christianity into a Christianity of our Korean minjung?

Faced with these major tasks, theology cannot be scientific or remain aloof as in an ivory tower. It must be a theology undertaken at the site of the minjung's life, a theology as a movement of the minjung. Theology has to be released from the monopoly of scholars to the hands of the laity. It has to become alive and working, providing lay people with directions in life and ministry. I alone cannot come up with all the visions of such a theology. This is a task for all Korean Christians. I believe it is the central task of Korean theology and churches to create a model of theology as a movement—an exemplar of Christianity of the Third World and, further, of the entire world.

Part 2

2
The Bible as the Book of Minjung

Q: I would like to hear your views on the Bible as the book of Minjung and, specifically, how to read the Old and New Testaments in the right way. Our topic is divided in four rubrics: (1) the traditional understanding of the Bible in the Korean church; (2) a critical examination of Western biblical hermeneutics; (3) biblical hermeneutics of minjung theology; and (4) recurring themes in the Bible. But we don't have to follow this order in our conversation. I will also ask other questions as necessary. For starters, can you talk a little bit about how Korean churches interpret the Bible?

2.1. The Conventional Understanding of the Bible in the Korean Church

A: How is the Korean church reading and understanding the Bible? I dealt with this question long ago in an essay, "The Korean Church's Understanding of Jesus."[1] In short, the Korean church presupposes doctrine before reading the Bible. Specifically, it presupposes the Westminster Confession of Faith and reads the Bible in order to justify it. Therefore, the Bible is simply a prooftext (*Referenz*) for the Westminster Confession of Faith. The Bible is nothing more than a tool for confirming what one already knows. For this reason, to an alarming degree, doctrine has become an ideology that subjugates the very meaning of the Bible. The resulting danger is that, despite emphasizing *sola scriptura*, the church uses the Bible as a tool to justify certain doctrines with biblical authority. And I judge that this kind of practice carries the possibility of spawning many different sects. For once you have submitted to a certain doctrinal system, you can alter the meaning of the Bible to conform to any system. Paradoxically, the more that biblicism flourishes, the more the Bible is abandoned and ignored.

---

1. Ahn Byung-Mu, "The Korean Church's Understanding of Jesus."

The term *conservative* is often used to mean preserving orthodoxy, but in the Korean church the label means, "Our doctrine is victorious."

A characteristic element of Korean Christians' attitude towards reading the Bible is an indigenous method of scriptural reading. With this method, you just recite the text without attempting to understand it. As with Confucian and Buddhist scriptures, the Bible is read in a manner exemplified by the maxim, "Read the text one hundred times, and its meaning will come to you of its own accord." As a child, I was forced to read and memorize *Analects*. The idea is that repeated readings will bring about awakening or salvation, but the act of reading itself is granted primacy over the awakening. This tradition has influenced the way Korean Christians read the Bible. Reading the Bible uncritically and by memory is itself a blessing.

This attitude of the Korean church was also shaped by early missionaries. Many of the first American missionaries to Korea were fundamentalists. Certainly they did not use historical criticism at the time. And in fact, their first and foremost concern was Christian mission. Above all, they took interest in how to propagate Christianity in a way that did not conflict with state power. Their basic premise was the separation of church and state. Since the last years of the Joseon Dynasty,[2] they taught that Korean Christians should be loyal to the state and that faith should not interfere with political or social problems. They taught Christianity in the form of simplified doctrines and used the Bible as a prooftext for these doctrines. The Bible simply confirmed the doctrines they taught.

However, the weakness of this approach became clear in the March First Movement.[3] It was revealed that many Korean Christians, deep down, did not accept teachings that advocated a separation of church and state or prohibited interference with social issues.

---

2. The Joseon Dynasty started in 1392 and ended in 1910. The first missionary of Protestant Christianity came to Joseon in 1884. The Catholic mission in Korea started much earlier. The first Catholic priest sent to Korea, Zhou Wenmo, was Chinese and entered the country in 1795.

3. The March First Movement was a nonviolent independence movement that started on March 1, 1919. Participants waved the Korean national flag shouting, "*Daehan dongnip mansae!*" ("Long live the Korean independence!"). It was the biggest national movement in Korea under Japanese colonial rule and the first large-scale independence movement that took place in a colony of victorious nations from the First World War.

Another major influence on the Korean church's understanding of the Bible was the revivalist movement. After the March First Movement failed, the Korean church moved in the direction of cultivating an inner spirituality. A great Bible study movement swept the country, and you could hear Christians shouting, "Bible! Bible!" everywhere. But the Bible played a small part in the sermons of the revivalist preachers. I myself attended many revivalist meetings and remember what they preached in a theatrical manner: a few doctrines as the frame for whatever they wanted to say. In terms of content, Confucian ethics were repeated, and the pathos was shamanistic. Certainly, dualism served an important function here. Whether the preachers preached the separation of church and state or humiliating ethics, there was an underlying dualism.

The doctrine of verbal plenary inspiration dominated the Korean church's understanding of the Bible. It claims that we must believe the Bible literally because every letter or stroke of it was inspired by God. This theory is directly related to biblical inerrancy. It didn't start in Korea, but it was a powerful tool that leaders in the Catholic church wielded and possessed. The pope monopolized the right to interpret the Bible and denied the same right to the laity. Church leaders asserted that the Bible itself was inspired by God, and this was, of course, intended to protect the authority of the Bible—and, more importantly, the authority of the interpreter. The word *inspired* here applies to the interpretive act; the interpreting act by the person with the interpretive right is inspired. Therefore, whatever interpretation is produced claims total authority and leaves no room for criticism. In Korea, biblical inerrancy was taken a step further. It was asserted that every *iota* and stroke in the Bible was dictated by the Holy Spirit, and therefore the Bible was to be believed literally as it was written. But in reality each denomination interpreted the Bible as it pleased, according to its own doctrines. As a result, ignorance of the Bible was rampant. For example, the Korean church set Paul up as the standard and made Romans and Galatians a hermeneutical key for interpreting the entire Bible, including the Synoptic Gospels. The gospels were read in a way that merely confirmed doctrinally formulated Christology. However, a closer reading of the Synoptic Gospels reveals problems with this approach. Comparing the Synoptic Gospels immediately reveals discrepancies. But since digging these out creates serious problems, the Korean church maneuvered around these difficulties and emphasized even more verbal plenary inspiration.

The same applies to the Old Testament. For instance, the Pentateuch has many problems. But the Korean church is unwilling to acknowledge the Documentary Hypothesis[4] and puts forward the verbal plenary inspiration theory. Let me emphasize again that the primary purpose of upholding this theory was to protect the right to interpret. In Catholicism, the pope had the right, and in Protestantism each denomination had the right. And if a new denomination branches off, the doctrine made by the denomination's founder takes the seat of the pope.

In the Korean church, the Presbyterian church stubbornly maintained its authority. It was Rev. Kim Jae-jun who finally stood up against it. He did not see anything new but could have a new perception when he became a little distant from church authority. For example, people like Han Gyeong-jik and Song Chang-geun studied in the United States at around the same time as Rev. Kim Jae-jun.[5] But when they returned to Korea, those who joined the mainstream became prisoners of church authority. Rev. Kim Jae-jun failed to join the mainstream and remained on the periphery. So he was able to say the right things freely. Human beings are all limited, and so our outlook is shaped by where we are situated. After returning from studying abroad, Rev. Kim Jae-jun worked briefly as a minister for a commercial school and was driven out to Jiandao. That is to say, he suffered harsh treatment by church authority and was pushed out to the margins. This created an opportunity for him to speak the truth. Rev. Kim cried out less for the freedom of biblical interpretation than the freedom of science, which meant freedom from church authority. Every reasonable person knew that the Pentateuch was not written by Moses. In the Pentateuch you read about Moses's death and his funeral, so it is nonsense to say that

---

4. Here, the editor of the original Korean text gives an in-text note to say, "The Document Hypothesis is the theory that the five books known to have been written by Moses are not in fact his works but later redactions of documents from various traditions, which include P, E, J and D and contain different contents and thoughts."

5. Han Gyeong-jik (1902–2000) was a Presbyterian minister who exerted great influence on Protestant Christianity and the culture and education of Korea. He was a conservative Christian leader who contributed to the remarkable numerical growth of Protestant churches in Korea from the liberation of Korea in 1945 through the 1980s. Song Chang-geun (1898–1950/51) was a Presbyterian minister who participated in and was persecuted for the movement of Korean independence from Japanese colonial rule. Later, in 1938, he became a collaborator for Japan. He was critical of legalistic faith and advocated internal, inspirational, and transformative faith. He cared for orphans in the red-light district of Busan.

Moses was the author. Anyone could say that much, but no one dared. Why? It wasn't because they didn't know, but because they wouldn't challenge the mainline church.

Q: During this time, church authority was visible and played a prominent role. But now, as with the Presbyterian church, individual congregations have a degree of independence. Still, when it comes to biblical interpretation, they are not free from traditional understandings. Isn't it possible that something else other than church authority is at work?

A: Absolutely, it's church authority. Korean Christians would not dare read the Bible beyond the doctrines taught by church authority. Since the Bible is our story, we have to be honest about where we currently stand. But we have not done that yet. The practice of reading the Bible is overpowered by church authority that tells you to read and believe doctrines. Even if they find the answers to their questions in the Bible, reading the Bible means nothing more than confirming the doctrines. Doctrines are extracted from the Bible, but the criteria for the extraction comes from a particular period of time, mixed with other motivations. Why should we be subordinate to such doctrines? The Bible consists mainly of stories and was written for over a thousand years. How could you possibly turn it into a timeless book of doctrines?

If we had a direct encounter with the Bible beyond the church authority, we would have already discovered its unique content. We would have discovered minjung facts in the Bible. For the core of the Bible is the minjung event, and we were standing right at the site of the minjung's real life!

2.2. The Unity of the Bible and Its Minjung Theological Meaning

Q: Then let's discuss the topic of the unity of the Bible. Do you see any unity in the Bible? If so, what could be its minjung theological meaning?

A: While studying in Germany, I was in great admiration of Bultmann. I read his thesis, "What Does the Old Testament Mean to Us?," and his conclusion was "It means nothing." He thought lightly of the Old Testament as secondary material for understanding the New Testament. So following his view, I didn't study the Old Testament. It was Bultmann's position that the Old Testament deserved our attention with reference only to Jesus Christ and that we didn't have to worry about Judaism or the history of the Jewish people. But Bultmann says that there is an unbridgeable gap between the historical Jesus and the Christ of faith. He says, "The preacher of the kingdom of God became the content of the preaching in the Christian church."[6] According to Bultmann, although the New Testament says that Jesus is the very Christ, the event of the historical Jesus and the Christ confession are two different things that have no relation with each other. Here, Bultmann seems to contradict himself when, with respect to Jesus Christ, he takes seriously the New Testament and thinks lightly of the Old Testament. For in order for him to be consistent, he has to recognize the significance of the Old Testament at least to the extent that is relevant to his claim.

At a conference on Bultmann, I heard a presentation by a New Testament scholar, Herbert Braun. He combed through the whole New Testament to identify representative passages in four categories: Christology, soteriology, ecclesiology, and pneumatology. He argued that there was no continuity or unity in any of them. In the end, he concluded, "Before God you are a possibility!" (*Vor Gott du darfst, du kannst*).[7] At that moment, I asked a question: "You teach at state universities and so can make a living with such ambiguous words. But we are living in the middle of a pluralistic religious setting and cannot afford to respond with ambiguity. We must have a definite answer. We must make a decision. As for such words as you have just uttered, Confucianism, Buddhism and *Daodejing* can say them very easily." That evening, after the conference, several scholars including Ernst Käsemann and Günther Bornkamm gathered around Braun and asked him to answer my question. At Bornkamm's request, Käsemann joined in and offered his critique. When the young people around joined, Braun lost his temper. Even in that situation, I asked him, "Then can you deliver to people of other religions a Christian sermon of evangelism?" He was reluctant to answer. Bornkamm urged him saying that it was an important question, and after a while he said, "Preaching a sermon of evangelism? I don't know but I can preach" (*Missionspredigt? Ich weiß nicht, aber ich kann predigen*). This was an important remark. There is a difference between evangelistic preaching and preaching as such. These words have long since remained in my memory, and I think he was being

---

6. Here I translate Ahn's direct quotation of what Bultmann said, but whether Ahn is quoting him verbatim in the first place is not certain. The same assessment applies to many of Ahn's direct quotations in this book.

7. Literally, this German sentence means, "Before God you are allowed to, you can!"

conscientious. Anyway, Braun's conclusion was that there was no unity at all in the Bible as a whole.

Here we need to reflect on what it means to inquire about the unity of the Bible. I suppose Bultmann would say that what matters is not whether or not there is unity in the Bible, but whether or not the Bible requires us to make a decision. It's an easy step from finding unity to systemizing the Bible. After all, the important question is what kind of unity is at stake here and why. Doesn't what we call doctrine come from what someone perceived as unity in their own judgment? When we are looking for unity, we have to be very cautious. Finding unity runs the risk of leading to systemization, organization, or unification. The Bible itself is a record of life that contains rich diversity. And if we make it monolithic by means of a certain doctrinal system, the Bible loses its vitality as a record of life. It is like capturing something living in a still frame.

If the unity we're talking about is not unity in this sense, but a certain tradition in the Bible, it is possible to see it. As Braun said, we are free to act before God. To use Bultmann's language, we can make a "decision" before God. His claim, "theology is anthropology," means that theology deals with the Bible as a record of life. The history of humanity is very long and diverse, and so is the history of the Bible. And just as our lives are complex and filled with contradictions, so the Bible has in it many contradictions that defy logical resolution. All the same, just as there is consistency in life, so there is in the Bible a wide flowing current. In this sense, we can point to one steady stream that runs through both the Old and New Testaments.

What consistency does minjung theology see in the Bible? When I speak of the Bible, I do not say "In the beginning God said" but "In the beginning an event took place." Take the exodus for example. First, there was the event of persecution by the powerful pharaoh, and then the event of the Hebrews' resistance and escape. The Hebrews suffered inhumane treatment and were groaning under the oppression of the powerful Egyptians. Finally they escaped. Similar events take place throughout the New Testament. In looking at this matter, Norman Gottwald's hypothesis on the revolution model of ancient Israelite society or George Pixley's perspective in *God's Kingdom* is very helpful.[8] After the Hebrews escaped

---

8. Norman Gottwald, *The Tribes of Yahweh: A Sociology of the Religion of Liberated Israel, 1250–1050 BCE*, Biblical Seminar 66 (Sheffield: Sheffield Academic, 1999);

Egypt, a monarchy was in place where those in power made people serfs in order to rule and exploit them. The oppressed minjung rebelled and connected with the Hebrews from Egypt to form amphictyony under the ideology of "God only" (mono-Yahwism). Here, mono-Yahwism indicates the position that, in addition to lifting up God above God's counterparts in the competing religions, rejects the human desire for taking the seat of God. Even though scholars in religious history view mono-Yahwism as the proclamation of the supremacy of one religion over other religions, the faith of "Yahweh only" expressed the notion that human beings must not absolutize themselves with power over others. The faith of mono-Yahwism and the event of having escaped from unjust rule are two sides of the same coin. I would like to highlight this as very important. The Yahweh faith of the amphictyony (what is called the twelve-tribe alliance) in ancient Israel was, I think, never purely religious and otherworldly, but contextually specific to concrete situations and events in life.

The system of this amphictyony lasted for about two hundred years until the Davidic dynasty, when things started to take a wrong turn. That is to say, another event happened. Saul before David was not much of an absolute monarch. With David, the monarchy was firmly established, and mono-Yahwism practically disintegrated. He virtually crushed mono-Yahwism by making Jerusalem the royal city, building palaces there, and enshrining the ark of covenant. The temple built by Solomon, the most corrupted king, functioned as a prison that incarcerated Yahweh. Here, Yahweh was degraded by the ideology of the Davidic dynasty. With the establishment of the Davidic dynasty, the history of the ancient Israel ended. It was the end of mono-Yahwism. Now the age of the prophets began.

2.3. Jesus—the Peak of the Prophetic Tradition That Maintained Mono-Yahwism

There were true and false prophets, but it was prophets such as Elijah, Isaiah, Amos, and Jeremiah that constituted the mainstream group. An important representative of this group was Amos. The mainstream prophets tried to restore the Yahweh faith debased by the royal power. Their faith in Yahweh was inseparable from the Hebrew social consciousness.

George V. Pixley, *God's Kingdom: A Guide for Biblical Study*, trans. Donald D. Walsh (Maryknoll, NY: Orbis Books, 1981).

The measure of a prophet, I think, lies in the power of the Hebrew social consciousness he or she had. According to this criterion, Jeremiah and Isaiah were fairly weak, and Amos was indeed the prophet of prophets. For example, Elijah defiantly stood up and cried out that God kept hidden seven thousand people who had not bowed down to Baal. These seven thousand belonged to the tradition that runs throughout the Bible. People like them preserved the laws of Deuteronomy and Leviticus, which handed down the commandments for the poor and oppressed. Although partly distorted by historians of the Davidic dynasty, the tradition that strove to preserve mono-Yahwism continued all the way through.

A similar understanding can be seen in Genesis. In my interpretation of the story of the tree of the knowledge of good and evil, privatizing the public was the sin and the beginning of the fall of humankind. The pattern continues in the stories of the Tower of Babel and of Cain and Abel, though in a considerably weakened form.

I think that the tradition of the prophets who preserved mono-Yahwism ran through the genealogy of Hasidim, the Essenes, and John the Baptist to reach Jesus. When we make a distinction between Judah and Israel, Galilee belonged to Israel geographically. Spiritually, it was inseparable from the Yahweh faith of ancient Israel. At the time of Jesus, Galilee was a region where the minjung lived, and Jerusalem was the region where, since the time of David, the wealthy had abducted God and swindled the minjung in collusion with the corrupted regime. It was in Galilee that Jesus first appeared and announced, "The kingdom of God has come!"

Jesus said nothing new about God—nothing at all indeed. But his life and actions were an expression of faith in God. I think Jesus restored the mono-Yahwism faith in its original sense. It showed itself in his life together with the Galilean minjung. He took Galilee seriously, living together with the Galilean minjung. He designated Galilee as the place to meet his disciples after his resurrection. These are things we can only correctly understand in terms of the mono-Yahwism tradition. In my view, the words in Mark 10:42, "among the Gentiles those whom they recognize as their rulers lord it over them, and their great ones are tyrants over them," are an important piece of evidence that Jesus denied a monarchic system. Another important reference is that Jesus rejected the view of Christ as coming from Davidic ancestry, which Mark first mentions. "If the coming messiah is the son of David, how could David have called him Lord?" (Mark 12:35–37). These words are very important. In this connection, Jesus going to Jerusalem was inevitable. You don't need to say something vague as Bultmann did. Jesus spent the last days of his life in Jerusalem with a definite purpose. Unlike the Essenes who wept for the Jerusalem temple, Jesus acted in whatever way suited him for the termination of the system that Jerusalem stood for. The Jerusalem built by David and the temple must end! This is the meaning of the last act of Jesus. We have to look at Jerusalem and Galilee from this perspective. After all, mono-Yahwism is embodied again in the days of Jesus. After Jesus, mono-Yahwism developed under the leadership of the Galilean minjung, who were inextricably linked with the faith of "Jesus Christ only" and the social liberation of the minjung. For at least two hundred years, until Christianity became the state religion of the Roman Empire, the Hebrews of ancient Israel appeared in history again. In this regard, I think we can speak of the unity between the Old and New Testaments.

Q: In one of your books I read your analysis of the antithesis between Galilee and Jerusalem, which looks into political history and socioeconomic history. The social relation between the Galilean minjung and the Jerusalem authorities was both political (rulers and subjects) and economic (exploiters and exploited). Therefore, with respect to the Galilean minjung, Jesus opposed the power of the political elites as well as socioeconomic exploitation. Some Old Testament scholars such as Gottwald employ a socioeconomic and historical method. They suggest that the mono-Yahwism faith began with the exodus, continued through the times of amphictyony and the judges, and disintegrated during the monarchy. They further propose that an uninterrupted series of movements arose to recover the ideology and the social system of the amphictyony. These movements were motivated by both political and socioeconomic visions, the latter recovering the egalitarian ways of production of the past. Earlier, you discussed mono-Yahwism with a political focus, but I suppose you also included a socioeconomic meaning in it, right?

A: That was certainly implied. Back in those days, too, power and economics were not separated. They are two sides of the same coin.

Q: Allow me to return to a previous point. Earlier you said that the unity of the Bible should not be pursued under the assumption of a certain doctrinal formula. How should we evaluate tools that biblical studies have employed so far, such as the formula of promise and fulfillment or typological interpretation? The names Old Testament (old promise) and New Testament (new promise) themselves imply theological assumptions.

A: Well, the formula of promise and fulfillment is not viable. I have no interest in reading the Bible through such concepts as promise and fulfillment or redemptive history. I don't accept the view that the Christ event was given in the abstract in the Old Testament as a promise to be fulfilled by the arrival of Jesus. The Christ event did not take place once two thousand years ago. It also occurred in the Exodus, the amphictyony of ancient Israel, the work of the prophets, and in Palestine during the time of Jesus. It is taking place now, too. I do not see it as a unique event that occurs once. The Christ event continues in the flow of history like a current of volcanic lava constantly erupting. Clearly, it had a decisive eruption in the Jesus event and therefore has great significance for our faith.

2.4. The Ideological Nature of Traditional Biblical Hermeneutics

Q: What are the hermeneutical contributions and limitations of historical criticism in Western theology?

A: Historical criticism is a very broad term for redaction criticism, form criticism, source criticism, and so on. Textual criticism is a method that was used everywhere for ancient documents. We do not have the autographs but only copies of ancient documents. There are many differences among these copies, and it has to be established which of them is closest to the original. And there is often lack of clarity due to lacunae and incomplete letters. So efforts have been made to reconstruct the original text. Textual criticism is not done only in biblical studies. But we can say it has been done most thoroughly in biblical studies. It was motivated by scholarly interests and religious fervor linked with the belief that the Bible is the Word of God.

In using the term historical criticism, the emphasis is placed on *historical*. A recent critique is that historical criticism is not entirely objective but rather involves the context of the critic. Even though it takes a historical orientation and a critical approach, it is not a neutral or objective methodology since criticism naturally involves the critic's standpoint and value judgments. There used to be the tendency to put blind trust in the social sciences as an objective discipline. There was a similar tendency with historical criticism. But that is no longer the case now. There are diverse methods under the name of historical criticism. However, a majority of them function as a way of justifying the basic premise set forth by the critic's subjective view. For example, consider the history of religions, which stemmed from historical criticism. Scholars in this area viewed the Bible as religious literature. They defined the linguistic expressions and concepts in the Bible under the assumption that religious language differs from the general language. By doing so, they were trying to discover the world that lies behind the biblical texts. But their problem was that the premise of viewing the Bible exclusively as religious literature made them look for the world picture in religions alone. They looked into Greek religions and the religions of the Middle East, Iran, Iraq, Babylon, Egypt, and so on. The research was fairly comprehensive.

Form criticism advanced beyond the history of religions approach. Form criticism classified units of biblical texts into different forms such as parables, epistles, sayings, and legends to identify what they had in common. It was the form itself, rather than its content, that mattered to scholars of form criticism. A prime example is apophthegma, a Greek literary genre that Bultmann used in his analysis. He perceived a story of a Jesus event in the form of apophthegma. Since he attributed importance to the words of Jesus, the meaning of the event itself became diluted. When this happens, the study of the Bible becomes estranged from its original meaning. After identifying certain forms, scholars debated which texts fit in these forms, forgetting that they came out of life itself.[9] They emphasized the words of Jesus and maintained that the church transmitted these words. But they did not inquire into the church's social status, class, or interests. They only viewed the church as a religious entity. That is, they upheld the church as a religious body but ignored the church as a sociological group.

Another step forward was redaction criticism. Though based on the achievements of form criticism, redaction criticism attempted to take a holistic view of biblical texts. Redaction critics examined the theological motives and intentions of the gospel writers. Yet, they do not give a clear answer to the question of whether the redactor was an individual or the church. For they only ask about the theology of Luke or Matthew without accounting for their social implications. Recently, biblical hermeneutics informed by sociological insights have emerged. This approach draws on form criticism and redaction criticism and complements these with

---

9. According to the editor of the original Korean text, Ahn here discusses in detail how form critics distorted the meaning of Jesus's disciples eating ears of wheat. The material was omitted because it was previously discussed in Part 1, Chapter 1, Section 5, "Theology of Event and Theology for Theology."

a sociological perspective. Gerd Theißen is the leading figure of this approach. Concerning the church, he does not speak of the church as a simple and unified entity but points out that there were several groups in the church. One of them was that of wandering preachers (*Wandercharismatiker*), who, following the radical teachings of Jesus, abandoned their homes and everything else to spread the gospel wandering from village to village. In the past, teachings of this nature were only understood as eschatological demands, but it is Theißen's understanding that Jesus demanded that they be followed literally in everyday life. He believes there were people who practiced them and that it was they who transmitted the teachings in question. In his understanding, the transmission of the radical teachings was possible because the transmitters really lived out the teachings.

The sociological approach became more thorough in what is commonly called material interpretation (*materialistische Auslegung*). It is an open question how to define material, but anyway this method is a product of Karl Marx's influences. Teilhard de Chardin thought that in the beginning God created the material world and thereby created the possibility of development in the world and human history. Also, Fernando Belo, a lay believer, interpreted the Gospel of Mark by means of a material methodology. Interpreting the Bible from a material perspective is less urgent for us Easterners. However, it is a very important task in German-centered circles of Western theology. For because they have a tendency to see everything ideally, an emphasis on material realities is radically different.

Thus far, I briefly surveyed the historical-critical method of interpretation. We must not overlook the fact that each interpretation is influenced by the ideological background of the interpreter. Without exception, the historical-critical method justifies the interpreter's own point of view and is not the exclusive way to objective truth. Here, we begin to feel skepticism. Do we necessarily have to follow in the steps of Western scholars? But we Korean theologians have already learned the method and so cannot help but work through it to overcome it. However, we have to consider whether we will pass this method onto the laity.

Q: You said that historical criticism is not an objective tool, but that the ideology of each age underlies it. But when it comes to form criticism and redaction criticism, isn't it the case that they are ideologically neutral in themselves? For example, the Japanese scholar Tagawa Kenzo uses redaction criticism for considerably minjung-oriented interpretations, whereas someone else uses the same method for right-wing interpretations.

A: No. Every method has an ideology. The historical-critical method as such is not an objective tool. The word *historical* itself means looking at the history of the given time period from a certain standpoint. The word *critical* means criticizing on someone's side. Therefore, it is not an objective tool, but there is a tendency to view it in that way. In historical criticism both optimism and dogma are involved. Historical criticism started as the effort to be objective and neutral. But what can ever be neutral in this world? For the claim to neutrality itself is taking a side. Neutrality has never been and will never be. It is impossible. We don't set out with partiality (*Parteilichkeit*), but in the end we cannot keep ourselves from taking sides.

This Bultmann knew, too. Trying to overcome historicism, he declared loud and clear, "Being part of history, we can never objectify history."

I am sidetracking a little bit, but I am of the opinion that historical criticism holds less significance for Easterners than for Westerners. The Eastern way of reading is quite different. There were times when the thinking of scholars in Confucianism and Buddhism came across to me as unorganized and unscientific. But later I came to a better judgment. At around the same time that I started Korea Theological Study Institute, Professor Yi Gi-yeong started Buddhist Study Institute in the same building. We were on close terms and sometimes talked about the Bible or Buddhist scriptures. On one occasion, I gave Professor Yi a passage from the Gospel of John, saying, "Please try interpreting this." His reading was not historical-critical. So I gave him an explanation from the historical-critical framework. But he never seemed to feel a need for this approach.

Let me give you another example, one from the days when I was under the influences of Mr. Yu Yeong-mo.[10] In contrast to a historical-critical interpretation, his understanding of the Gospel of John was more subjective. Concerning the verse, "I am the way and the truth" (John 14:6), he said that "I" referred to himself, that is, Mr. Yu himself. I said, "Sir, even

---

10. Yu Yeong-mo (1890–1981) was an educator, religious philosopher, and comparative religionist. He is regarded for developing a unique synthesis of Christianity, Buddhism, Confucianism, and Daoism. Influenced by Tolstoy, he was a non-orthodox Christian. He identified himself with the nonchurch movement. He influenced Ham Seok-heon and Kim Gyo-shin (1901–1945), a renowned historian.

if such an interpretation could be acceptable, the text explicitly refers to Jesus himself. Don't we have to make this distinction in the first place?" He responded, "I am a person who interprets the Bible now before an impending death." With this response, he stopped me from saying anything more. He meant, "I am not joking. I don't need historical criticism." So I thought to myself, "Aha! He has no need of it!" The same was true of Mr. Ham Seok-heon. I talked with him about a Bible passage, "Sir, these are not the words of Jesus. They were made up according to the need of the church." Mr. Ham responded, "Could it have been really the case? Do we really have to think so?" Then I realized, "He, too, has no need of it!" So I came to think carefully about why we needed historical criticism. The conclusion is that we use historical criticism because we have been forcibly taught Western methods. Otherwise it may be possible to develop non-Western hermeneutics. The West needed that particular method. With the rise of the Enlightenment, a rational interpretation of the Bible based on reason became very important. But it's different for us. Words such as *do* (way) and *hak* (learning) do not correspond to the Western science (*Wissenschaft*). *Hak* is always *hak* and not *Wissenschaft*. Therefore, using the historical-critical method is an unnatural thing for Easterners to do. We do it because we have no other choice when we try to connect with the traditions of the Western science. But if we look at our problems with our own eyes, there is no need to adopt the method. That is not the only way!

2.5. Tension between Text and Context

Q: The issue of scholarly methods is closely related with the development of modern science and historiography in the West. For this reason, it is an extraordinarily complex matter. The ideological nature of Western methodologies warrants closer inspection. Recently, Latin American liberation theology and North American black theology have helped bring about new approaches to biblical hermeneutics. A central feature is starting with the context of the interpreter. Please tell us about the hermeneutical contributions and problems of this approach.

A: Let me first talk about something tangentially related to that topic. When I was in Germany, I met Heinz Eduard Tödt and then Günter Brakelmann—both were Christian social ethicists. Later I became close with Moltmann, a systematic theologian. Tödt and Moltmann opposed one another hermeneutically and criticized each other at every opportunity. Tödt said that the method of proceeding *from the text to the context* didn't work because the former was too narrow compared to the latter. As a result, he changed his field of study from biblical studies to social ethics in order to move from context to text. As a biblical scholar, he received his degree under Bornkamm with an important and well-received study on the Son of Man. In spite of being an important New Testament scholar, he changed his area of study in order to begin with the context. Brakelmann thought in the same way as Tödt. However, Moltmann said that, despite claiming to move from context to text, Tödt and Brakelmann never did so. They began with the context, but never fully came to a sufficient analysis of the text. Meanwhile, Tödt derided Moltmann saying, "Moltmann's text is dogma. There is a genealogy of dogma in systematic theology, isn't there? He is imprisoned in that framework and cannot escape." Some time ago, when Moltmann came to Korea, he repeated the same criticism: "When did Tödt ever engage the text?" So I said to him, "They say you are held captive by dogma and so can never address the context, the site of real life. I agree with them. Hearing what you say feels like scratching the shoe while feeling an itch in the foot."

This kind of conflict is not new with liberation theology or black theology. From antiquity to the Medieval Age, allegorical interpretation was mainstream, wasn't it? The allegorical method employed symbolic language and was therefore useful during times of persecution. Later when the church became the supreme authority and monopolized the right to interpret the Bible, this method became a weapon to render the laity powerless. No matter how the priest interpreted the Bible, he could say, "This is an allegorical interpretation. It contains a spiritual meaning that you do not know." In other words, they used symbolic language to advance their own agendas on the Bible. Martin Luther emphasized *sola scriptura*, believed that anyone could read the Bible, and rejected the allegorical method. The belief that anyone that can read can understand the Bible played a significant role in liberating Christians from church authority. Luther said that anyone can interpret the Bible and that the right to interpret the Bible is granted to everyone—not just the privileged few. But is it true that "the meaning of the Bible is self-evidently revealed by its letters?" No. We may think we read the Bible with an open mind and take the words of the Bible as they are. But that is not what really happens. We interpret the Bible based on preconceived beliefs and assumptions. The Bible is called a sacred text, but in reality, the doctrinal assumptions I already possess function as the sacred text. This, in turn, shapes my criterion for selecting certain passages from the Bible over others. Here, it would be helpful to think about the expression "from the context to the text." Your Christology comes from outside the Bible, that is, from the doctrines or inclination of your church. Therefore, when it is considered in relation to the Bible, it is not the text but the context, right? Merely putting this context into the Bible and pulling it back out, you mistake it for the words of the Bible, namely, the text. Going one step further, we can say this: "'From the context to the text' is nothing new at all. In fact, it is correct to say that the allegorical interpretation and Luther's approach took this path. They also set out from the context (*Sitz im Leben*) as the church or the context as the doctrines and proceeded to the text of the Bible. However, we can say conversely, 'My Christology, Jesus Christ as I know him, I have received from the text, and therefore I have come from the text to the context.'" This is a classic example that illustrates what came first: the chicken or the egg?

Concerning the question of the text and context, some people speak of the difference between Rev. Suh Nam-dong and me. They say that Rev. Suh moves from context to text, whereas I begin from text to context. Recently, some German theologians have sent me a list of questions on minjung theology and made the same observation about Rev. Suh and me. When Rev. Suh was still alive, we promised not to speak of our differences for the time being. We agreed that now was the time to talk about our commonalities, rather than talk about our differences. We didn't want to weaken the strength of our concerted efforts. Now I regret that we didn't discuss our differences and criticize what deserved criticizing or clarify what needed clarifying.

Professor Song Ki-deuk recently wrote an essay on Rev. Suh's minjung theology in the *Hanshin Daehak Hakbo* (Hanshinn University Newspaper). He said, "The object of minjung theology is not Jesus but minjung." If Rev. Suh had said the same thing, it would be one of the differences between him and me. At an earlier occasion, Professor Song said that, even though both Rev. Suh and I did minjung theology, I stressed theology while Rev. Suh stressed minjung. Rev. Suh said at a meeting one day, "Why should the Bible be the text? Why not us?" His question suggested that we ourselves were the text and that the Bible was in fact the context. Now I believe the time has come for me to clarify my position on this question. Where do I stand now? I am concentrating my attention on the Bible for the time being. My work is grounded in the Western theology in the historical-critical tradition, and so I study the Bible, if only to break away. Rev. Suh started with nonbiblical sources in the first place. But this does not mean that his analysis of legends and folktales was done with no connections to biblical texts. Although he did not cite biblical texts, his perspective was deeply influenced by the Bible. That is to say, biblical texts informed his perspective on the minjung. Rev. Suh did not think that my reading of the Bible was separated from our context. He thought that I foregrounded context as a lens for my reading of the Bible. Rev. Suh knew this. If the question determines the answer, it is only natural that the questioner's standpoint shapes how she or he views the Bible. Minjung theology insists that it arises from the site of real life. When we fully embrace this idea, it would be no problem to say that my theology goes *from text to context*. Even if I adopted the context-to-text approach, someone might ask, "Why do you see the context in that way?" I would respond saying, "Because I know the text." Therefore, it is my conclusion that it is wrong to divide the context and text as two polarities. How can you tell the two apart? Even as we cannot objectify history while living in history, I cannot objectify the context or text when I am reading the text from my context. We see in Bultmann a pattern of thinking that separates and opposes text and context and then bridges the two with a third entity. In his thesis collection, "Contact and Contradiction" ("Anknüpfung und Widerspruch"), Bultmann addresses the possible frictions and connections between the Bible and some other entity.[11] But I think we have to renounce this kind of question as such. My own experiences tell me that the text and the context are impossible to separate. These two are a single indivisible reality. Trying to separate them, I think, is artificial. So I oppose the subject-object scheme that separates context and text.

When the Swiss theologian Fritz Buri visited Korea, we had a long conversation. He said the reason he travelled to Korea and Japan was to see if there was any solution in the East to overcome the subject-object dichotomy. I said to him, "We don't have a clear distinction between the subject and the object as you do. Western influences have made us make the distinction, but it was not the case in the past. In the East, *hak* (learning) does not objectify things in that manner. The distinction between text and context does not exist in the East. 'You' and 'I' are not sharply differentiated as it is in the West. More important than the singular 'I' is the collective 'we.' Perhaps our family system is responsible for that. In the same way, in the everyday language, it is not subject or object

---

11. Rudolf Bultmann, "Anknüpfung und Widerspruch: Zur Frage nach der Anknüpfung der neutestamentlichen Verkündigung an die natürliche Theologie der Stoa, die hellenistischen Mysterienreligionen und die Gnosis," *TZ* 2 (1946): 401–18.

but the verb that matters. We do not say, 'I love you' but simply, 'Love,' and then it is understood. Germans say, 'I come out of your house and go to my house,' but we say, 'Go.' It is not necessary to make the subject and object explicit. However, the dichotomy became a bigger issue after Western influences. Dividing context and text into two separate entities and debating which comes first is a Western question, not ours." That is what I said to him.

Q: You criticize separating text and context as coming from a Western dichotomy in contrast to Eastern ways of thinking. If we take one step further, is it possible that the Bible itself is not purely a text but a state of fusion in which the context and the text are indivisibly one? Take for example Jesus's actions. They are not distinguishable from their situations. And to use your language, they took place as a single *event*. With the Old Testament, too, the history and law of covenant are not two but one. In this regard, even if we look at the text only, we cannot speak of the text as separated from the context. Making this distinction seems to stem from a misunderstanding of the text.

On the other hand, however, it seems worthwhile to pay attention to the context-to-text method. Historically, text-to-context was upheld as the orthodox position until the modern age. Here, the context-to-text method served as an iconoclastic function against traditional biblical hermeneutics. This contributed to a new way of reading the Bible. When we look at the Korean church, however, text-to-context is still maintained as the orthodox position. For this reason, in the Korean church, the context-to-text method is a new approach to biblical interpretation. So I think it worthwhile to emphasize this method for its enlightening and iconoclastic function. Although Western theology is said to have already addressed the question of the text and context, the context that Western theology assumes seems to differ from what is assumed in the Third World. In our case, simply taking up the context-to-text method is not sufficient to solve our problems. So we are trying to answer other questions such as, "What is the nature of the context?," "Whose life setting?," "In which life setting did Jesus live?," and "At which life site is the event taking place?" For this reason, I believe we need to lift up the context-to-text method in our own church situation in our own way.

A: That's right. Biblical hermeneutics of the Third World is qualitatively different from that of Western theology. Biblical hermeneutics of minjung theology and liberation theology involve a fundamental question that cannot be incorporated in its entirety into the text-context framework of Western theology. The statement that minjung theology did not begin in an armchair means that it began on the site of real life. This site is neither a religious site nor the inside of the church. The context minjung theology looks into is the very life and context of the minjung. At a theological symposium, Professor Jeong Jin-hong said that minjung theology had a strong *pathos*, and this is only natural. Minjung theology is all about pathos. It is never about objective science. It is a struggle. It is a fight for overcoming something on the site of history. Therefore, the deep pathos of minjung theology is to be expected. The context minjung theology speaks of is different from Western theology. And employing the expression, "the convergence of two stories," Rev. Suh Nam-dong speaks of the encounter between the minjung tradition in Korean history and in the Bible. But I don't intend to pull the minjung event into the text—an apparently unnecessary move. The events of the Bible are already taking place in the minjung events. We only need to testify to them.

2.6. What Is the Context of Minjung Theology?

A: That's right. They are impossible to separate. For example, there is a debate on if the Gospel of Mark was written before or after the Jewish War. But I believe that the *ochlos* appeared while the Palestine minjung were wandering after the war. Therefore, there was no separation between the life setting of Jesus's minjung and that of the gospel writer. In other words, Mark was now writing his own stories, and they were at the same time Jesus's stories. In a different kind of life setting, Mark would not have been able to write what he wrote about Jesus. Mark's own life situation helped him see Jesus's life situation accurately. The same applies to us. Our life setting enables us to see clearly the life setting of the text. Without one, you cannot see the other.

Q: Is it accurate, then, to identify Jesus's life setting with that of today's minjung?

A: I don't want to use the word *identify*. As a minjung theologian, I focus my main attention on interpreting the Bible. But when I witness an event, I don't try to go back to the Bible. So reflecting on and writing about the event produces a writing on the Jesus event. But I have no conscious intention to connect the event with Jesus, although I would eventually link the two in a future scholarly work.

Q: If we adopted the position of taking the story of the minjung event to be the story of Jesus, wouldn't the canonicity of the Bible break down?

A: It's a question of whether the Bible is the only canon, right? When Rev. Suh Nam-dong was at his most radical, he stated emphatically, "Canonization itself is a problem. Why should the Bible alone be the canon?" This was his question. He was not happy with me going back to the Bible all the time. He freely made his own assertions without seeking agreement with the Bible. Compared to him, I am likely to come across as a biblicist or a canonist. Let me give you my opinion on this matter. What we call the canon—the sixty-six books we have of the Old and New Testaments— are these alone the truth? Are these alone the criterion of the truth? First, when we set the contents of these books aside and only consider external authority, doesn't historical criticism break down all of this authority? Next, we need to consider internal authority. The canonicity of sixty-six books of the Bible is established when you acknowledge church authority. But since I don't acknowledge this authority, I don't recognize the existence of the canon itself. Only sixty-six books became the canon not because they alone were the truth, but because church authority drew a line to that effect. It was through a long process that the list of canonical books as we know it now became fixed. Here, Athanasius played a significant role. Pope Damasus I fixed the New Testament canon at the twenty-seven books, no more or less. For example, the Syrian church still has only twenty-two canonical books. Does the Egyptian church have thirty-eight? Having twenty-seven books for the New Testament canon holds only for the Eastern and Western Churches. Until this final decision was made, Hebrews was constantly in flux, and the canonicity of James was always called into question. The same happened to Revelation, and 2–3 John were always a source of trouble. Additionally, 2 Peter, Titus, and Philemon were problematic. After a complex historical process the church authority put an end to the controversies. But later Luther excluded Revelation from the New Testament when he challenged church authority. James stayed in the canon, but Luther said its contents did not belong in the Bible. Such is the true nature of the canon, which Christians hold as an absolute.

Rev. Suh Nam-dong and I do not acknowledge the concept of the canon. For me, the external authority of the Bible is not important. All the same, we basically have to respect the history that has developed around the canon. We cannot bring this history to naught.

It is true that historical criticism has done a lot in tearing down the external authority of the canon. However, it has failed to show that the dominant ideology covered up or distorted the original meaning of the Bible.

Minjung theology is successful in this regard. It reads the Bible through the eyes of the minjung. This statement is consistent with Luther's remark that he criticizes the Bible with the Bible. From the perspective of minjung theology, the essence of the Bible lies in the minjung event. This constitutes one current that runs throughout the Old and New Testaments. Reading the Bible in reference to this current helps us to identify what the dominant ideology of each age covers up. What Westerners fail to see, namely, the minjung-centeredness of the Bible, Korean minjung theology clearly foregrounds. This is truly miraculous. I often think that minjung theology in Korea is a special gift from God. It amazes me how perfectly the perspective of the minjung aligns with the Bible. This is a gift we have acquired on the site of the Korean minjung's life. The meaning of the Bible is clarified through this perspective. It feels like the wall between the Bible and the site of our life breaks down, and a whole new vista opens up before our eyes. Even though I am pained by the distance between my own reality and that of the minjung in the Bible, I am no longer afraid when the things I hold dear break down.

Q: Regarding the question of canonicity, Rev. Suh Nam-dong mentioned "the Bible as a reference." How does that differ from your view on the matter?

A: Sure. I should address that question before going on to other ones. That Rev. Suh calls the Bible as a reference doesn't mean that the Bible is the only reference for him. He treats other materials such as the history of Korean minjung and church history as references. However, the Bible is my sole reference. I seek agreement with the Bible on every occasion. This is where I stand. Whether I read the history of Korea, see the events of the minjung, or look into the history of the Korean church, the reference I use is the Bible. That's why I am not a scholar in minjung studies but a minjung theologian. This does not mean that I am against studying or developing thoughts on the minjung with a different method. Such a work is possible from the standpoint of minjung studies, and I can discuss minjung studies with those who do that work. As a theologian, however,

I consider it my duty to make theological contributions by utilizing the Bible. However, if a certain minjung event conflicted with the Bible, I might try to explain it by means of another kind of reference. In that case, I would be doing that not as a minjung theologian but as a scholar in minjung studies. I am a minjung theologian because, whether I deal with the history of Korea, church history, or any other type of material, the Bible serves as the reference for my reflection and agreement. In this respect, Rev. Suh and I clearly differ.

Q: Then what about this case? There is a diversity of areas in theology, and it is possible to approach the question of minjung in terms of systematic theology or church history. Is this not minjung theology?

A: Any theological pursuit, whether in systematic theology or church history, is only possible when your eyes have been opened anew by the Bible. Whenever I hear a Korean systematic theologian or church historian, it worries me that their perspectives sound too Western. I come to think, "The Bible doesn't see it that way" or "Minjung traditions of the Bible do not say so."

Q: What do you think of the views advanced by Juan Luis Segundo in Latin America? He says that, although revelation is absolute, it says nothing specific about the concrete problems of our lives. Therefore, we need something to function as a bridge between our problems and the Bible as the source of absolute revelation. He also says that ideology functions as a bridge. Ideology alone helps illuminate concrete realities and thereby allows us to reflect on political and social experiences. What do you think of his claim?

2.7. The Bible Only Asks Us to Make a Decision

A: I don't like the premise that revelation is absolute. Is that really so? I am not sure. Perhaps we need to use another expression for what Segundo has in mind. This is what I know. The Bible does not give specific directives for specific situations. There is a temporal distance, and it is not really possible. It is not possible to draw behavioral or ethical guidelines directly from the Bible. On this point, I agree with Bultmann. The Bible demands that we make a decision. It does not allow us to be indifferent. It demands a response. However, it is silent about what specific actions we have to take. It is I who must decide. In what ways do we fight? What kinds of strategies and tactics do we employ? How do we protest? Looking for the answers to these questions in the Bible is a laughing matter. I am the one who must find the answers in my own real-life situation. Does this mean becoming estranged from the Bible? No, it does not. The Bible continues to require me to act with love and justice. There can be no estrangement. Let me repeat: Carrying out a labor movement in a biblical way or solving the problems of farmers in a biblical manner is nonsense. You must protect the rights and interests of laborers and farmers—the Bible says this much. But when it comes to organizing a movement for laborers or farmers, we all, Christian or not, must decide for ourselves.

For instance, suppose two people interested in organizing a labor movement are talking at the same table. One is a Marxist, the other a Christian. The two are sitting face to face. They can talk all they want with one another. Which method is the best? Is the use of violence permitted? We are not supposed to put these questions to the Bible. Making a choice about policy is up to people. In the words of the German theologian Braun, whom I mentioned earlier, "Before God you are allowed to, you can" (*Vor Gott du darfst, du kannst*). Nothing more or less than this.

Q: Segundo says exactly the same thing. You cannot look for policy programs in the Bible.

A: I haven't read Segundo, but that's what Bultmann says. Jesus doesn't propose programs.

Q: So far you have deferred giving answers about what specific strategies to use, responding as though you were not concerned. Even in the theological dimension, you have not given definitive answers on the use of strategies. But those who are doing ministry or fighting together with the minjung in the field are urgently asking for Christian guidelines.

A: Here is the deal. As I say repeatedly, I do not distance myself from these issues on purpose. I simply don't believe I have all of the answers. If anything, I think that those in the field are better positioned to come up with strategies and policies based on minjung theology than I myself could. So I am being humble in this regard. It is those who are in the field that have to do this work, but I have the feeling that they are putting it off. I don't think that theologians should monopolize the work.

2.8. The Consistent Theme Minjung Theology Sees in the Bible

Q: Lastly, please point out the essence of and the consistent theme in the Bible from the perspective of minjung theology.

A: In my view, the essence of the Bible is the event of liberation. Bible passages that minjung theology has mentioned most frequently belong to the consistent theme of the event of liberation.

Luke 4:18–19 is a passage that attracted our attention from the very beginning. Mark thought of the essence of Jesus's proclamation as the advent of the kingdom of God (Mark 1:15). But Luke understood it precisely as liberation. The word *aphesis* is used in the expressions "proclaim release to the captives" and "let the oppressed go free" (Luke 4:18). The word comes from the verb *aphiēmi* and means "to set free a slave," "to exempt from a debt," and "to forgive sin." In short, it means liberation. Verse 19 says, "to proclaim the year of the Lord's favor." This refers to the institution of jubilee. So it would be appropriate to say "the year of the Lord's favor" is the year of liberation. Jubilee is the year when you are set free through releasing prisoners, liberating slaves, and returning the extorted lands. By the way, this passage is a quotation of Isa 61:1–2. Isaiah actually reflects the historical situation when the people of Israel were released from Babylonian captivity, returned to their lost land, and built a new country. We used this passage again and again. We lifted it up like the flag of our fight for human rights at sites where many people were executed.

Making liberation central naturally led us to see in the exodus the foundation of the biblical value. (Only later did I learn that liberation theology does the same.) The significance of the exodus became all the greater for the knowledge that the exodus was the Hebrews' liberation movement. When we took "Hebrew" to be not the name of a people but the name of an oppressed class, the meaning of the escape from Egypt became clear. The exodus was precisely the event of liberation from economic exploitation and oppression by the powerful.

Also of importance is the nature of the alliance of the Canaanite tribes. As another dimension of the Hebrews' liberation event, this points to the serfs who were subject to the Canaanite monarchs and fought successfully for independence. Since they achieved this precisely through forming an alliance, the community rejected monarchy as a form of government. The claim, "There can be no human being above a human being," found expression precisely in the mono-Yahwism faith. This amphictyony in ancient Israel lasted for two hundred years.

However, this form of ancient Israel degenerated. The one who was responsible for it was no one other than David. Although Saul is called the first king, he was not yet an absolute monarch, and the foundations for an absolute monarchy were set up during David's reign. He was the enemy of ancient Israel. David joined together Israel and Judah, but the latter did not belong to ancient amphictyony. David joined these two into the nation of Israel. In order to install a centralized government, he robbed the Jebusites of their city Jerusalem, placed it under his personal rule, and built palaces there. And in order to support his royal authority, he obtained the ark of covenant, the symbol of liberation, by force and placed it in Jerusalem. By doing so, he turned Yahweh into an ideology bound to a certain place and royal power. The story culminates with Solomon, the son of his adultery, who built the temple in the style of a palace chapel subordinate to the palace and imprisoned Yahweh. Then the priestly aristocracy emerged. During the Davidic dynasty, the historians for David's royal family contaminated the traditions of Israel. The glorification of David, his covenant with Yahweh, and drawing a direct connection between the messiah, the Davidic family, and Jerusalem—these events set in motion antiminjung violence. This history influenced the New Testament, and so there remains an attempt to link Jesus to the bloodline of David. Minjung theology has been diligent to fight against this ambush in the Bible.

In addition to putting up this fight, minjung theology detects the legacy of the Hebrews in the prophets' struggles. Some prophets defended the royal power, and others absolutely denied it. But one thing was clear: they always proclaimed ancient Israel as the true meaning of Israel and therefore insisted on God's sovereignty. They fought unrighteous power and passed judgment on the exploitative forces against the poor. The legal codes they revised were important for us. Genesis, I believe, consists of folktales set in the time before the Davidic dynasty but convey interpretations of the issues since the dynasty.

Next, minjung theology has concerned itself with the history of the intertestamental period, which is not included in the Protestant canon. This interest originated in the awareness that understanding Jesus requires background knowledge of the intertestamental history. I taught a class called "The History of Jesus's Age" repeatedly, and this effort was based on an ongoing interest in political, social, and economic dimensions. The greatest benefit of this work, I believe, was that I developed an interest in the region of Galilee and uncovered the antiminjung nature of Jerusalem.

It was inevitable for minjung theology to reconfirm the importance of the Gospel of Mark in the New Testament. Not only is Mark important as the earliest gospel; it is also significant because of its minjung-centered character.

Discovering Mark had a profound influence on me personally. On the one hand, the discovery helped me to reject the perspectives of Western theology. On the other hand, and more importantly, it played a decisive role in my understanding of current minjung events.

The first words I paid renewed attention to were "the beginning of the gospel" at the opening of Mark. This phrase does not refer to the gospel as a discrete idea but to the entirety of the Jesus event—all of the minjung events in which Jesus participated.

The next passage that caught my attention was Mark 1:14. Western biblical scholars ascribed importance to Mark 1:15 as a summary of Jesus's preaching. But they dismissed verse 14 as the work of redaction. But this verse was riveting: "Now after John was arrested, Jesus came to Galilee." Why did this expression strike me like a bolt of lightning? It was our situation. At the time, the Yushin (Revitalizing Reform)[12] government was in a period of political unrest, which made me read the Bible with a sense of urgency. I read about the arrest of John the Baptist in parallel with the imprisonments that were taking place all around us. Simultaneously, we could not help but ask, "Where can we go in this situation? Is not Galilee, the scene of the arrest, the only place we can go?" And right then the words, "Jesus came to Galilee," was decisive. Galilee was the region ruled by Herod Antipas who arrested John the Baptist. Against this background, Jesus proclaimed, "The time is fulfilled, and the kingdom of God has come near; repent, and believe in the gospel!" (Mark 1:15). As I made this connection, I regretted what form and redaction criticism made us blind to. Adherents to the so-called theology of the Word analyzed the Jesus event scene by scene by appropriating the Greek literary genre of apophthegm. They contended that the event in each scene was no more than the frame (*Rahmen*). They refused to give it any more meaning than as a set up to the saying. For example, with the Sabbath controversy, Jesus and his hungry disciples are described as plucking and eating ears of wheat on the Sabbath.

---

12. See above ch. 1, n. 13.

The opponents criticized them for violating the Sabbath. In response, Jesus declared, "The Sabbath was made for humankind, and not humankind for the Sabbath" (Mark 2:27). These words are truly important. But when seen against the background of eating ears of wheat out of hunger, they do not convey a universal truth. They become a proclamation to protect those who are treated as sinners for being hungry as well as a proclamation of protest against the evil forces that degrade and exploit people.

By entering the territory of the ruler who arrested John the Baptist and proclaiming that the kingdom of God has come near, Jesus makes a declaration of war.

When I looked at the Bible from this standpoint, the notion of *ochlos* became prominent, and I began to part ways with Western biblical hermeneutics. Jesus did not preach into the thin air. He lived among and together with the minjung. In short, the gospels do not intend to develop a formal Christology; they intend to report the event of Jesus's minjung movement. Jesus and the minjung are not in a subject-object relationship. They are *we* who make the event happen together. They do not appear in a peaceful scene but at the site of minjung's life, which is like a cauldron of white hot anger—the anger of the deprived, destitute, and corruption-resisting minjung. I picture it this way: Many angry minjung set up footholds in mountain caves and are preparing for a final battle. Young men in every village are participating and come under the surveillance of the authorities. Those who wander aimlessly on the streets are stopped and interrogated. In a situation like this, Jesus moves together with the minjung—they were hungry minjung. Someone said that it was the honeymoon days of Jesus and the minjung, but they never enjoyed a bed of roses.

At last, the minjung charge into Jerusalem together with Jesus. There, the event of Jesus's execution takes place. This event constitutes not the fate of Jesus as an individual but the minjung event. If you do not join the event, you cannot comprehend its meaning.

The core of Christianity is a theology of the cross. But this theology must accurately view the cross as a political and minjung event. Then the present-ness of that event will reveal itself, enabling us to join in it. Resurrection was not experienced or recognized by those who had nothing to do with the Jesus event. This is a recognition that makes possible the experience of the present manifestation of the cross event. In the same vein, only participants in the Jesus event experience minjung events that occur in the present.

2. The Bible as the Book of Minjung

Seeing the stories of the Bible as an event opens up new angles and perspectives for reading the Bible. We have tried to understand Paul in this way. Above all, we paid attention to the "advance of the gospel" Paul mentions in the Epistle to the Philippians (1:12). We discovered this notion in the flash of light created by the meeting between Paul's imprisonment and our imprisonment. It surprised Paul that the fact of his imprisonment, not his preaching, helped to advance the gospel. Here, he is referring to the theology of event, not the Word.

The event precedes the Word. It is like "the owl of Minerva" that Hegel mentions. The event happens by day, and the owl recognizes the site of the event by night. But why do people turn the event into the Word? This is like hiding the event beneath a cotton blanket. Paul's arrest in Jerusalem and transfer to Rome was also an event. Indeed, Paul's life was full of events. Why do people exclude them from an attempt to understand Paul's thoughts? While discussing Paul's so-called prison epistles, why do they not mention the reason for his imprisonment? We are having a similar experience as Paul. We are not free to publicize the events we know and experience. So they are communicated in the form of a rumor.[13] We have to pay attention to Paul's life and think earnestly about why the cross was central to his faith. He emphasizes the cross—not Jesus's death. As a mechanism for executing political criminals, the cross represents the political event that led to the execution of Jesus.

And we continued to take interest in the question of where and how Christ's presence exists. It is our conclusion that Jesus is present in the suffering of the minjung. In this regard, the parable of the last judgment in Matt 25 and Heb 13:12–13 are two crucial texts. Hebrews says: "Jesus suffered outside the city gate in order to sanctify the people by his own blood. Let us then go to him outside the city gate and bear the abuse he endured."

Christ suffered outside of the city gate! This was the Christ I met while I endured all kinds of humiliations and pains in prison. The early Christians, like Paul, were challenged by numerous sufferings: they were put into prison, beaten, robbed of their property and the lives of their family (Heb 10:32–34). According to Heb 11:36–37, they "suffered mocking and

---

13. The Korean word Ahn uses for "rumor" is *yueonbieo*, which literally means "flowing language and flying language." It refers to a groundless and widespread rumor and usually bears a negative connotation. Here, Ahn reclaims the word and uses it in a positive way as a truth-bearing medium of minjung's communication.

flogging, and even chains and imprisonment. They were stoned to death; they were sawn in two; they were killed by the sword; they went about in skins of sheep and goats, destitute, persecuted, tormented." This was the state of suffering Paul endured, and I believe that enabled him to achieve such incredible insight on the presence of Christ.

Lastly, if you ask what then is the key to reading the Bible, I will answer, "Being on the side of the minjung!" More specifically, it is looking at everything through the perspective of the afflicted. I believe the main current of the Bible is exactly this. And I believe the liberation of those afflicted is the essential purpose of the Bible. True interpretation is only possible through participation in this event of liberation.

3
The Minjung Jesus

Q: Today I would like to ask you to do the following three things in the given order: (1) offer your critique of Western Christology, (2) examine Christology as shown in the Bible, and (3) discuss minjung Christology. Western Christology focuses on the person and work of Christ, that is, who Christ was and what he did, the latter being a soteriological question. There seems to be a one-sided emphasis on his divinity, though Jesus is said to possess both divinity and humanity. His humanity functions more like a safety net that prevents him from becoming a mythical being. Recently, this tendency has found acute expression in kerygmatic Christology. Consequently, the question of how Jesus actually lived, which is important for minjung theology, has become insignificant. So to begin, I would like to hear your thoughts on Western Christology of this nature.

A: In my judgment, the Christology that has been dominant up to this point has not developed from the conclusions of interpreting the Bible. Apologetic demand has preceded the need for conveying Christ as he appears in the Bible. Discussions of Christology have been shaped by this demand and continue to serve as the basis of Christology. This Christology produced a Christ from the Hellenistic world for those who are philosophically inclined. But it was a Christ who is foreign from the Christ of the Bible. In the Greco-Roman world, Christ was depicted in a way that demonstrated how superior and special he was. For this reason, the doctrine of the dual nature of Christ was put forward. This doctrine attributed humanity and divinity to Christ as the God-human (*Gott-Mensch*). The image of the God-human was never Christian, but a tradition common in the Greco-Roman world was placed on Jesus. Bultmann also acknowledged that this process occurred in the formation of Christology. For this reason, I wonder whether this Christology is even biblical.

This Christology persisted for so long in the Western world. It set the stage for the development of Christianity as the Greco-Roman system and worldview dominated the Western world. Now, since this system has diminished, there is no longer a place for such a Christology. Nevertheless, this Christology is still maintained to preserve the institutional church that is built upon it. Because such a Christology has less appeal, we only have the exterior of a church, which is being ignored at the real-life sites of history. I believe that there is no reason to accept and repeat this kind of Christology. But this Christology was planted in the Third World in a different environment under the sway of other religions, such as Korea, where diverse religions such as Buddhism, Confucianism, and Daoism already took deep root. And so it ended up being something very disparate and unappealing. But surprisingly, this Christology has become the basis for preaching and dogmatic theology. Earlier, I mentioned the divinity and humanity of Christ, and this notion was intended to answer the question "Who and what is Christ?" However, I don't believe this question exists in the East. Western theology drew a dividing line between God and human beings. It then struggled with the dilemma of identifying Christ as divine or human, before finally reaching the mistaken conclusion of calling him the God-human. Now it contends that denying the divinity of Christ is not Christian, but there is no such representation in the East.

3.1. The Christology of Western Theology That Must Be Overcome

Q: Western Christology has focused its attention on the personality of Christ neglecting the actual life of Christ. It understands his death in terms of the doctrine of atonement. Concerning the resurrection, it has been debated whether the resurrection was a historical fact and what it means. Can you tell us about how the doctrine of atonement understands Christ's death and resurrection?

A: First of all, Western Christology has omitted the life of Jesus, namely, his deeds and words. As Bultmann said, "Jesus preached the kingdom of God, but the church has preached Jesus is Christ." That is to say, the content of preaching has changed. Among the events of Jesus, only the death on the cross is included in Christology. The cross is defined as the event of atonement. Behind this definition lacks the Greco-Roman way of thinking—though it is not confined to Greece and Rome—the so-called legal-ritual (*juristisch-kultisch*) paradigm. The thought that sin must be punished, even vicariously, underlies the legal thinking and plays a central role in the ritual religion. Blood is a symbol of life. This is true not only of Greco-Roman society but also of religion in general. Legal and ritual thinking serves an important function in Western Christology. But we have to ask if interpreting Christ in this frame is the only way to understand him. In Christianity, even God is confined by this frame. This God is also said to punish a sinner without fail. A person who has made someone shed blood must shed blood, and a person who has killed must be killed. In the Old Testament, God appears as a God of vengeance. Therefore, Ernst Bloch says that the God of Christianity is bloodthirsty. The belief that someone must shed blood for the sinner constitutes the essence of Jesus's cross. Does such a legal-ritual thinking fit with Jesus's life? Jesus never said such a thing. But this legal-ritual frame of thinking has become the foundation of the established order. Surprisingly, this thinking constitutes the core of Western Christology. The ritual thinking in Judaism relates to Jesus's death as a sacrifice for atonement. However, this kind of understanding only explains a part of the issue. It is surprising that Christology of this nature has virtually become the criterion of the Christian faith. We must inquire whether the legal-ritual view of God was accepted as such in the life and teaching of Jesus. I don't think it was from Jesus's point of view. If we respect his point of view, the event of Jesus's cross has to be understood from a different perspective, and there has to be a significant change to the current expression of Christology.

Another issue that dominates Christology is messiahship in the Jewish tradition. Western theology did not designate Jesus as the messiah after looking into his life; they fit him into existing ideas about messiahship. In Jesus's days, there were various representations of messiah, but none of them fits particularly well with Jesus's life. The word *messiah* means "anointed," and this was translated into the Greek word *Christ*. But Greek-speaking people could not understand the meaning of anointed, and so Christ became the proper noun for Jesus in the end. If the original meaning of messiah was preserved, Christology as we know it would not have been formulated. Turning Christ into the proper noun for Jesus resulted in great confusion. All of the Jewish representations of messiah were bound up with Jewish nationalism. Since the salvation of the Jewish people was the primary concern, there was no representation of messiah separated from power. Therefore, a messiah was thought of as a powerful person, a judge. But Jesus does not match this description. For this reason, the early church fit elements of Jewish messianism into Christ who was to arrive.

They explained Jesus's existence using Greco-Roman language and the cross using legal-ritual ideas.

During a lecture given a long time ago, Braun caused a stir by saying that there is no unity at all in the Christology of the New Testament. He was right: New Testament Christology, as a whole, is inconsistent. There were many attempts to explain Jesus through ideas from Judaism and the Greco-Roman world, none of which corresponded to Jesus's actual life. According to traditional Christology, God in the passion of Jesus is under the bondage to legal-ritual rules and is not a God of grace or freedom.

An understanding of the resurrection depends on an understanding of Jesus's passion and death. Since the resurrection and the cross are two sides of a single event, a different interpretation of the cross means a different interpretation of the resurrection.

Q: You have discussed the legal-ritual thinking in a negative light. Are there any positive considerations? Does it have any historical validity? A community requires order for its existence, and order requires restrictive force. So shouldn't the legal-ritual thinking have any validity for minjung?

Protestant evangelical theology explains the death of Christ in the doctrine of atonement. But it considers Christ as having overcome the ideas of atonement and retribution from Judaism. We would like to hear your opinion on the claim that Christ becomes the sacrificial lamb but forgives all of humanity freely and unconditionally.

A: I acknowledge the existence of legal-ritual reality. But if it explained all of life, we would have no need of God, grace, or Christ. Legal-ritual thinking plays an absolute role in maintaining the existing order. Even the church is made to support this order. We need to think seriously about whether Jesus's role is to confirm this order or to liberate people who are bound to it. In some respects, the evangelical doctrine of atonement is self-contradictory. It says that God killed Jesus instead of punishing the sinner and that Jesus was the substitute for God. If that is the case, God is also bound by the law of retribution. The God that has to kill God's son for the requirement of killing someone is not the God of Jesus. I don't know about the people who are immersed in doctrines, but I myself do not find such a God believable.

Another issue is distinguishing between good and evil—that is, the question of who defines sin and how. The definition of sin, in legal or ritual terms, determines the way it is punished. So what is sin? If it is an action

3. The Minjung Jesus

that violates something, then what is this something? Ritual sin would be violating a regulation on rituals. The criteria would be something like temple, and a priestly class would declare what is sin. The legal paradigm would view sin as anything that disturbs the social order. So who made the social order and for whom? The social order is created by the powerful for themselves. They define sin and impose punishments for their own benefit. There is little debate regarding some sins. For example, everyone accepts that murder is sin. However, while some forms of murder are punished, others are not. For example, it is not considered murder when the ruling class starts a war resulting in the deaths of the multitudes.

Q: Preaching based on the doctrine of atonement is very difficult. Still, when you are feeling very troubled after committing a moral sin, you sense an underlying comfort from the knowledge of being forgiven through Jesus bearing our sin.

A: Having a sense of moral or ethical sin is a problem. Your attitude towards a sinner is a crucial key here. Jesus stood up against the legal-ritual reality condemning people in absolute terms. Traditional Christology does not bother to see Jesus's resistance. In fact, it is not resistance against such a reality but obedience to it.

3.2. Christ the Suffering Servant

Q: Now we need to address Christology as it appears in the Bible. First, I would like to ask you about the relationship between the Christ event and the Old Testament.

A: Bultmann treated the Old Testament merely as secondary material. I used to think this way for a while. But engaging in minjung theology led me to take the Old Testament more seriously. I resolve to read it anew. The whole Bible is a stream of volcanic lava, and the Jesus event is the climactic explosion of the lava. If the Old and New Testaments flow in the same direction, I think their deepest origin is suffering. The history of Israel begins with suffering—a suffering that is caused by structural power. In the narrative of the exodus, the pharaoh of Egypt was not an individual but a symbol of state power. The Hebrews groaned under this power, and the history of suffering caused by the powerful has persisted. This is not a natural suffering like birth, aging, illness, or death. It is a political suffering. Liberation from political suffering is presented as the supreme goal in the Bible. Fighting for liberation and freedom from this suffering occurs in a fragmentary way. The Old Testament legal codes attach considerable importance to the suffering of the poor in particular. The Ten Commandments are a summation of the legal codes, which apply to those who are afflicted by the powerful. The ulterior motives of the Ten Commandments are to prevent the exercise of absolute power in the name of God and to alleviate the suffering of those suppressed by such a power. What the escapees planned to achieve in the land of Canaan after the wilderness was a communal life not ruled by a single power. But it was not achieved. Instead, the powerful regime of the Davidic dynasty was established and brought about a lot of suffering. The prophets resisted. Ever since, the minjung continued to endure a double suffering at the hand of foreign powers and at the hand of the ruling class that served as a pawn to the empires. At last, Jesus was born under the reign of the Roman Empire. The relationship between the Roman Empire and Jesus is no different from the relationship between the Egyptian Empire and the Hebrews or the Davidic dynasty and the poor people oppressed by it. Jesus stood against the problem of suffering caused by state power. How Jesus opposed state power should be the starting point in our efforts to develop Christology.

Specific images of the messiah are found in the apocalyptic literature. But I don't think there are any in the Old Testament. It was only natural that the minjung who suffered oppression by the powerful were longing for someone who would save them. It is inevitable that persecuted people have a picture of the messiah. Some sects deemed Moses the messiah, others the prophet of their time, and for others even David. There were many ideas of the messiah, but most of them reflected the idea of those under oppression that they themselves must possess power for liberation. It is natural that those who suffer at the hands of the powerful desire liberation by someone more powerful. This person must be the messiah.

However, there was an exceptional image of the messiah that appeared in Deutero-Isaiah: the suffering servant in Isa 53. It is imaginable that the Jewish people, after a long history of being trampled on by foreign powers, were boiling with a desire for revenge. This expressed itself in the thought of judgment. Eschatology and messianism went hand in hand; the end of the world meant the end of Israel's enemies. The people of Israel believed that the end would bring judgment for the gentiles and the arrival of a new world where Israel would take the center stage as the chosen and true people of God.

Was the suffering servant the messiah? In fact, this notion of messiah didn't play a notable role in Judaism. But Jesus's minjung saw in the suffering servant Jesus as Christ. This was an event like a revelation, and how could it have been possible? I believe that it was not theology but the life and death of Jesus before theology that made this possible. Above all, Jesus's suffering reminded the minjung of the suffering servant. Therefore, it is not the case that the narrative of the passion of Jesus was created according to the preexisting image of the suffering servant, but vice versa. The image was connected with Jesus retrospectively.

Jesus's passion was not a heroic death in the Greco-Roman world. The Jewish messiah who was supposed to judge the whole world was not expected to undergo such a death. And you cannot just interpret Jesus's death away in the legal-ritual terms.

By the way, the minjung of Jesus inherited something important from apocalyptic literature. It was eschatology and it served as a framework for understanding and explaining the event of Jesus's cross. This move of interpretation, I think, made it possible for the apocalyptic image of the messiah to be called for again. However, because such an image never conformed to the life of Jesus of Nazareth, they came to project it onto the one who would come again. For this reason, the image of the messiah from apocalyptic literature shows up only in a fragmentary way. The Christ of kerygma was formulated in Greco-Roman society for a missionary purpose. But the minjung tradition carried an image of Jesus that was the closest to the actual fact. It differed from the Jewish image of the messiah, the Greco-Roman idea of the God-human, and the legal-ritual view of the world and history.

Q: Inasmuch as suffering makes up the deepest undercurrent in the history of Israel and the Old Testament, we can see the link between Jesus and the suffering servant. We could say that the minjung are able to save themselves and others through suffering, but do they have to suffer all the way to the end?

A: Let me defer answering this question. But I want to make one thing clear. The suffering servant is an image of Israel who kept suffering and was met with contempt and disparagement. When you keep taking beatings, it is a common response for you to grow stronger by all means or wish for a superhuman messiah's vengeance. The people of Israel, however, went beyond this kind of response. They came to understand that, in the middle of suffering, they were fulfilling the role of the messiah in the world. In terms of spiritual history, the response is worthy of a king. And the minjung realized that Jesus's execution, an absurd defeat, was for the sake of all humanity; and through this realization they became resurrected themselves. Here, the continuity between Jesus and his minjung was created. This was a great event and a continuous movement.

As the Marxist Mihailo Marković said, if Jesus's minjung had acted in vengeance or joined forces with the Zealots, the Jesus event would have been interrupted. For in reality they would be unable to withstand the Roman Empire. Most importantly, it would not save the world from evil; instead, it would repeat the vicious circle of taking vengeance against others.

In his study of the commandment for loving the enemy, Gerd Theißen examined cases of loving the enemy in Jesus's time. He discovered without exception that loving your enemies was an expression of generosity and magnanimity by a kingly being to display his kingliness. Therefore, "Love your enemy" was in the language of the time, "Act like a king." It was not the expression of nonviolent resistance by the cowardly or weak. It actualizes another level of self-consciousness: "We who are beaten are on a higher dimension than you."

This is a conclusion consistent with the understanding of Jesus's passion. It is of a higher dimension. That is to say, the true messiah is the kingly messiah who seeks to break the vicious cycle of evil by eliminating the persecutor's sin and evil through being beaten and killed. Jesus's minjung brought about a similar outcome of saving themselves from their weakness and saving others, because they prided themselves on their membership in Jesus's messiah movement despite persecution. With this understanding, we see continuity in the suffering of Israel, the passion of Jesus, and the suffering of his minjung. Therefore, the messiah we have here is not powerful and invincible but minjung-like. This contrast accords well with the contrast Mr. Kim Yong-bok makes between the messianism of power-driven domination (political messianism) and the messianic reign fulfilled with peace and *koinōnia* (messianic politics). The suffering minjung begin to break the vicious cycle of vengeance by thinking that they are suffering for the world. By doing so, the ultimate kingdom of God, the rule of the messiah is fulfilled. In this sense, the suffering minjung is the messiah.

3.3. Salvation Comes through Minjung

Q: Now, please tell us about the representations of Christ and the minjung in the Bible, especially in the gospels. We would like to know how the work and passion of Christ can be interpreted in relation to Christ designations and messianic self-consciousness.

A: I dealt with this question in the thesis, "The Subject of History Seen in the Gospel of Mark."[1] First, we should presuppose that Jesus himself didn't have a messianic self-consciousness. There are a variety of messianic designations for Jesus: Christ, the Son of God, the Son of Man, the Son of David, Lord, and so on. Of these, Jesus used "the Son of Man" to refer to himself, but I don't believe this description carries a messianic significance from the book of Daniel or elsewhere. This designation, as in the book of Ezekiel, means that he was a mere human. Therefore, as Bultmann says, it is just a designation of humility. If Jesus considered himself to be the messiah, I would not think of him as the true messiah. Based on his behaviors, he does not appear to fit himself into a traditional understanding or preexisting image of the messiah. In fact, the life of Jesus as narrated in the gospels does not fit neatly into any understanding of messiah during his time.

William Wrede characterized the Christology of the Gospel of Mark as the messianic secret.[2] But we don't have to think that Jesus concealed his messiah identity. Perhaps Wrede came up with the concept in order to explain the discrepancy between Jesus's behavior and existing images of the messiah. I hope you don't take it that I am underestimating Jesus by saying that he was not the messiah. I am not! If anything, we should believe that he was so full of life and of a higher dimension that he could not be limited to such a frame.

As for the Son of God title, Jesus did not apply it to himself alone but to all true human beings. Above all, Jesus called God the "Father of human beings." Western scholars claim that Jesus put the expression "my father" in the plural when he was using it for people in general, but this point is far-fetched. We have to ask again who is the Father in the Lord's Prayer (Matt 6:9). Anyway, I don't think he performed miracles with the consciousness that he was the Son of God. It is undeniable that those who transmitted the facts about Jesus described his miraculous acts to demonstrate his supernatural powers. But it doesn't make sense to draw from this the conclusion that he was the messiah. Above all, from whatever angle

---

1. Ahn Byung-Mu, "The Subject of History Seen in the Gospel of Mark" [Korean].
2. William Wrede, *The Messianic Secret*, trans. J. C. G. Greig (Cambridge: James Clarke, 1971).

you see the narrative of Jesus's passion, you cannot ever fit it into the idea of the divine Son of God or the Son of the Almighty One.

Then how can we characterize the life of Jesus as Christ? Interpreting his death merely in reference to vicarious atonement is an over-simplified dogma. At least Jesus himself did not center his attention on sin. For him, there did not exist what you call a sinner. Who on earth defines sin? You are a sinner if you get caught up in the net cast by the existing order, or strictly speaking, the ruling class. Jesus didn't see them as sinners but as the people he had to liberate. And he leveled his criticisms at exactly those who criticized sinners.

Since it is always the case that the strong ascribe sinfulness to the weak, a sustained emphasis on sin leaves the weak with the short end of the stick. Those who were groaning under those who controlled and dominated the legal-ritual system came rushing to Jesus in large numbers. Jesus proclaimed to them, "Blessed are the poor, for theirs is the kingdom of God" and "You are sons and daughters of God." He didn't try to instill these ideas into their minds. He just perceived the weak people in this way. He did not see them as sinners but as human beings and formed together with them a community of sharing. Jesus did not respond with deliberate plans or try to save the downtrodden with a messianic self-consciousness. He lived in their midst and gave all he had. Of course, Jesus shared his consciousness with them too. With no strings attached—or like Li Taibo who plunged in for the moon forgetting about the water[3]—Jesus entered among the minjung who were sinners in the eyes of the legal-ritual order of the time. He befriended and shared with the minjung; and to them, who were caught up in the legal-ritual net and treated as subhuman, he said, "You are the master. Yours is the kingdom of God. You are the true sons and daughters of God." These are not expressions for changing the consciousness of the minjung; they are his honest beliefs. He did not merely stand on their side; he believed that they were the only source of salvation (the kingdom of God.) He repeatedly told the elites to take note of them because he

---

3. Li Taibo (701–762), whose real name was Li Bo, was a Chinese poet from the Tang dynasty (618–907). He and Du Fu (712–770), another Tang poet, are regarded as two of the best poets in Chinese history; they are often jointly represented by the designation *Li Du*. His poetry bore the Daoistic influence in their fantastic elements of transcending humanity and seeking freedom. He was a wanderer throughout his life and is known to have been a lover of wine. Legend has it that he drowned diving into a river while drunk in the hopes of catching the reflection of the moon on the water.

believed salvation could only be opened through the minjung. Jesus lived in exactly the same way as the minjung. He died on the cross in order to proclaim that the salvation of all humanity could only be achieved through them. And this death on the cross indicated the height of the minjung's suffering. The death of Christ on the cross signifies not the death of an individual (*individium*) but that of the minjung who were being crushed to death by the rulers. And those who are killing the minjung can afford to be saved only when they properly recognize the meaning of Christ's death they have caused. No other path to salvation is available.

At the risk of sounding abstract, let me bring up these words of Jesus, "All who take the sword will perish by the sword" (Matt 26:52). This means that those who wield power will perish by power. Jesus did not think that all of the problems created by power could be solved with a greater power. There is a different solution: the suffering minjung, instead of buckling in resignation or in the sense of defeat, are finally able to end the tyranny of the powerful through suffering in the awareness that they are the masters of history. The minjung of Jesus were a group of people who had, instead of the sense of sin, the awareness that they themselves, despite being thrashed in this way, were truly the sons and daughters of God. Salvation comes through the minjung who are abused and dying on behalf of the world.

Q: Then it is liberation of consciousness and not liberation of real-life suffering, right?

A: Confucius found his ideal government in the rule of Emperors Yao and Shun,[4] for they did so little that their people didn't even know they governed. In other words, they used so little power as to create this impression. The more you try to create order by means of power, the more despotic you have to become. The fallacy of utopian ideas is that they involve dictatorship. To rule, to dominate, or to govern has been the cause of pain, and so the salvation of humanity is only possible when we do away with it. For this reason, Confucius sought not a rich and powerful country but a benevolent royal government implemented by means of virtues.

However, Lao-tzu and Juang-tzu, especially the latter, criticized Yao and Shun, for their way was simply another way to rule people and there-

---

4. Yao and Shun are legendary sage kings in Chinese history who are supposed to have been active between the 2300s and 2100s BCE. Shun succeeded Yao. Their virtue and wisdom serve as a model for later Chinese rulers.

fore unnatural. That is to say, harboring the intention to make people happy in such-and-such a way is a wrong thing to do. The idea of helping someone itself originates in the consciousness of those in power. You have to be liberated from power as well as the hope to change the world for the better. This is doing nothing, and even doing nothing is harmful if you are conscious of it. Think about it this way. In relation to the liberation of minjung, you have wondered if liberation is not of consciousness alone but also for life of the minjung. I don't think that is the case. If the minjung persevere in suffering and realize in their consciousness that they are the master of history, power will lose its place in the end. Power loses its force and meaning. Then the world changes. We have thus far intended to use a sword to take out the sword-holding power, but now I am talking about ignoring the sword in the first place. By ignoring the sword, you incapacitate it. Usually, we dismiss it as an idealistic fantasy, and this is precisely our limitation. We usually think that, dictated by economic principles, people will not voluntarily lower their standards of living or that the powerful won't give up their power of their own accord. Gandhi of India came closest to realizing this ideal. He didn't hold a needle to drive away one million British troops. His disciple Vinoba witnessed that, despite political liberation and driving out the foreign power, the economic problem remained. So he decided that the first priority was to distribute the land to the minjung and set out on a pilgrimage. He travelled all over the country inquiring into people without land and pleading with landowners to share their lands. The communists criticized him, saying, "Why are you wasting your efforts on what could be done overnight by legislation and land reform?" He responded, "To reform society by means of violence is not true revolution. You cannot expect a good new age to come about from such a revolution. I believe in the human heart. When we touch exhausted hearts and turn them into gladly-sharing hearts, there is true sharing, and this ushers in a new world." It is not material alone that matters. Material distribution must be accompanied by sharing. Therefore, Vinoba appealed to the human heart for voluntary sharing. But I don't speak of doing nothing. Suffering does not merely refer to humiliation due to powerlessness and cowardice. True suffering comes to the one who says that what is wrong is wrong and that what is right is right. Resistance against injustice is both a right and a duty. I cannot give up the belief that this kind of resistance will bring an end to injustice. Wasn't Jesus's passion a form of suffering from this kind of resistance?

However, it is hard for us to maintain this belief. We are stuck with the thought, "What kind of a ruler would voluntarily give up his or her power?" or "Isn't taking the ruler's power away the only viable option?" I am not an exception. But Jesus was different. He didn't appeal to violence but shared himself and looked forward to such a world. Jesus's minjung believed so. They never meant to continue to live in affliction just believing themselves the children of God. They were expecting the transformation of the world. Jesus's minjung didn't think of Jesus's death as a miserable defeat. They believed, "Jesus died for the whole world. He is transforming the world. God's *eschaton* event is taking place now." The *eschaton* event is a complete transformation of the world. So Jesus's minjung never took up weapons or thought of organizing in order to avenge themselves and conquer the world. This was true of Jesus's minjung. Even though they were not immune to the infiltration of the will to power, most thought of themselves as being on the frontlines for reforming the world, even while acknowledging their lack of power. It was a peaceful movement. This movement gradually changed the world until it toppled the Roman Empire. Although it was not the reality yet, Jesus's minjung believed he had already brought about the end of the world. Jesus himself concentrated all of his strength on preaching the kingdom of God. While in reality violence was rampant and the Roman Empire was in power, he proclaimed, "The kingdom of God has come near. Blessed are the poor." He was really convinced of it. That the poor are blessed does not mean they will become rich; it means the poor will be the masters of a new order. The poor can become agents of change and transform the world. Since the early Christians had this belief in the experience of resurrection, they took no arms in their hands and formed a community that, unlike the existing power system, brought Rome down to its knees through service.

Q: What is the difference between sharing and showing solidarity?

A: Westerners often use the word solidarity. They are unable to take another step beyond this. As far as I know, the Third World began to use the word *sharing* at an assembly of the World Council of Churches. Here, the emphasis is specifically on the sharing of material. As a matter of fact, we cannot really expect the First World to use the word realistically, for they cannot share. Instead, they like using the word *solidarity*, and I believe this word is an abstraction of sharing material goods.

Q: In the minjung movement, we do not see the minjung unquestioningly sharing and being afflicted, but rather claiming and fighting for their shares. Do you think what you've just mentioned can account for such an aspect of the minjung?

A: First, I would like to make this point clear. What I have been discussing so far is the picture of Christ in the Bible. Above all, it is important that we acknowledge this picture of Christ. For the way things are in real life cannot ever change the picture of Christ in the Bible. Samuel Brandon's interpretation that links Jesus to the Zealots does not explain this picture.[5] True, the minjung of today do what they can to take their share. They can succumb to instincts and be selfish, and sometimes they go astray. I don't glorify the minjung. But I view them in a different light. The minjung can transcend themselves. We only have to remember recent events we have witnessed. A young man, Jeon Tae-il,[6] not minding his own hunger, pleaded for help about the unfair treatment of his coworkers. But in 1970, after hitting a dead-end wherever he turned, he burned himself and stunned the world. This turned our full attention to the working conditions of laborers in the Pyeonghwa Market[7] where Jeon worked. He offered himself as a sacrifice. To say it another way, he shared himself. We have witnessed a series of martyrdoms that have been taking place at an accelerating rate over the last fifteen years. We have seen countless events in which laborers sacrifice themselves for their coworkers' rights and interests. I am confounded that these events of self-transcendence are not taking place in the church but

---

5. Samuel G. F. Brandon, *Jesus and the Zealots: A Study of the Political Factor in Early Christianity* (New York: Scribner's Sons, 1983).

6. Jeon Tae-il (1948–1970) had to quit school in the fourth grade due to poverty and started working to provide for his family. In 1965, at seventeen years of age, he began to work in the Pyeonghwa Market in Seoul as a tailor's assistant. The next year, he became a tailor and later a garment cutter, a relatively well-paid job. The Pyeonghwa Market belonged to a garment-manufacturing complex. Working conditions at approximately five hundred small factories were very poor. Young female laborers had to work fourteen hours a day in a crowded and unventilated room with no natural light. Jeon made efforts to improve the working conditions of the laborers by pressuring employers to meet the Labor Standards Act. At a rally in front of the Pyeonghwa Market on November 13, 1970, Jeon set himself on fire and shouted, "Observe the Labor Standard Act!" and "We are not machines!" At the hospital, before passing away, he said to his mother, "Please accomplish for me what I have failed to accomplish."

7. *Pyeonghwa* means "peace."

in the midst of the minjung. Isn't it the continuation of the fire that Jesus started?

3.4. Jesus's Presence in the Lives of Minjung Today

Q: Now let's turn to minjung Christology. Traditional Christology holds that Christ is present in the sacraments and preaching, but minjung Christology holds that Christ is present in the suffering minjung and in the robbed person of the Good Samaritan story. I'd like you to tell us about minjung Christology with a focus on how and where Christ is present today.

A: Representative biblical texts are the Parable of the Last Judgment in Matt 25 and the passage about Christ outside the city gate in Heb 13. Prior to discussing the question of where Christ is today, let's think about the problematic nature of the proposition that Jesus is Christ. In his last lecture at Heidelberg University, Bultmann criticized his disciples' writings in different aspects, to the effect that there was no continuity between Jesus and Christ. This does not mean that the early Christian mention of Christ did not presuppose Jesus, but that there was no substantial (*sachlich*) continuity. For while Jesus preached the kingdom of God, his disciples preached Jesus. Therefore, it was not Jesus himself but his disciples that made him Christ. In this sense, the continuity was superficial. I don't agree with Bultmann, however. True, an autobiographical account differs from someone else's account of you. The emphases would be different, but I believe the fundamental facts remain the same. I think the messianic stream of the volcanic lava erupted in the active volcano of Jesus of Nazareth. The Christ event did not take place only once in Jesus of Nazareth. So we don't need to go back to the event two thousand years ago for the messiah experience. Even as the stream of volcanic lava continues to erupt, the Christ event continues to take place in history. In this sense, I don't think the Jesus event is qualitatively unique and unrepeatable. The Christ event did not take place only once in Jesus of Nazareth but keeps taking place.

Jesus died. If he was resurrected, then he disappeared from the realm of history. Here a problem emerged. Jesus's minjung were not content with missing Jesus and waiting for the messiah. Here, they had a present-time experience of Jesus largely in two forms. One was the Holy Spirit, which signified the presence of Christ. In the Gospel of John, the expression "spirit of Christ" appears. Although Trinitarianism keeps blurring it, I'd like to see the Holy Spirit as the mode of Christ's presence. If the Holy Spirit indicates that Christ is present in a supernatural manner, the other experience indicates that Christ is present in everyday life. The Christ event is taking place all around us. This experience appears in Matt 25, and Christ is present in the actual life site of the imprisoned, the naked, the hungry, the poor, the captive, and so on. In my opinion, a thought like this was not formulated overnight but grew out of the minjung's own experiences. Hebrews 13:13 says, "Let us then go to him outside the city gate and bear the abuse he endured." The expression "bear the abuse" says something very important and is open to multiple interpretations. Visiting him outside the city gate is a shameful thing to do. But right there, where they are deserted and alienated from the world, Christ is present. Let's go there. Christ is not within the city gate now. This means that Christ is not in the realm this world acknowledges. By the way, at first I described the Holy Spirit as supernatural; but I don't consider that the activity of the Holy Spirit and the everyday occurrence of Christ's presence are two separate events.

Let's take another step and look into the Gospel of Mark. This gospel was written approximately forty years after Jesus's ministry. But its location was certainly the actual location where the minjung of Mark's time were living. It recognized the site of the minjung's life as the site of Jesus's presence. After a sound defeat in the Jewish War, the people of Israel lost their country and wandered around hungry and naked like a colony of ants scattered after losing their tunnel. Mark took note of these people. According to the Gospel of Mark, Jesus took pity on the crowd who had been hungry for three days and wandering around like sheep without a shepherd (Mark 6:34). This could describe the minjung forty years earlier. But it refers to the minjung where Mark was now standing. Mark portrays Jesus sharing bread and his own self with the hungry minjung. Likewise, the scene of Jesus's death on the cross is a representation of the darkest place of divine absence where God does not answer the endless cries. It describes both Jesus's suffering and the suffering of the minjung in Mark's day. The life settings where Jesus of Nazareth was situated forty years earlier and where Mark was writing his gospel are inseparable. Therefore, I believe that Mark was writing his gospel in view of the Christ present in the lives of the minjung, the site of God's absence, where they were dying a helpless and undeserving death and wandering hungry.

In this way, Mark saw Jesus standing in the life setting of his own age. He saw Jesus's suffering and death not as an individual but as the minjung. By portraying Jesus, he portrayed the life of the minjung.

Q: Should we stop with identifying Jesus's suffering and death with the realities of today's minjung? Mark's preaching only comforts the minjung and doesn't lead them to active resistance, does it?

A: We are indeed left with that question. Whereas the Zealots fought and died in the Jewish War, Mark preached to the minjung as if to say, "As Jesus said, 'My God, my God why have you forsaken me?' at the moment of his death, you should trust only God all the way to the end. As the children of God, call God Father, and there will finally be a time when Rome will throw away the sword." If Mark preached to us like this today, we would not be able to accept it. But Mark actually preached in this way. In the midst of the suffering reality of the minjung, he presented a picture of Jesus who was dying in a helpless way. The Marxist Marković responded favorably to this depiction of Jesus. As I said earlier, he held that if Jesus had done as the Zealots did, he would not have had any success and would have disappeared from history. He took a wise course of action. Even in social-scientific terms, Jesus fought a strategic fight. The Zealots simply disappeared from history. All things considered, they were responsible for the premature demise of Judah. It is true that they were meaningful, impressive, and well-received. But they accomplished nothing. In contrast, Jesus's movement, or Mark's portrayal of Jesus, would have been hard to accept at the site where people were dying an unfair death fighting against Rome. In such desperate circumstances, Mark's preaching may have resulted in stoning. Not every church held the belief that Jesus was fully present in the lives of the minjung. If we look at church history, some churches maintained this conviction. Others contended that you could only experience the presence of Christ in official church organizations during corporate worship. Of these, the latter gained ascendency and gave rise to the idea that the church was the body of Christ. This idea eventually developed into the idea that the church fulfilled the role of Christ's representative—a far cry from the minjung Christology as presented in Matt 25, Heb 13, and the Gospel of Mark. Perhaps the notion that Christ is present for those who are suffering in the site of minjung's life is inconceivable for those who are not Jews.

Let's think about two anecdotes from history. The Nazis ferreted out Jews upon entering Poland. A group of Jews were hiding at a Jewish cemetery. Under the circumstances a woman in the group gave birth to a baby in the midst of the graves. No one was able to help her but the old grave keeper who took up the baby and looked up to the sky. The grave keeper prayed, "Oh, God, are you sending us the messiah only now? Otherwise, how could a new life be born in the midst of graves?" This is an experience of the messiah's presence that was possible for the Jews who had lived a history of suffering for thousands of years and were now facing death. The child itself could not be the messiah. However, the messiah experience took place at the site of the minjung's suffering, a place of graves in this case.

The other anecdote comes from the novel *Night* by Elie Wiesel, this year's winner of the Nobel Peace Prize.[8] It is about the execution of Jews in a concentration camp. The Nazis were habitually hanging a few Jews at a time. On one occasion, they hanged two adults and one young boy at the gallows. The two adults died immediately, but the boy was writhing in anguish. One of the Jews watching the scene whispered in despair, "Where is God now?" Then someone behind him answered, "God is dying at the gallows there now." God was not outside of the killing. He was right there in the scene. The answer does not mean that the dying boy himself is God, but that God is there where he is dying an unfair death, that the God event is taking place there. This is an observation which it is impossible for a non-Jew to make. The Jews were capable of such a confession of faith because they had always lived in the suffering of this kind. I believe that experiencing God in Jesus's death is made possible due to the existence of a deep spiritual tradition.

3.5. The Institutional Church Has Rejected Christ among the Minjung

Institutionalized Christianity has given up on the claim that Christ is present in the suffering of the minjung. So there was an increasing emphasis on the church. Protestantism maintains that Christ is present only in the proclamation of the Word and the administration of the sacraments. For example, in the Eucharist it is said that the bread and wine are the living blood and flesh of Christ. But this is wrong. This is nothing other than a religious ritual designed to avoid the difficulty of following Christ.

Is it the case that Christ is present only in the administration of Word and sacrament? Not at all. Christ is present at the site of the minjung's suffering, even where the name of Jesus is not known. The theology of

---

8. Elie Wiesel, *Un di Velt Hot Geshvign* (Buenos Aires: Central Union of Polish Jews in Argentina, 1956), translated as *Night* (New York: Hill & Wang; London: MacGibbon & Kee, 1960). The author won the Nobel Peace Prize in 1986.

the Word is possible when someone witnesses to the presence of Christ in the minjung's suffering. It is our task to witness to this. Our task is not repeating what the Bible says or preaching but saying that Christ exists at the site of the minjung's suffering and that he is speaking at this site. In the works of Dostoevsky, we hear words of truth pouring out of the mouths of drunkards. In the same way, we find and bear witness to Christ in unexpected places. It is precisely Christians who bear this kind of witness, and only by witnessing can you recognize Christ. However, the witness of a mere observer of the minjung event cannot be a true witness; a correct interpretation of the event alone would never suffice. Witnessing is connected with martyrdom. By sharing in the suffering of the minjung, a true witness will eventually bring about the event of Jesus again.

Q: You say that we Christians have to testify that Christ is present in the suffering minjung. But are we actual witnesses? Are we bearers of such a witness? For example, I would like to ask if Jeon Tae-il or the poet Kim Yong-taek, who wrote *The Seomjin River*,[9] is not a much greater witness than those who do theology, believe in Jesus, or go to church.

A: Your view is not different from mine. Testifying that people like Jeon Tae-il and Kim Yong-taek are true witnesses to Christ is what theology is supposed to do. The word *Christ* itself is not important. But we have to say it. That's exactly what theology has to do. Merely describing facts about the minjung is nothing more than minjung studies. We must show that Christ is present in the minjung facts. That is the primary goal of minjung theology.

Q: Up to this point, we have discussed Western Christology, Christology in the Bible, and minjung Christology. Western Christology developed the doc-

---

9. Kim Yong-taek (b. 1948) was born in Imsil, Jeollabuk Province, an agricultural area in the southwestern Korea and has lived in this region all his life working as an elementary school teacher. He made his literary debut in 1982 with a series of poems each entitled "The Seomjin River." His poetry links traditional values of the agricultural region with changes of the modern day. The poet's first book, *The Seomjin River*, was published in 1985. One of the major rivers of South Korea, the Seomjin River flows from a southwestern region of the Korean peninsula southward into the South Sea. This river serves as an important natural element for the people of Kim Yong-taek's home region. Kim's early works faithfully represent the lives of the farmers of this place and voice criticism of the injustices the farmers face.

trine of the dual nature of Christ under the influence of the Greco-Roman idea of the God-human. Western Christology also depicted the Christ-to-come under the influence of messianic ideas in Jewish apocalyptic literature. However, Christ in the Bible is different from the Greco-Roman God-human and the messiah of Judaism; he led a life full of suffering and shared his life with the minjung. Jesus did not see the poor as sinners or intend to atone for their sins. He saw them as the children of God and proclaimed that salvation for all of humanity comes through them. It is the task of Christians and theology to testify that the Jesus event is not a singular event but continues in the life of the minjung today. Christ is not so much present in the church, the Word, or the sacraments. Rather he is present most fully where the minjung live. The Christ event is taking place at the site of the minjung's life. Next, we would like to present three facts or events related to the minjung and focus our subsequent conversation on them.

Case 1

To consider Jesus's presence in the minjung event, we must first attend to the cries of minjung farmers of this land. Like the Psalms of the Old Testament, *The Seomjin River* is a book of poetry by Kim Yong-taek that contains the laments of today's Korean farmers. The farmers identify numerous problems: the government purchases agricultural products at a price that falls short of the production costs, various kinds of taxes, and farmer's household debts. Approximately 60 percent of the lands tilled by the farmers are tenant land, 46.4 percent of farming households are tenant farmers, and the rate of tenant farming is 50 percent. Additionally, farmers are plagued by pollution-related diseases caused by industrial sewage and agricultural pesticides. Faced with these problems, the farmers began a movement to gain reasonable purchase prices. If successful, the movement will develop into a land reform movement. However, in the current situation of the division of the two Koreas, various laws prevent these basic demands being met.

The problems that trouble farmers are well represented in *The Seomjin River*. Reading a representative piece of this book would allow us to hear the voice of Jesus Christ crying out together with today's farmers. Among the several representative works of this book are "The Seomjin River 20 (A Chronicle of the Persimmon)," a description of how the farmers felt when they earned a low wage for persimmons in good harvest; "The Stage is Crooked, but Beat the Drum Right" and "The Meal Prices," a testimony to society's responsibility for the farmers' misery and a criticism of unfair policies dependent on foreign countries; and "The Seomjin River 16 (Moving House)," a moving portrayal of a farmer's family moving out of their home village and the gloomy and tired farmers who deal with the loss. I will read the last example:

> After an early dinner we all gathered together and helped the family pack for the move. A mirror, a broken wardrobe, a few rope-bound crocks, a bundle of used clothes, and dirty cashmere blankets. It was absurd that these household goods, more fitting for life on the countryside, without a common thing such as a black-and-white TV, would be in Seoul. But we silently packed and loaded them on the three-wheeler in the yard of the community hall. The wife of the head of the leaving family was in tears, wiping her nose with her skirt hem. Other women in the neighborhood tried not to look at one another in the face or talk to one another. She hastily sold other items to the neighbors or gave them away for free—things like a *hwakdok*,[10] a used *deokseok*,[11] a *mangtae*,[12] and a *jeolgutong*,[13] often forgetting herself as if from having a lump in her throat.
>
> The land where the fathers of our fathers and their fathers lived working hard; the rice paddies and the dry fields and all kinds of fruit trees; the several-hundred-year-old zelkova tree on the rear mountain; the flat field and the flower field across the river; the Temple Valley; the *Duru*[14] Rock and the Lightening Rock at the boat mooring—these are places that are familiar to our eyes and whose names are familiar to our bodies. There we cut firewood and caught fish and played while growing up. These places filled with memories crossed our minds mixed with unfamiliar names in Seoul such as Gurodong, Seongnam, Shingil-dong, and Myeongdong.
>
> The small bonfire in the yard was dying away, and the *Saemaul* slate-roofed house[15] was completely emptied. In the yard of the village

---

10. A mortar for grinding grains or pounding things such as chili.
11. A straw mat used for covering an ox's back.
12. A straw rocksack.
13. A large stone mortar for grinding grains or making rice cake.
14. *Duru* seems to mean "overall."
15. The expression "the *Saemaul* slate-roofed house" suggests that the house was built during the *Saemaul Undong* (New Village Movement). This movement started in 1970 by the initiative of then president Park Jeong-hui for the development of local communities. In its early stage, the movement centered on environmental improvement with cooperation from local residents. Included in this undertaking were mending fences, revamping village roads, and replacing thatched roofs with slate or gal-

community hall the whole neighborhood had come out to bid farewell. The women were not able to hide their sorrow: they were in tears and took out crumpled notes from their skirt pockets and said, "Buy your kids some bread or something on the road." This incident didn't feel like just someone else's concern. Whenever it happened, we became fewer in numbers and felt very sorry. Now, everyone that had to go back home was gone. In the yard of the community hall was a dim light. Some old folks and kids were standing around with nothing to do, their faces fallen and tired. After exchanging farewell wishes with the village folks, the head of the moving family drank with us. He was wearing an old-fashioned dress shirt stained with rice-paddy water and grass sap, a crumpled suit custom-made for his wedding, and worn shoes. His kids were happy, sat behind the wheel, and pestered him to leave soon. But we silently emptied our cups of rice wine, awkwardly shaking hands cut by a sickle and torn by thorns and thumped by a shovel or pick; at a loss for words and so only saying, "Wish you the best," "Safe travels." From time to time we saw the pitch darkness beyond one another's shoulders. As if tearing himself away, he hopped in the rear seat of the loaded car and looked away from us. The women in tears picked up the ends of their skirts to wipe their tears. The kids were standing holding onto their mothers' skirts. I felt my throat tightening thinking that his family would be in the cramped space surrounded by the household goods throughout the evening. When the car was pulling slowly out of the yard of the community hall, a loud sound of rushing water turned around the river bend in the distance ahead. The headlights threw a brief light on the Stepping-stone Street. The howl of the river swept through our hearts as a wide current.

 The land with which he mixed his blood and sweat and flesh; the land on which he, while deserted and despised, did everything he was told to do by the state; the land that he nevertheless loved and lived on—this is the land he was forced out of at age thirty-five.

 Having passed the pavilion tree at the entrance of the village, the car ran smoothly on the wide *Saemaul* road shooting its lights here and there. Even after the red tail light of the car was out of sight on the path leaving the village, the people remained forlorn in the yard of the community hall—looking away from one another, brightening their cigarette lights while sitting or standing, looking ahead at the black mountain or looking down at the ground, and thinking of the days when they had lived with him rubbing fleshes against one another. Unable to help their hollowed hearts, clearing their throat, they broke away in

---

vanized iron sheets. The phrase "the wide *Saemaul* road" that appears later is also a product of the New Village Movement.

dark forms one by one. The lights of the community hall went off one after another behind our backs, and a deep and large darkness filled the neighborhood. We passed the empty house with our eyes consciously turned away. Thinking of this neighboring home that was blackened and unlighted that no one will ever move in now, hearing the tweeting of a scops owl and the sound of the river, we will be turning and tossing and sleeping only fitfully for some nights. Someone else will leave, too. Someone else will leave, too.

The sound of the Seomjin River's water stopped with a big sigh and breathed again with difficulty.[16]

Case 2

I am going to tell you a story of a woman who is a little over forty. Since the 1960s the economic development plans were the single most important factor for the economy as a whole. A serious problem arose for those who lost their land in agricultural areas but were unable to adapt to urbanization. This woman was one of those people. She left her hometown for an urban area at a young age but couldn't settle down in any particular place. After a period of wandering, she temporarily settled down in the vicinity of a US Army base near the Imjin Pavilion[17] of Paju, Gyeonggi Province. She got married, and, after the death of her husband, she married again, this time to a man who was good for nothing. Her husband was jobless, drank too much, and beat her. She had no choice but to work as a dog dealer and live like a beggar for five or six years. Upon the withdrawal of the US Army from the area, she lost her means of living there and came to Seoul. In Seoul, living in a tent hut, she and her husband barely eked out a living. Her husband worked as a construction worker on a daily contract, and she worked at a bottle-stopper factory. She was illiterate and didn't have an elementary school education. This made it even harder for her to make a living, and she began to run into debt. She took out usurious loans, ending up with a debt of ten-million won and going to a detention center for failure to pay. In this bottomless pit, she struggled with whether to live

---

16. Kim Yong-taek, "The Seomjin River 16 (Moving House)," in *The Seomjin River* (1985). Translated into English here by Hanna In.

17. The Imjin Pavilion is located about fifty-four kilometers (thirty-four miles) northwest of Seoul right below the demilitarized zone. It was built in 1972 for the South Koreans who had come down from North Korea before or during the Korean War who could not return home after the war.

or die before falling asleep. In her sleep, she had a mystical experience: something like a red fireball grazed her face. Later on, after being released from the detention center, she had the same experience again and decided to press forward. Then, at a revival meeting she attended, she saw a vision of her family members suffering pitifully. And then she began to speak in tongues. Afterwards, she began to attend Full Gospel Church,[18] became actively involved in the church activities, and confessed Jesus as her savior. Going through these experiences, she became a new person, and her relationships with her mother-in-law and sister-in-law improved. In addition, she led some people in her neighborhood to her church. She worked hard to reduce her debt down to four million won or so. I think we can gain new insights for creating a different order if we take seriously the experiences of this woman's change grounded in social-scientific thinking.

Case 3

I would like to mention a case in relation to poor people. This story was shared by a pastor. It is about the death of a man who was hired as a day laborer in an agricultural region. The laborer lived in abject poverty with a wife who had a speech impairment for fifty-three years before becoming bedridden with a serious illness. He was barely surviving on government provisions. One month before his death, the pastor visited him. After seeing him in critical condition, the pastor took him to the community health center. But the doctor refused to treat him because he didn't possess a yellow card for the destitute. The pastor got the card issued and had the doctor treat him. The doctor said he needed to go to a bigger hospital, so the laborer and the pastor walked twenty kilometers to the hospital. But the ill man was denied treatment because he was visiting past eleven o'clock, the cut-off point for receiving patients who could not afford to pay. They had to walk twenty kilometers back home. Later on, they went to the hospital again, but the sick man was denied treatment again because he

---

18. Full Gospel Church here refers in all probability to Yoido Full Gospel Church, a Pentecostal church located on the Yeoui Island in Seoul. It belongs to the Assembly of God of Korea. It was founded by Jo Yong-gi in 1958 and has achieved a remarkable numerical growth. The current membership is approximately 500,000 members, which is the largest church in the world. YFGC offers its own Full Gospel Theology, which emphasizes blessing in the worldly dimension. Among Korean Christians, YFGC is often criticized as a champion of the prosperity gospel.

had no identification card. While the pastor was acquiring the card, the ill person passed away. His wife told him to believe in Jesus before death if only in consideration of the pastor's help. But he said, "Who the hell is Jesus? There's no Jesus." Who could possibly say to this man, "You are not saved," only because he didn't believe in Jesus?

A: I read Kim Yong-taek's book of poetry. The poet not only suffers, but also speaks on behalf of the minjung in the place of the minjung. I have no problem taking his poems to be a contemporary version of Psalms. The poet is an individual but at the same time not an individual. A witness does not merely complain of what they have suffered as unfair. The instant you recognize what you have suffered as the concern of the whole humanity, you become the messianic minjung in the true sense of the term. When you see a certain hardship of the minjung, you should not define it with existing ethical, religious, or legal notions. Rather the proper response is to experience in sadness something totally different, something you don't have yet—a messianic experience. This experience is something that goes beyond you on the individual plane. I refer to this experience as a messianic cry. In the poem of Kim Yong-taek, the problem does not remain an individual's problem alone but becomes a problem of all farmers. He utters their agonized cry; therefore, this cry becomes a messianic cry. In the case of the latter two stories, we should consider them beyond ordinary considerations, beyond ethics or law, or even religious norms. We should view the sorrows and pains of the people in question to be those of all humanity. This in itself is a messianic experience.

On the contrary, if we only place these stories on the personal plane, the woman's story could easily receive an ethical judgment. For being in a debt of ten million won could be an ethical problem. The life of the woman as an individual doesn't move me at all. Only when the uneducated woman takes a stand with the utmost tenacity, I experience power from her life and feel, "Wow! She has a power that I don't have at all!" If experiencing power from her situation is salvation, then we can say that salvation comes from minjung. In *Crime and Punishment* by Fyodor Dostoevsky, this kind of messianic experience or messianic witness is evident.[19] According to the memoir by a woman who was like a sister to him, Dostoevsky was a

---

19. Fyodor Dostoevsky, *Crime and Punishment*, trans. Richard Pevear and Larissa Volokhonsky (New York: Vintage Classics, 1993).

person who was cunning, doubtful, and fond of drinking and gambling. In spite of not being an exemplary person, he was capable of looking beyond the realm of his own life. He saw the problems of one class or the whole humanity and reported them. In so doing, he was bearing witness to Christ beyond ethics, law, and even religion. Sonya was a quiet, uneducated girl and registered prostitute. By letting her represent the quintessential Christ minjung, I have long since thought, Dostoevsky was the witness to Jesus who knew him best in the era prior to the communist revolution. In miserable poverty, Sonya's father lived in the past in a drunken stupor. His second wife was a proud and harsh woman, who tried to keep up the old life even in near-starvation. In this hopeless situation where they could only expect to starve to death, Sonya became a prostitute and brought some money home. At the same time, she held the Bible in one hand yet felt no pang of conscience. She finally overpowered Raskolnikov who was an intellectual. In this way, Dostoevsky lets Sonya embody the Christ minjung who escapes religious and legal measures. In other words, the story of Sonya illustrates that Christ is present in the minjung.

The same goes with Kim Yong-taek, the poet we read earlier. He is not a farmer who tills the land, but he is doing important work as a witness. It is not easy to connect the single issue of persimmon to the broader concerns of farmers in general as a critique of the flawed social structure. Similarly in the case of Jeon Tae-il, it is not important that he personally went through a lot of hardships. It is not important, either, that he found money someone else had dropped to buy a pear to eat instead of returning it to the owner. What is important is that Jeon Tae-il with little schooling felt the need to report the reality of the laborers and, having no success, burned his own body as a sacrifice to bring attention to the issue. He didn't confine the problem of his pains to the personal level but sublimated it into the collective plane of all laborers. Here the image of the minjung-like messiah emerged. We don't need to say that Jeon Tae-il is the messiah. But we can say Christ is present in Jeon Tae-il in this way.

Once again I feel how vastly different the attitude is from that of Jesus—the attitude that tries to define or criticize the life of the minjung religiously, ethically, or intellectually. Jesus unconditionally received the sick—especially the mentally sick—prostitutes, and tax collectors as friends and the children of God. Prostitutes are in actuality sacrificial offerings, but the church today defines them as bad, licentious women. But Jesus befriended these women and embraced tax collectors, who were branded as traitors from a nationalistic and political standpoint. This is difficult and not easy to digest. Jesus's life was remarkable. We can say that an enormous stream of volcanic lava erupted in Jesus. Earlier there have been some appearances of smoke and some earthquakes, but the eruption took place for the first time with Jesus. And later, the same kind of eruption took place in various forms even if not necessarily related to the name of Jesus. So we say that the event of Jesus Christ keeps on exploding even now.

3.6. The Minjung Event Is the Jesus Event

Then how does the event of Jesus Christ, namely, the minjung event, take place? I heard Mr. Ham Seok-heon once went to the tuberculosis sanitarium in Masan and said rudely to the patients there, "You sick bastards!" He meant to say, "Cry the pains in yourselves somehow. Pierce the hearts of us healthy ones with that cry. Our hearts are dried up, and their spring of love is exhausted. And your cry could make something come out of them." This rude language is a prophetic expression. I also say to patients not "You pitiable ones" but "Cry from your deepest pain. Your cry can save those who are healthy." Out of the pain comes poetry. The cry itself becomes the answer. The cries of farmers become the sound of salvation to those who are not farmers, that is, the city dwellers of Seoul. Christ is not a problem solver who single-handedly solves complicated problems. Rather, he is a person who cries out. His cry pierces our hearts and breaks us out of our comfort zones and breaks up our own logic. Christ is someone who liberates us in doing so. Reading a poem like the one we read earlier shakes me at the core. Stories of exemplary and reasonable people pose no problem to me. I can rationalize around these stories, dodging this way and that. But a stark cry of the minjung confounds me and throws me for a loss. What confronts you in such a situation makes you cry, "Indeed you are more capable than I am. I am really ashamed. Now I must do something." This is the messiah movement. This is what may be called the winds or waves of the messiah that continue to take place. For example, with the student movements, young people who worked hard to gain admission to college are throwing away their lives. How is it possible that young people are presenting their bodies as a living sacrifice in that way? Paul's words, "Present your bodies as a living sacrifice" (Rom 12:1), are being realized right now. The church is failing to live up to them. But with students, miracles are happening now. We have to take them as a truly touching messiah experience. Now the Christ event keeps exploding, but the church has clouded our eyes. Doctrine has blinded our eyes and deafened our ears, so we must be liberated. This liberation is not possible through preaching but only by the minjung event. We should be able to say to those who are having a worship service at church, "Let's go out to the site of self-transcendence. Christ is present there." But the atmosphere of the church never allows that. Can we say that Christ is present for those who are suffering now, for Jeon Tae-il or Song Gwang-yeong?[20] Jesus's minjung already did so two thousand years ago. As a matter of fact, Matt 25 is not Jesus's story; it is the confession of Jesus's minjung. This is the confession searching for the Christ of presence. The presence of Christ has been estranged from us because of the church's brainwashing.

Q: You say that the experiencing and witnessing to Christ do not take place individually but collectively. However, in hymns and in the faith consciousness of believers, Christ is thought of in very individual, religious, and personal terms. I would like to hear what you think of the reality that, while many Christians of our country, including members of Full Gospel Church, are minjung, they by and large experience Christ individually and spiritually. You have also said that theology should not stop with describing the life and suffering of the minjung but testify that Christ is present there. If Mr. Suh Nam-dong and you differ by any chance on this point, can you please elaborate?

A: Let me answer this question by saying what I intended to say earlier but couldn't. The cries in the Psalms differ from the cries of the poetry book we read from earlier. In the Psalms such words as "my enemy," "evil," and "injustice" appear frequently, and this probably has to do with the social structure of their times. Words like these have a thick political connotation. There must have been a lot of hunger at that time, too. But there are many spiritual, rather than economic, concepts expressed then. Today, however, it appears that an increasing number of material expressions are used. This

---

20. Song Gwang-yeong (1958–1985) was born in Gwangju and entered Gyeongwon University in Gyeonggi Province in 1984 to study law. As a college student, he actively participated in the democratic movement against the Jeon Du-hwan dictatorship. On September 17, 1985, he set himself on fire and ran shouting, "Abolish the evil laws about the universities, and down with the dictatorship!" and "Jeon Du-hwan, be responsible for the Gwangju slaughter and resign!" before collapsing. He was transported to the hospital and died on October 21. Ahn speaks of Song in more detail in part 3, chapter 12.

change is only natural in the modern society. It is not an accident that we see the emergence of materialist interpretation (*materialistische Auslegung*) these days. Because modern people are bound by material, a language that reflects material concerns is fitting. Since language reflects the worldview of the given age, it is an authentic approach to use the language of the age. Now we can change even God into a material expression without difficulty. But the church today would not understand. It thinks that only singing the sorrows of the psalms two thousand years ago is religious; otherwise you have gone astray. But the lives of Christians themselves are completely bound up with materials, and therefore their faith and life are separated. Given these circumstances, we must come up with material interpretations. I don't mean that we need to be slaves to material, but that we must interpret materially because modern language is material.

3.7. Salvation Must Be Expressed in Material Language

I am still thinking about the first question. I don't have a definite answer yet. In this age dominated by a material worldview, our task is to find material language to express the idea that the messiah saves us. We have to express the word salvation in a material language. However, to do so is nothing really new. Even though spiritual language was used in the past, there was contained in it material liberation, the liberation from famine or economic plight. Never were the spiritual language and material liberation separated from each other. Now it is being revealed that even God is this way. Now that our eyes are more open in material terms, we are able to see the Old Testament with more clarity. The same applies for the minjung, who are viewed by modern people in material terms.

Ironically, the traditional church uses spiritual language even though it has become enslaved to material goods. On the contrary, at a church like Full Gospel Church, they are boldly using material language to convey the gospel. But the problem is that their motivation is misguided. The material desires of those who gather at that church are thoroughly of a personal nature. And the church's witness to personal material difficulties does not connect to the collective plane of humanity at large. It only defines the problem individually and personally. Therefore the members become increasingly enslaved to personal desires—this is wrong. The church should say not only "You can live well by doing this. You can be rich by doing this" but also "If you alone are rich, other people will be poor." They must turn their eyes from addressing individual poverty to collective poverty. Preaching so that an individual person would turn his or her eyes collectively to all of humanity is the messianic testimony. Those who gather at Full Gospel Church do not follow the community of Jesus in sharing a meal but go in the opposite direction of individualism. The result is division among its members and the Jesus community.

I cannot say anything definite about the second question. I don't think Rev. Suh Nam-dong said all he had to say. The poverty of our generation was greater, which I experienced mostly in Jiandao or in my own home. The farmers of Jiandao were in a truly miserable situation. So it takes much more than a typical description of poverty to shock me. During and after my college years and up to the point of going to Germany, I made a lot of efforts to help poor people around me. "I could end my own life here for the fate of this one person" was the attitude I had. "Living for you as a single person is living a qualitatively good life, and living according to a plan is not right" was the philosophy I lived by. I strove to embody the principles of sharing, nonpossession, and participation. I didn't do such things as saving money, buying furniture, and obtaining two sets of clothes. Therefore, having a family made no sense to me. This was my experience. Looking back, this kind of experience originated from Jesus. Even though I experienced many tragedies as a young boy, it was only through Jesus that I was able to experience them poignantly as something public and collective. Through the Jesus event I came to see everything anew, and I think of this as my new birth. It was my original experience (*Urerfahrung*) and original revelation (*Uroffenbarung*). I can never leave this. Poverty does not become salvation for us. Being poor by itself does not provide salvation. Salvation is bestowed when my poverty is sublimated as our poverty and our problem. This is something I experienced in Jesus. In this sense, the doctrine of atonement back in those days gave me an increasing assurance about "we." If it wasn't for my encounter with Jesus, I would have taken what I experienced not as the Christ event but just as an everyday event. I would have thought "Well, why don't I make money, too?" The attitude of seeing the poverty of one person as a problem of humanity and recognizing your own involvement in it; the attitude of not escaping from the painful site of the minjung's life for worldly gain; the attitude of changing my perspectives after hearing this experience—this is precisely the evidence of believing in Christ. If I had not known Christ, I would not have been able to testify that Christ is present at the site of the minjung's life. I am pretty sure Rev. Suh thought so, too. But he didn't say so for some reason. Possibly he agreed on the post-Bonhoeffer view that, since words such as "God," "Christ," and "Jesus" became so common as to lose meaning and value, it was better not to use these words for the time being. People with this view were perhaps afraid that uttering "Jesus" and "the Christ event" too easily might exclude the reality of the minjung and take us back to where we used to be. I have the same concern. But I still think I must say these expressions. Perhaps this is all the difference there is between Rev. Suh and me. I don't think there is any essential difference between us.

8. The Role of the Holy Spirit Is to Liberate Humanity

Q: At a place like Full Gospel Church, they use experiences of the Holy Spirit and other supernatural experiences as tools of evangelism. If these experiences were used to raise and spread the awareness of collective pains, how would you assess that?

A: Let's think about the language of the Korean minjung. Take shamans for instance. If we call Jesus a shaman, the most important reason is his exorcism. Today's exorcism differs greatly in that Jesus's exorcism was eschatological in character. Jesus believed that exorcism signified not merely curing the disease of one person but expelling the devil or the old force that keeps humanity in structural subjugation. We must keep in mind Jesus's words, "If it is by the Spirit of God that I cast out demons, then the kingdom of God has come to you" (Matt 12:28). These days, the church's exorcism and curing of illness just satisfy the personal desire to be cured of one's illness.

We can say the same to speaking in tongues. Jesus didn't speak in tongues. Paul said, "In church I would rather speak five words with my mind in order to instruct others also, than ten thousand words in a tongue" (1 Cor 14:19). This is practically an exhortation against speaking in tongues. Speaking in tongues is something private: "What is the use of saying unintelligible things in a personal ecstasy? It is meaningful when publicly shared." Therefore, Paul's injunction to make what is received communicable to others through interpretation is a warning against speaking in tongues remaining private. Although Jesus was a healer, how many sick persons could he actually have cured? Jesus treated the problems of individuals in terms of the social structure. For Jesus, the person in question is not an individual. The role of the Holy Spirit, too, has bearing not merely on individuals but on the liberation of all humanity. That the role of the Holy Spirit is eschatological, in today's language, means that it entails the transformation of the whole system. The word *eschatological* means that all humanity should liberate itself from the current system that is interwoven with ethics, religion, law, and so forth, by overturning it. The role of the Holy Spirit lies in the transformation of the system and the liberation of humanity.

In reevaluating shamanism today, we have to keep the same point in mind. Shamanism is short-sighted because it stops with relieving a personal *han*. Jesus never relieved the *han* of individuals but tried to relieve the *han* of humanity or of a certain class. In our reevaluation of shamanism, we must rethink its self-centeredness. To some, communication through a shamanistic (religious) language is effective, while for others a material language is more effective. Either way, it doesn't matter.

Q: Lastly, please tell us about the relation between cosmic Christology and the minjung Christology. Do you think minjung theology can accept the cosmic Christology or theology of culture?

A: I once said that the God of the Bible is not the answer to a cosmic riddle. By and large, a metaphysical God functions as the solution to the riddle of the universe. That is to say, God had to be postulated as a hypothesis that solves the unsolvable problems of the world. However, the Bible never mentions such a God. For this reason, I think the idea of the cosmic Christ is not biblically grounded. This doesn't mean, however, that the cosmic Christ is absolutely impossible to conceive. Although we find it urgent to expect salvation from the minjung event, I don't think it is an eternal and unchanging truth. I only mean that, for those of us who are living in this age, salvation through the minjung event is the truth.

Q: Then do you mean minjung theology loses its utility when playing becomes the main activity of life as futurology claims?

A: No, that has nothing to do with it. What I mean is that I don't believe my current experience is the eternal and unchanging truth. The only thing I have the right to do is to bear witness in our age. The language of theology of culture is not born of labor but in currency in an intellectual group disconnected from labor. Theology of culture is, it seems to me, what privileged people do who have no connection with the land or labor. They simply enjoy music and talk about God, the world, and Christ to come up with logical explanations for intellectual problems. Someone who lives in this kind of atmosphere could use theology of culture. But even for these people, it would be beneficial to read them Kim Yong-taek's poems and tell them about the minjung. But explaining the cultural or cosmic Christ would not lead them to salvation. Music was originally connected to the rhythm of labor, but the current classical music is either royal music or church music. This is music from a totally different world separated from labor. Since we are now far removed from the site where labor produces things, we may be more inclined to this music. The cosmic Christ belongs to a theology advocated mainly by elite Indian intellectuals of high social status who studied abroad in Britain. I am skeptical that these people would be saved by upholding such a theology. If anything, it seems they have an even greater need to listen to minjung Christology for their salvation. Conversely, I am not sure if those bound up with the harsh reality of life would need the cosmic Christ. If you take people who feel sorry about one persimmon into the cosmic realm, they might be liberated only a little bit. However, the cosmic Christ wouldn't make much sense to them as they would only see the persimmon at this very moment. Moreover, since they don't understand the language employed for such an explanation, they would not be able to understand that theology anyway.

Q: According to the minjung Christology you have expounded thus far, Christians and theologians can recognize the presence of Christ at the site of the minjung's life and attain salvation by participating in that site. But how can the suffering minjung themselves be saved? Who can save them?

A: Moltmann once asked, "If Christ and minjung are identical, who saves the minjung of that description?" What underlies this question is the presupposition that the savior of minjung should come from somewhere out there. I believe that minjung save themselves in the minjung event. But even if we leave out the doctrine of atonement, the term *salvation* becomes problematic. If you view poverty and pain as negative and consider breaking free of them, then transforming pain into joy and poverty into wealth would be salvation. But I think we have to be liberated from this kind of logic. Jesus didn't fall for this logic. The words "Blessed are the poor, for theirs is the kingdom of God"[21] do not mean that the poor

---

21. This quote is based on Luke 6:20, "Blessed are you who are poor, for yours is the kingdom of God."

will become rich. If I use the word *liberation* instead of *salvation*, which is vague, liberation is achieved by the minjung themselves. The minjung obtain power for liberation when they recognize their own pains and realize that their pains are not unique to themselves but are shared by others—and so carry their burden together. I don't think that people who are not minjung should discuss the strategies of liberation for the minjung. Minjung liberation is what minjung do for themselves, and they identify strategies for themselves, too. Turning individual sorrows of poverty into collective sorrows of poverty will naturally lead to a movement of salvation and liberation. Kim Yong-taek and Park No-hae[22] are engaged in the salvation movement right now. This movement differs from communism, in which the ideologists develop strategies, present certain visions, and lead campaigns for liberation. It appears to me that arrogance lurks in this way of thinking. Minjung theology claims that the messiah event and salvation event are taking place in the midst of the minjung right now. No one standing apart from the minjung ought to discuss salvation with their own prescription.

The poet Kim Yong-taek is an elementary school teacher. He is not a farmer who tills the land. Although he has keen observations, bears witness diligently, and participates in the experiences of the farmers, there still appears to be some distance between the farmers and him. Jesus, in spite of traveling around agricultural areas, was not a farmer who worked on the land. A person who does not participate in and suffer with the minjung is unable to fully understand. In this sense, I agree with the basic observation in theological language that salvation is not what you create but what arrives.

Let's go back to Moltmann. When he was asking who would save the minjung if they identified with Jesus, he was evidently assuming that he knew the minjung. But we had not yet discussed with each other who the minjung were. I don't view minjung merely as the pitiable, the miserable, and the exploited. "The minjung are miserable, but I am well off. So I feel sorry"—I don't think in just this way. It is important to change the under-

---

22. Park No-hae is an alias for Park Gi-pyeong (b. 1957). Here, *nohae* is a reference to *nodong haebang* (labor liberation). Park started to work as a laborer in Seoul at age sixteen, and later worked on the frontline of labor movement and democratic movement. He published his first book of poetry, *The Dawn of Labor*, in 1984 and organized the Socialist Laborers' Alliance of South Korea in 1991. In the same year, he was sentenced to life in prison on the charge of heading an anti-national organization. He was granted pardon in 1998.

lying value system. It would be more appropriate to say, "If anything, I am such a nobody. I am pushed to the periphery. The minjung are standing at the center of history. They are the agents of production." Minjung are pitiable only in the sense that they are alienated from participation in the outcome of production. They are great when they are recognized as agents of production. From this viewpoint, it is the exploiters who are pitiable. It is problematic to disregard this aspect of minjung and only take pity on them and view them merely as the object of salvation. We need to take a different perspective and see the minjung in the position of the messiah who saves. But Moltmann objected by saying that the passage "the Lamb of God that takes away the sin of the world" (John 1:29) refers to Christ and not to the minjung. Nevertheless, it seems unwise to define minjung simplistically.[23]

Q: The minjung of Jesus's day and the minjung of today suffer in pain. As long as there are minjung, there will be pain. I believe that it is right to say that we see the messiah in the pains of minjung and that by participating in their pains we are saved. However, even though Jesus can be identified with the pain of the minjung, isn't it possible to perceive Jesus as the liberator who brings the joy of community to the minjung buried in their own pains and desires and causes them to start a movement for liberated community?

A: So far I have been discussing the liberation of Jesus and the minjung as the same event. Jesus's life itself was the minjung's liberation, and through Jesus the event of the minjung liberation is taking place. In Jesus's pains and death on the cross, the minjung suffered and died on the cross. But we do not possess sufficient language to adequately express this idea. We should find the right language. If we are trapped in the subject-object frame, we cannot build a bridge between Jesus's death and the minjung. We might even say that what takes place in the identification of the robbed person in the parable of the Good Samaritan with Christ is the minjung event and messiah event. There is no separate messiah. We say this in order to avoid the separation of the two. It is not just that Jesus liberates the minjung, but

---

23. For Moltmann's account of the debate with Ahn, see Jürgen Moltmann, *Experiences in Theology: Ways and Forms of Christian Theology*, trans. Margaret Kohl (Minneapolis: Fortress, 2000), 249–67; trans. of *Erfahrungen theologischen Denkens: Wege und Formen christlicher Theologie* (Gütersloh: Gütersloher Verlagshaus, 1999).

also that the minjung in a way liberates Jesus, too. It was not the case that, despite being self-sufficient, Jesus made a plan and started a movement for the minjung. Rather, his life itself became a life that liberates the minjung. Jesus was not a strategist. Indeed, like a person of incarnation, he lived life to the fullest, so his life was precisely the life of the minjung, and his death was precisely the death and liberation of the minjung. In this sense, in claiming that minjung save themselves, we are not leaving Jesus out.

4
The God of Minjung

Q: In the past, the existence of God was taken as a self-evident premise. But these days we encounter the opinion that the assumption of God's existence is not necessary. This way of thinking is exemplified by the perspective that God is dead. How can we recognize God and the meaning of God in this age?

4.1. "God Is Dead"?

A: The existence of God was taken for granted in the past. Now this belief is no longer self-evident. People think they can live without God, and this is a problem. This is a problem that originates in the West. Friedrich Nietzsche is famous for declaring "God is dead." Prior to Nietzsche, Jean Paul already talked about a similar phenomenon. But their declaration was inseparable from the collapse of the traditional Western worldview.

Theism is a worldview. That is to say, God was a hypothesis designed to explain the world, life, and so forth. Theism expressed answers to life's most difficult problems by means of the concept of God. Therefore, God is a product of contemplation. But once such a worldview has broken down due to the development of science, the concept of God automatically has lost its place.

Of course, the God of contemplation is a philosophized God. In the West, faith in God is transmitted through the Bible. This philosophical-biblical faith in God came to form the Christian culture. This culture is the product of the Christian system. This system was supported by the Western worldview with God at its zenith. Therefore, the death of God only applies to intellectuals, not ordinary people who have not incorporated the Christian faith in God into their worldview. Such a God explained this world. But this God, who was only intelligible within a particular worldview, became subject to the very same worldview. Therefore, this God had to share the same fate with it.

There is another aspect to the declaration that God is dead. It derives from the realization that the traditional idea of God cannot solve the problems arising out of the reality. Internationally, the Cold War came into being between East and West, and subjugation of the South to the North intensified. Dictatorship arose in the national or ethnic units, thereby causing a clear division and intensified conflict between classes. However, past experience led to the judgment that physical power alone was a viable solution. This judgment has, I believe, led to the rejection of even the God of Christianity.

However, this is a problem of how God is represented, not a problem with God as such. Christian doctrine has used expressions such as "God is omnipotent," "God is omniscient," "God is ubiquitous," and "God is the arbiter of the human destiny." But did Christians believe in such a God in reality? No. If they really had believed, their lives would have been different, and so would the course of history. In other words, their concept of God and their faith in God were different.

Then, either of them had to be corrected. Do these expressions really describe the God of the Bible properly? These expressions seem to convey human values in the name of God. But such a God does not really exist. Therefore, before discussing the omnipresence of the Christian God, even within theistic Christianity, it should be stated that such a God does not exist. So "God is dead" is a funny thing to say. For such a God never existed!

Perhaps Martin Heidegger was right when he said that "God is dead" is not so much a factual declaration as the cry, "God, where are you?" Marx considered that the removal of God was the precondition for destroying the existing order because it would eliminate what forms a class-based society and justifies exploitation. On the contrary, Nietzsche envisioned that he would experience total chaos in which every distinction disappeared since the death of God would lead to the collapse of the existing value system. He pictured a person searching for God with a lamp in broad daylight. Before Nietzsche, Jean Paul crafted a story as follows: After the execution of Jesus, people flocked to the church because they believed that the Second Coming of Jesus would happen in the church. (Based on this traditional belief, cemeteries were installed in the churchyards. Big abbeys became a cemetery for the bodies of famous persons.) Those who gathered at church were expecting Christ to come, and sure enough the executed one descended to the altar of the church. So the people rushed there in a crowd with joy and expectation. But Jesus, his face pale and dejected, confesses that there was no God anywhere in the other realm beyond death—nothing but a void. At that moment, the corpses that had been waiting for resurrection in the graves died again—that is, forever. But after mocking theism in this way, Jean Paul ends the story with the following words: "I woke up startled and realized it was a dream. Oh, what a relief!"

These last words are similar to Nietzsche. Since the death of God destroys the existing order—and this in turn means exactly the end of the world—he hoped reality would be otherwise.

Doubts such as "Where is God?" and "God is dead" come up because of a discrepancy between the representation of God and the reality of life. A worldview with God at its zenith was designed and used to explain everything away. But it turned out unable to answer the questions of life, incapable of solving anything. Even worse, this view of God turned out to be serving the superstructure that placed people in chains, which caused rebellion.

4.2. Western Theology's View of God

Regarding notions of God we have had up to now, I believe the subject-object frame is the greatest fallacy. Both theism and atheism have mistakenly objectified God, turning God into an object of contemplation. Can something that has become an object of human contemplation be God? Here, the fundamental fallacy was to postulate God as the answer to the riddles of the world. And the idea itself is problematic that we are the question and that God is the answer.

Human beings automatically took the seat of God, or God came to serve for human beings' ideologies or institutions, in the wake of the overflowing optimism in the infinite progress of humanity. This happened because human beings were confident in solving all the riddles of the universe. However, after World War I, optimism in humankind rapidly gave way to pessimism. At this point, works like *The Decline of the West* by Oswald Spengler came out, and they were like a dirge for the age of reason.[1] At this time, young theologians proclaimed "No!" (*Nein!*) to all of the efforts to rebuild civilization on the foundation of human power. It was declared that the God based on human religiosity was an idol. The

---

1. Oswald Spengler, *The Decline of the West*, ed. Arthur Helps and Edward Werner, trans. Charles F. Atkinson (New York: Oxford University Press, 1991). Translation of *Der Untergang des Abendlandes*, 2 vols. (Munich: Beck, 1918, 1922).

assertion, "God is an absolute other!" (*Gott ist ganz Anders!*) sums up their point. This is at once a cry about the crisis and a confession about human limitation. They held that, in the ruins of destruction, human beings must not set out on any project but wait. It meant that they had to hand the initiative over to God and wait for God's command.

The names given to the theologians who advocated this view—the school of crisis theology, dialectical theology, and Neo-orthodoxy—reflect the characteristics of their age. Barth, one of these theologians, claimed that "God said" (*Gott hat gesagt*) had to be made the new starting point, and this means a dialectical return to orthodoxy. Their discovery of Kierkegaard was not an accident. Kierkegaard was a Christian thinker who opposed the Hegelian view of God, was thoroughly conscious of the limitations of human existence, and proposed unconditional obedience to the God of the Bible.

However, the emerging theology failed to become the answer of the age. A solution to the problem was in demand, but this theology advocated silence and waiting. It prevented access for those who were seeking God in a new way. It eliminated any possible contact between God and humans. God was useless. If God is the only actor on the stage of the world, what on earth are humans supposed to do?

Barth's proclamation of God as an absolute other, against his intention to unify everything under the sovereignty of God, intensified the Western dualistic thinking. God's reality and human's reality existed independently; each was used to explain the other. But Barth exploded the bridge between them. He thought that reason could be neither human religious representation nor the bridge between God and human. He destroyed what deserved to be destroyed. But since he placed God outside the human realm, he created the possibility of being able to say God is dead or absent.

Bultmann, who made the same shock his point of departure, refused to identify God with reason or religious representation but did not accept a faith that forced the sacrifice of reason. Even though God is the object of faith, this faith has to be something that human beings can understand. He stood by the human capability of understanding. Faith is a religious concept, but he thought it could be explained in ontological terms. It was his belief that faith was religious language for the ontological view that "Humans are relational beings" and "Humans are limited beings." Bultmann believed that Heidegger's definitions of Being-in-the-world and Being-towards-death were fitting because they expressed exactly what theology tried to state about humanity. However, even Bultmann failed to escape from the dualistic frame of thinking. In his thesis, "What Sense Is There to Speak of God?," he confessed that you cannot speak of God because speaking of humans requires speaking of God and vice versa.[2] The inability to speak of God leads to the inability to speak of human beings and vice versa. What underlies this view is his claim, "Theology is anthropology," or "Humans are relational beings." But even as Western ontology failed to escape from the dualistic frame of thinking, Bultmann's view of God failed to overcome the subject-object frame. In this regard, I believe Western theology has something to learn from Eastern thinking. It has to look at the Bible with different eyes. Even though Eastern thinking and the Bible are different in their nature, I think they can come together in not dichotomizing the world.

4.3. The Eastern View of God

Q: In the East, we do not perceive division in conceptualizing God. Instead, God is expressed in terms of truth, the Buddha nature, and Dao, which are understood as the universal reason, a psychological level, and the natural principle, respectively. However, in the Bible, God appears as an object you yearn for and cry out to, personified in language that is personal and individual. God is depicted as capricious, angry, and quarrelsome just like humans. Since God appears this way in the Bible, Christianity later accepted the view of God as object and person. Please share your opinion about this matter.

A: Eastern thinking either does not mention God or, when it does, refrains from speaking of God as an absolute other or absolute transcendent. There is no dichotomy in which God and humanity run eternally in parallel. Buddhism does not mention God. But we would be wrong to view it as nontheistic. Confucianism uses words such as "heaven" and "the Highest Deity" to refer to God. However, this God, unlike in the West, does not develop into a persona. For this reason, Confucianism does not fall neatly in the category of theism. Christian evaluations of these religions based on linguistic expressions should be seriously checked. Christianity has committed the great fallacy of defining religion mainly in terms of

---

2. Rudolf Bultmann, "What Sense Is There to Speak of God?," *The Christian Scholar* 43.3 (1960): 213–22; translation of "Welchen Sinn hat es, von Gott zu reden?," in *Glauben und Verstehen* (Tübingen: Mohr Siebeck, 1933), 26–37.

theism. For example, Buddhism does not have the word *God*. But Buddha stands in its place. Confucianism has a conception of heaven and the Highest Deity, and Daoism has Dao in the place of God. But technically they are not theistic or atheistic. Confucius is judged to be nonreligious based on the following examples. When asked about the spirits of the dead, he answered, "If you are not able to serve humans, how can you serve their spirits?"³ He did not discuss "extraordinary things, feats of strength, disorder, and spiritual beings."⁴ This judgment, however, is made after putting him in the category of atheists. Confucius was sincere about sacrificial rites. According to *Analects*, "He sacrificed to the dead, as if they were present. He sacrificed to the spirits, as if the spirits were present. The Master said, 'I consider not being present at the sacrifice, as if I did not sacrifice.'"⁵ Also, the Chinese character 禮 (*li*) is a pictograph that represents the two-way interaction between above and below. This 禮 is a religious act and one of the central elements of Confucianism. What is even more important than this is Confucius's idea of heaven or heavenly calling.⁶ When his most beloved disciple Yen Yuan died, he wept, "Alas, heaven has forsaken me, heaven has forsaken me!"⁷ On another occasion he says, "I do not complain against Heaven, nor do I blame humans. I study what is lowly and so get through to what is exalted. Only Heaven knows me."⁸ Confucius knew his heavenly calling at the age of fifty and took this calling as his fate. The simple reason Confucianism of this nature is not acknowledged as a religion is that it contains no faith element. Yet, we need to be critical about this from at least two points of view. First, to

---

3. Confucius, *Analects* 11.11.1. Translation by James Legge, *Confucian Analects, the Great Learning, and the Doctrine of the Mean: The Chinese Classics*, vol. 1, rev 2nd ed. (Oxford: Clarendon, 1893). Legge's translation has been slightly revised for inclusive language.

4. Confucius, *Analects* 7.20.1.

5. Confucius, *Analects* 3.12.1–2.

6. This idea appears in *Analects* 20.3.1. James Legge translates the same idea into "the ordnances of Heaven"; Robert Eno translates as "your destiny" in *The Analects of Confucius*, version 2.21 (Bloomington: Indiana University, 2015), http://tinyurl.com/SBL3812b.

7. The given sentence appears in *Analects* 11.8.1. The English translation is my literal rendering of Ahn's Korean representation of the Chinese original. James Legge translates the sentence into "Alas! Heaven is destroying me! Heaven is destroying me!"

8. Confucius, *Analects* 14.35 [trans. Eno] (37.2 in the Legge translation). Eno's translation has been revised for inclusive language and harmony with Ahn's diction.

define the meaning of faith only in Christological terms narrows the biblical faith and distorts our understanding of other religions. Second, the emphasis on faith is the tradition of the Western Church. But the Eastern Church emphasizes experiences. A similar emphasis is found in the Bible. The *pistis* of the Bible not only has the narrow christological meaning, but also signifies a commitment to an Absolute. In this regard, for example, the Buddhist attempt to escape the self is an act of surrendering oneself. The Daoist emphasis on nothingness and doing nothing is a way of removing all reliance on human functions or techniques. This could be a form of faith construed in different terms. I am of the opinion that Eastern attitudes of faith deserve a higher evaluation than Western approaches since it is free of the subject-object dichotomy. "Believe" or "surrender" is better than "believe *in*" or "surrender *to*" something. Buddhism and Daoism do not refer to God as an object! Judging them to be atheistic is based on a superficial understanding.

4.4. How Does the Bible Speak of God?

There are various descriptions of God in the Bible, but essentially they point to a God that causes an event to occur. An event takes place in history. More specifically, it takes place in life. Therefore, the God of the Bible is never estranged from life. Since God is the power that makes an event happen in life, God cannot merely be an object of contemplation. Since people live in the event, they cannot objectify it.

God does not exist as a responder or problem-solver in another realm beyond this world where humans are groaning and crying out in the middle of life and events. God exists right here in the midst of the crying out. Therefore, the God of the Bible is not the answer to a riddle of the universe or life but is the question from the conflicts and contradictions of life itself. The God of the Bible is not perfection and harmony but conflict and contradiction. Rather than harmonizing the world, God causes problems. God keeps making events happen. And God takes contradiction to extremes. Every story is full of contradictions beginning with the stories of Adam and Eve and Cain and Abel. The God of the Bible abounds in prejudice, anger, pleasure, even sadness—in this sense, God is conflict itself. Here, I think we have to notice how Yahweh and human beings or the world resemble each other. At the same time, God is not dependent on human values or ethics, but is free from them. Why did God allow Abel to be killed? Why did God love Jacob more than Esau? Why did God let the Israelites wander in the wilderness after liberating them from Egypt? Why did God let the history of Israel be full of tribulations? It is difficult to explain these questions by means of traditional ethics or values. But these qualities of God began to morph after the establishment of the Davidic monarchy. It is not the metamorphosis of Yahweh as such, but that of the view of God. This was explained in the age of the New Testament in terms of the Greek thinking. It became the God language that constitutes the base of the dogma. As a result, instead of a God who is or reveals God's self in conflict and contradiction, God became the object of our ought-to (*Sollen*)—a being who always achieves peaceful harmony and resolves conflicts. For example, we read in Matt 5:48, "Be perfect as God is perfect." This is an expression rooted in the Greek cosmic view of God and cannot be understood in Hebrew. (In Luke, instead of "perfect," "merciful" is used.) I think it is our task to shed away the view of God that has degenerated due to the Greek way of thinking and to understand the original God of the Bible anew.

Q: This seems to be suggested in what you have already said. But if we believe that the God of the Bible is conflict and contradiction and that this reflects contradictions in history or society, does this mean that this view of God reflects the characteristics of social class? In other words, do you think that the God of the Bible reflects the social position of the people who spoke of God in that way?

A: Yes. Yahweh of the Old Testament reflects the contradiction and conflict of the people of Israel. The Yahweh God was not formed in the contemplation of Israelites but reflects their very history. Therefore, it is neither possible nor desirable to understand Yahweh apart from the history of Israel and its social conditions. This does not mean, however, that God can, according to Feuerbach, be treated according to the simple formula that God is a reflection of human hopes.

Yahweh is active, not passive. As I said before, the premise that Yahweh is the answer to human questions is wrong. Yahweh is not a being who responds to the questions of the universe arising from human intellectual interests. Neither is Yahweh a being who listens to the stories of humans and hands out solutions when they cry out from the corruptions and conflicts in the midst of their lives. We do find these descriptions of God in the Old Testament. But there is no fantastic description of Yahweh in the other realm. Yahweh is not an omnipotent genie in a lamp or a being like an unchanging principle. If these are the attributes of God, the Old Testament could be characterized as more atheistic than theistic.

Modern people do not simplify life as people of the past did. They do not attempt to explain life with simple logic. They don't think life is only possible when they overcome conflicts and contradictions because these are an anti-peace and anti-divine reality. On the contrary, they believe that conflicts and contradictions themselves are part of life, perhaps even an important impetus for the formation of life. That is to say, they don't take a passive view. In order to speak to modern people about God, we have to explain that God exists in this very reality, in conflicts and contradictions. I believe this is possible.

Q: Still, the Old Testament shows God as a liberator who constantly goes beyond contradictions and conflicts to save and liberate. Can we gather any clues from this representation of God as savior or liberator?

4.5. The God of Liberation

A: Certainly, Yahweh of the Old Testament can be characterized as a God of liberation. The exodus is the original starting point of the Old Testament. It speaks of Yahweh precisely as the God of liberation. Yahweh beats Egypt, the powerful dominator, and liberates Israel, the weak party groaning under the dominator. It was not until the exodus that Israel had its first collective encounter with God. A recent Old Testament study offers new insight about Hebrew: that Hebrew was the name of a class, not a tribe. In opposition to the Canaanite conquest theory, it proposes the theory of the insurrection by Canaanite farmers (Gottwald).[9] Either way, it seems to be an established theory that ancient Israel started with amphictyony as an autonomous community built by Syrian-Palestinian Hebrews. The Yahweh faith has to be reassessed based on this premise. That is to say, the Yahweh faith is the driving force for an antimonarchy revolution. We should not view mono-Yahwism in terms of rivalry between Yahweh faith and other religions but as a declaration of an absolute denial of the rule by a deified human. From this point of view, Yahweh was the God of the Hebrews, namely, the minjung, from the very beginning. It is not an accident, therefore, that the central conception of Yahweh is as one who

---

9. Gottwald, *Tribes of Yahweh*.

always sides with the weak. This is a God that cannot be conceived in the East or in the Hellenistic worldview. A God that makes the exodus happen and takes sides with the Hebrews—this kind of God is partial and so fails to be a God for those who seek a universal God. This God is extremely crude. This God is conflict. Why does this God suppress Egypt and stand on the side of the Hebrews? This itself already exposes the contradiction. This is not a solution. The exodus is liberation for the Hebrews, but it is loss and defeat for the Egyptians. A universal God is good for you and me both, but Yahweh is not such a God. Liberation is not a solution under the assumption of the existing order. Liberation is an event that simply destroys the existing order. In this sense, Yahweh is not a solution. Could the liberation of the Israelites as one people be the solution to the problems concerning the whole world? That Yahweh loved the people of Israel in particular does not conform to the notion of a universal God. Such a God cannot be the answer to the questions about the world and the cosmos.

4.6. The God Imprisoned by Temple Religion

Q: Then what is the difference between the God who appeared in the Old Testament and the God who appeared in Jesus?

A: You are asking about the difference between the God of the Old Testament and the God as shown in Jesus. To answer this question, I think we need to expand our scope by surveying the Old and New Testaments.

First, we need to establish that the God of the New Testament is not intended to be different than the God of the Old Testament. Nowhere in the New Testament is there a conscious effort to establish a new concept of God. However, the representations of God change considerably. Even in the Old Testament, different images of God show up in different types of sources: J material, E material, P material, and so on. The differences here are intertwined with geopolitical conditions and the resulting differences in modes of life that accompany historical development.

I believe we can divide the representations of God in the Old Testament into two main categories. Chronologically, they correspond to the periods before and after the Davidic monarchy. Since the Old Testament scriptures were edited by the historians of the Davidic dynasty, it is difficult to sort out precisely when the final form of the text was produced. But tradition criticism has made it possible to some extent. Because the historians of the Davidic dynasty edited and interpreted various ancient historical and literary texts, different spiritual traditions were included in the texts they compiled. However, since they did not invent or fictionalize history but used historical sources, fragments of the sources are preserved. A representative example is the story of David. There was a covenant between God and David, which included the promise of the blessings for a thousand generations. But what is important is the fact that David pursued the ark of covenant that led Israel and enshrined it in Jerusalem. Solomon his successor finally built the temple, and the temple centralized Jerusalem as the holy city and established the ideology of the Davidic monarchy. God, the creator of the world and the arbiter of history, became the patron God of a monarchy and was imprisoned in the temple. This introduced in the Old Testament a new pattern of representing God. God could no longer be met outside of the temple. So Israelites scattered around the world had to go to Jerusalem to meet God, and this gave rise to the custom of pilgrimage. Even in Jerusalem, in order to be allowed an audience with God, rituals had to be performed by the priestly class, including offering sacrifice. Now, meeting with God involved geographical limitations and economic conditions as God became an object of ritual. Of course, religion became the handmaiden to the power of the monarchy. Therefore, in principle no priest would challenge the royal authority. If anything, the royal power possessed the right to appoint priests.

This ritualistic religion stratified society. A prime example is the purity laws. The purity laws were mainly sanitization laws by modern standards. These laws divided the haves from the have-nots and the employers from the employees. For laborers could not stay in a clean state all the time. The same was true of the sick. Laborers with a stubborn stench in particular became unclean persons automatically.

Consequently, the God of liberation became a restrictive God, and the God who used to be ubiquitous all over the world became the God of the temple. The God of love became the God of judgment.

There were a group of people who resisted it: the prophets.[10] The prophets were not religious aristocrats within the existing institution. They fought against the powerful who abused royal power in the name

---

10. Here the editor of the original Korean text gives an in-text note to say: "*Nabi* is the Hebrew term for prophets. For further discussion, see John Bright's 'Prophets of Israel,' the introduction to his commentary, *Jeremiah*, volume 27 of Korea Theological Study Institute's International Biblical Commentary Series."

of religion and exploited the minjung. Some of them criticized aspects of the existing system; others brought the entire system into question. A representative of the former group was Isaiah, while Amos represented the latter. The lonely cry, "God desires mercy, not sacrifice,"[11] is quoted in the New Testament (Mark 12:33) and reveals the prophets' attitude against ritualistic religion.

Some organized and launched collective resistance. While not denying temple religion, they denounced the ruling class occupying Jerusalem out of anger that the religious leaders, in collusion with the powerful, used the temple for exploitation and maintaining power. A sect called Hassidim appeared before the Maccabean Revolt and decided not to identify with Jerusalem. The Essenes and the John the Baptist sect followed suit. The Pharisees also rose up in resistance. They made their resistance movement a people's movement by making the law a way of life.

Under the leadership of the Pharisees, legalism was established. In collusion with the rabbis, they made the law the norm of everyday life. This finally resulted in a legalized system becoming equated with the will of God. The law served as a dividing line between the sinful and the righteous. A sinner was "a person punished by God" who failed to fulfill the duties of the legal system. The poor, the sick, and the oppressed could not help being in this place. Therefore, the God who initially stood on the side of the poor minjung had changed into their judge.

The appearance of Jesus brought about historical transformations. The culmination was the eradication of the temple religion and the collapse of the ruling system centered in Jerusalem. This is not what Jesus intended. It was rather the result of the revolt of the Jewish minjung in the year 66. But such an event is impossible to consider apart from the Jesus event. As a result, Christianity became liberated from Judaism both regionally and institutionally and developed beyond Palestine. Roman rule was dominant outside of Palestine both politically and culturally through the influence of Hellenism. But Christians who had been expelled from Palestine and wandering in the gentile world became, along with other Jews, minjung in the literal sense of the word. The minjung who joined the Jesus movement spread out "like an epidemic" (Acts 24:5)[12]

---

11. This quote is based on Hos 6:6, "For I desire steadfast love and not sacrifice, the knowledge of God rather than burnt offerings."

12. This quote seems to be based on an expression in Acts 24:5, "a pestilent fellow," a description made by Tertullus about Paul for Felix the governor.

with the sense of calling that they were the main actors in the salvation of the world. Despite not having any security, they dug into Roman Empire like moths and finally brought it down.

4.7. God after Jesus

God after Jesus was surely different. Strictly speaking, God did not change; the understanding of God changed. The change in representation was effected, above all, by changes in historical conditions. Let me offer a few examples. First of all, the conditions for constituting a country changed. After the invasion by Rome in 66 CE, Jerusalem fell in 70 CE. The leadership, who represented the people, now caved in, and the temple, the ideological center of Israel, was destroyed. The Jews were expelled out of the lands of Israel and Judah. This shook the foundations on which the faith of Israel rested.

Second, most Israelites became wanderers in gentile territories, where they had to survive by any means in foreign environments. Under these circumstances, it became increasingly difficult to maintain nationalistic and exclusivist notions of God. Now they had to explain God in the language and cultural framework of Hellenism. Additionally, temple religion and the legal system collapsed, which caused Christianity to emerge as a new religion in different circumstances.

Yahweh could no longer remain the God of a single people, the Israelites. Yahweh was now the God of the cosmos. How could you demonstrate that the Yahweh of the Old Testament was the God of all humanity? Paul answered this question with a teleological view of redemptive history. Paul knew he was called to be an apostle for the gentiles. But he did not deny the special relationship between Yahweh and Israel. On the one hand, he spiritualized the concept of the people of Israel. He asserted that Christians were the offspring of Abraham. The true Israel is spiritual, not physical or based on blood ties. On the other hand, however, he could not abandon the idea of the superiority of Israel as a people. Even though the people of Israel had betrayed Yahweh, God would fulfill God's promise with them. This conviction would be preached to the gentiles first. This would provoke the envy of Israel, and then Israel would finally repent and be saved—a reality that would be fulfilled in the *eschaton* (Rom 11:25).

At any rate, it was a big task for the first Christians to bring God out of Israel. For it was the first of the tasks that would prove that Yahweh was the God of the whole world. But they did not Hellenize Yahweh. God was never an idea or principle as the guarantee for preserving the existing order. No! This God is the reality that makes events happen in order to liberate humans from the world gone wrong. They believed that such a teleological act had found its concrete manifestation in the Christ event. Therefore, they concentrated their efforts wholly on Christology instead of the development of the doctrine of God. There was another peculiarity. Even though God has to be universal and rational, this God was partial. In this respect, this God is the same as Yahweh of the Old Testament. However, whereas Yahweh of the Old Testament was partial to Israel as a people, the God that appeared through Jesus appeared as a God partial to the oppressed, the poor, and the unfortunate—namely, the minjung. Jesus's origin, deeds, and fate all demonstrated this point in the most dramatic way.

Then is this a totally different God? I think I have to answer this question in two respects. This God is precisely the same Yahweh of the Hebrews. Yahweh created conflict by choosing the people of Israel. The God of the New Testament created conflict by unconditionally standing on the side of the minjung. Both are identical in standing on the side of the weak. But the difference was that the God of Jesus cuts a straight-line path of love, while the God of the Old Testament cuts a parabolic path of love.

4.8. The God of Minjung

Q: You have pointed out the difference between the God of the Old Testament and the God as shown in Jesus through the difference in the shape that the paths of their love take: a parabola versus a straight line. But according to the teaching familiar to us, the two Gods are identical because the God of the Old Testament achieved complete revelation of God's self in Jesus. Couldn't it be that the difference between the two Gods stemmed from the distortions made by court historians to reflect the interests of the ruling class during the transition from the covenantal community (Israel) to the monarchy?

A: Yes, I don't deny that. But we have to be cautious about one thing here. The premise that we can clearly differentiate between God, history, and the interpreter is problematic. Are we right in thinking that God exists as an objective reality independent of history and the interpreter, and that both history and interpretation are clearly separate from God? Can we speak of a God other than the God who appeared in the Old Testament and in Jesus? Can a God outside of history, a God who exists independently, enter our consciousness? I wonder what this God has to do with us and if we can even speak of this God. I answer all these questions, "No." In short, the only God we know is the God we experience. But here another question arises. In the Bible, a variety of Gods are recorded according to different historical conditions. Which of them is the true God? In your question you mentioned distortions in representations of God. But doesn't this presuppose certain criteria? You have a God that is dependent upon your own experience.

The God I am referencing is the God as shown by Jesus. After meeting the God in Jesus who stands on the side of minjung, I observed a pattern in the diversity of representations in the Old Testament. Since Jesus's love toward the minjung is direct and unconditional, I have come to see it as the way God truly is.

But there is a problem with this. In the New Testament, there is a diversity of ways in which Jesus is introduced as Christ. The Gospel of Mark is central to my understanding. Many scholars have studied this short text and understood it in various ways. A prominent motif that is identified is the messianic secret or the idea of the imminent *eschaton*. The narrative of Jesus's passion was thought to be central to the gospel and was interpreted from the Christological perspective. I once shared this approach. But at some point I began to see the minjung as central to the Gospel of Mark. It was not because I discovered a new version of Mark, but because I was blind to the minjung at the time. What healed my blindness? Although I started reading Mark with an interest in the minjung in the late 1960s or the early 1970s, the decisive moment was the event of the suffering minjung. It was nothing but a great shock. How was it possible to speak of salvation and liberation, while looking away from the suffering minjung? It was because I had been brainwashed by the ideology of the dominant system. Because royal and paternal authority were supreme in the patriarchal system, I bought in to a view of Jesus from this point of view. I failed to see the minjung who lived with Jesus.

But Jesus was not a ruler in any sense of the word. No! He was a poor and oppressed person. His life and death were no different from the fate of the minjung. There can be no Jesus without the minjung. My eyes were opened to the plain truth not by reading the Bible but by encountering the minjung event that was happening where I was living. The Jesus event and the minjung event are two different stories from two different places and time periods. I saw them as successive explosions of one identical event.

Now it is only natural that the question arises, "Then isn't it the case that the minjung event, not the Jesus event, is what matters?" But without the Jesus event, it would not have occurred to me that the minjung event was the very site of God's self-realization. Without an encounter with the minjung event, I would not have realized that the Jesus event, as the minjung event, became the God event. Therefore, they are inseparable.

4.9. The Reference for the God Event

Q: It has become clear that Jesus is the reference in discerning the God event. Is it possible to experience the God event in a different religion or in ordinary events? Mr. Suh Nam-dong makes the Bible, church history, and the history of Korea references for his minjung theology.

A: I experience the God event in the Jesus event. For me, therefore, the Jesus event is the sole reference. But I cannot assert that there is no way to experience the God event outside of Jesus. For I have not tried other ways! For me, the God of Christianity is the true God. But this doesn't mean that I have the right to say other religions do not know God or are false. If a person of a different religion experiences God on their path, there is no reason to deny it.

But I don't think that I encountered God only through Jesus. The moment I discovered myself in Jesus, I discovered that I had already been in God. Before then I was not a religious person. I grew up in an atmosphere of Confucianism and had some familiarity with Buddhism. But I wasn't a religious person. The name of Christ was new to me. Nevertheless, I became convinced that I had already been in God. Therefore, I am not hindered at all from thinking that a Buddhist, a Muslim, or an atheist can be in God—or, more specifically, a son or daughter of God. What hampers this kind of thinking is theism. I believe theism belongs to the same category as atheism. In theology, there is the logic that distinguishes between general history and redemptive history. Similarly, there is a distinction between the sacred and the secular. These distinctions may be useful for protecting the vested interests of religion but they diminish God in the end. After all, the desire to monopolize reaches all the way up even to God. I believe it is possible to experience the God event in other religions, books of philosophy, literary works, works of art, and so forth.

Q: The Gospel of Mark says that Jesus has come to lead people to repentance and shows his partiality with sinners with such ideas as "I have come to call sinners" and "I am on the side of sinners." But isn't it true that there are numerous understandings of God in the New Testament?

A: That's why I put special emphasis on the stories of Jesus. If we separate "The Kingdom of God is being fulfilled now" from Jesus's behaviors, we cannot explain the relationship between Jesus and the minjung. For Jesus, God is inseparable from the fact that the kingdom of God is arriving. Surely the conviction that "The kingdom of God is being fulfilled now" opened up the possibility for Jesus to draw a straight line to God's love. But living in Jesus means the complete destruction of the existing order. When this conviction diminishes, you come to worry about maintaining the status quo and the institutional church. Leaning too far towards one extreme is not desirable. In other words, order becomes a necessity. So you come to establish ethics and order again. This already started with Paul. It started in the 60s, no, in the 50s. The process of development is revealed by comparing the gospels, the early epistles of Paul, and the later epistles of Paul, including the Deutro-Pauline epistles. When the earliest church was convinced of the eschatological advent of the kingdom of God, communities freely gave up personal possessions. But once these expectations disappeared, the ways of life changed. A different order called the church was created, and then other institutions were created.

The church came to establish itself on earth in place of the kingdom of God. But with Jesus, "The kingdom of God has come near" (Mark 1:15) was the conviction. Yet this conviction did not presuppose the formation of the church and was even antiethical. After the conviction died down, everything changed. Therefore, we must read the New Testament again by the criterion of the event of Jesus's minjung. For example, during the Reformation, the Reformers reassessed the whole Bible in light of the criterion of *sola fide*. Now we must do the same using the criterion of the minjung event. This could be a new movement. I suggest that we look at the whole of the Old Testament and New Testament in this way. The gospel is not Jesus Christ having died for us. It is the event Jesus brought about with the minjung.

Q: I would like to go back to an earlier topic. Previously you said that you did not come to be in God through meeting Jesus, but that meeting

Jesus confirmed that you had already been in God. What is the qualitative difference between believing in God and not believing in God? And if I could add another question here, what is the difference between a discussion that does not presuppose God's existence, as in materialism, and one that operates on the assumption that God exists?

A: Let's look at this example. Bultmann understood human beings through assuming God's existence and through reading the Bible that assumes God's existence. But he was surprised that Heidegger reached a similar understanding and expressed it in nearly identical language with a different assumption or methodology. In his literary works, Dostoevsky approaches the reality of Jesus more accurately than modern New Testament studies. But his insights don't seem to come from faith or a thorough study of the Bible. He likely had no more knowledge of the Bible and Jesus than the average Russian of his time. But I believe that his intense life experiences enabled him to see the world and humans in an entirely different way. I believe he interpreted Christianity from this perspective. In the epilogue of his book, *The Behaviors of Jesus*, the Japanese author Arai Sasaku expresses his awe that young people in Korea understand the reality of Jesus with an amazing degree of accuracy.[13] Yet he himself arrived at an understanding of the historical Jesus by means of a different methodology. He adds that there is no single correct methodology. The same conclusion can be drawn irrespective of method. We have to admit that the conclusions we have arrived at through Jesus can be reached by others without Jesus. So is there no difference between what you attain with faith in Jesus and what you attain without faith in Jesus? There is a difference. Perhaps it is the same kind of difference that exists between how you would respond to someone when you know they love you and how you would respond when you don't. I can only say as much.

In response to the second question, I don't believe we can say that only those who presuppose the existence of God can have the right understanding and live in the right way. It is not my place to judge. God makes the final judgment. I think it is possible that a person can comprehend and fulfill God's will in a more open-minded way, despite being unconscious of God, than someone who assumes the existence of God. For example, someone who does not confess or even despises Jesus may actually be

---

13. Arai Sasuku, *The Behaviors of Jesus* [Japanese].

more advanced in the minjung event. Therefore, we cannot say they are outside of Jesus. Taking one step further, it is possible to confess that Jesus is working with them rather than someone who calls on the name of Jesus. In this sense, I am not monopolizing God or Jesus. Can you monopolize Jesus by calling his name? Can I monopolize Jesus by being conscious of him? Jesus may be hidden in the most unexpected places. I believe this is fundamentally the *missio Dei*.

Q: Then let's say that talking of Jesus or God is only a matter of utility. If there is no difference between a person who presupposes Jesus or God and a person who doesn't—and, if anything, the latter can be better, does the utility of speaking of Jesus or God only concern you as an existential being?

A: When I was in Germany, Braun once gave a lecture on Christology, soteriology, and ecclesiology of the New Testament. He argued that there is no continuity in any of these. And concerning the question of what is the thesis of the New Testament, he offered the following conclusion, "Before God you are allowed to, you can." This stirred controversy among those who were present. At one point, I asked him, "Can you preach a sermon of Christian evangelism (*Missionspredigt*) with such an outlook?" But he was silent. Then Käsemann and Bornkamm around us urged him to answer, saying it was an important question to answer. Only then did he say, "*Missionspredigt? Ich weiß nicht, aber ich kann predigen*" ("Preaching a sermon of evangelism? I don't know, but I can preach."). That is: "I cannot say, 'You should not believe in Buddha. You can be saved only through believing in Jesus.' But I can preach." This means that he can witness to Jesus according to his experience. At the time, I didn't like his answer. But now I think it was a sincere remark to make. Experience matters to everyone. So I can say, "I am having this particular kind of experience and recognizing God in this particular way." But I cannot say, "You're wrong. There is no other way." I believe this is possible before Jesus.

Therefore, we cannot claim, "I have (or the church has) a monopoly on God." We can only say, "According to my own experience, God is such-and-such." Further, we should be able to bear witness and say, "God is working there" or "Christ is working here," wherever the minjung event is taking place.

Q: I would like to ask you a similar question. In different religions or even within Christianity, there seems to be various ways of recognizing

God. Some perceive and worship God in nature; others perceive God as the being who defines one's view of or attitude toward life; and still others perceive God through pious feelings experienced in one's psyche. Where can we, in today's reality, see the God who appeared in Jesus and the Bible?

A: I am not interested in nature for the sake of nature. I do not experience God in nature. Even when I am reading a novel, I don't feel interested in descriptions of nature but prefer descriptions of people. For example, I am more attracted to the writings of Dostoevsky than Tolstoy. Tolstoy gives lots of descriptions of nature. I see a Dostoevsky-like aspect in Jesus. Despite living in nature day and night, he does not start with it but looks at people. Even though you can experience God through nature or have a mystical experience, I myself am not interested in it. Only through events happening in my interactions with other people do I encounter God.

Now, in connection with the second question, I agree with Bultmann when he says, "Theology is anthropology." Here, anthropology means that we can only see human beings. We cannot see God. We cannot look straight at the sun but can only see the things illuminated by it. We can go further to see the sun in all of the things that it enables us to see, and this is like seeing God in human beings. In other words, the attempt to explain human beings by necessity ends up speaking about God. This is what theology is all about! Anthropology looks exclusively at human beings not in relationship with God. The claim "Theology is anthropology" looks into human beings as beings who are not independent, but who stand before God together.

All I know is that we, together with our neighbors, can see God in joy and sorrow and through an event. But the Old Testament says that you die upon seeing God directly, and God's actual presence means the *eschaton*. In this sense, we need to consider the diverse manners in which people live as the sites where they meet God. A theological explanation has to come into play here. If we consider the cross and the resurrection event as the culmination of the Jesus and minjung event, we can see God's true and ultimate presence and revelation in the resurrection of Jesus and the minjung taking place while they were falling and being trampled upon. I believe the cross event and the minjung event are directly connected. If we see them apart from one another, the cross is merely a magical object or an object of ritual. It follows that we can meet God less in the formalities of a worship service, such as the sacraments or the sermon, than in the struggles of the minjung for liberation.

Now, in the theology of the Word, whether it be Bultmann's or Barth's, the place of the proclamation of God's Word is the only site for meeting God. But I believe that preaching and the sacraments as such are meaningless. When preaching makes an event happen in history, when the sacraments of Jesus' flesh and blood transform into an event in which we share a meal, there we can meet God. The same, I believe, applies to prayer.

Q: Here the historical event surely means the minjung event, right?

A: Certainly. It's the event of the minjung's liberation in which resistance arises, the social structure changes, and liberation takes place.

Q: If we consider your earlier quote, "Before God you can," with regard to the minjung, it becomes a proclamation of true liberation and grace. But if those in power interpret it to their own advantage, it becomes a terrifying proposition. In *The Brothers Karamazov*, Dostoevsky said through Ivan that without God anything is possible.[14] For example, those who have nuclear weapons and monopolize the wealth of the world would like it better if God did not exist. For the God of the past is accepted as the God of the law and ethics. But even if God existed, wouldn't they be pleased with the phrase "you can"? There seems to be a problem here. If Western theology's affirmation, "Before God you can," does not assume a minjung-oriented position, namely, partiality to minjung, it would be an irresponsible statement.

A: For this reason, I need to mention that it was those in power to whom Jesus spoke. He told them the minjung facts. This is especially clear in the Gospel of Luke. And the content of these facts is the minjung event. Only when they accept these facts, does salvation become possible. But they do not come to Jesus.

---

14. Fyodor Dostoevsky, *The Brothers Karamazov*, trans. David McDuff (London: Penguin, 2003).

Q: So, is it a matter of proclaiming liberation to the minjung and proclaiming judgment for those who are wealthy and in power?

A: Of course. Jesus told his followers to give up everything and follow him only. Most of them did not, so he said that it is more difficult for the rich to enter the kingdom of heaven than it is for a camel to go through the eye of a needle. Bultmann says Jesus's command was proclaimed to individuals, but I don't agree.

Q: Let's take a further step from Christology. What do you think of the doctrine of the Trinity?

A: I do not deal with the doctrine of the Trinity. It is not in the Bible, and I believe it is nothing more than a convenient tool for explaining God. We can find language for the three persons of the Trinity in the New Testament but not the language for their unity. It doesn't matter to use such a tool if it is needed for the development of your thinking. But it is unnecessary to explain the Holy Spirit with the concept of personhood. It is preferable to see in Christ both the Holy Spirit and God. If we view Christ and the Holy Spirit as events, rather than falling for an ontological view of them as persons, then they are different expressions of various aspects of what the minjung do. Minjung as such are not anything great when considered individually or collectively. What is remarkable is the event of self-transcendence. I believe we can refer to this as *missio Dei*, the continuation of the Jesus movement, and the presence of the Holy Spirit.

5
The Church as Community of the Minjung

Q: Many of those engaged in congregational ministry wonder if minjung theology on the whole has an ecclesiology. I am wondering what you think of the church from the standpoint of minjung theology. First, what is the essence and function of the church according to minjung theology? Who does the church consist of? Second, can this ecclesiology accept traditional models or the ecclesiology of Western theology? If so, what kind of church would we have as a result? Third, what structural and organizational forms should the minjung church adopt? Fourth, the aim of minjung theology is liberation. Participants in secular minjung movements have the same goal. What is the difference between the minjung church and the community mentioned by the secular minjung movements? If there is any relation between these two, what is the nature of this relation? Finally, is the minjung church in a conciliatory or hostile relationship to the existing system?

A: It is only natural that minjung theology should have its own ecclesiology. But since our first priority was to develop minjung theology, we did not treat ecclesiology properly. The development of minjung theology itself serves as a criticism for the existing church, and it will simultaneously highlight the true shape of the church. Since what underlies the whole of minjung theology now is the critical spirit against the West-formed ecclesiology, it naturally has a different ecclesiology. However, it is not putting its ecclesiology into specific terms. But the church does exist, and so minjung theology cannot just stay silent to the request for clarifying its attitude toward the church. So, in order to discuss the ecclesiology of minjung theology, I need the qualification of "If you insist that I respond to such a request." But I will not necessarily respond to your questions in the order you asked them.

The word *ekklēsia* is used forty-six times in the Pauline epistles. This means that the church has increased in importance for Paul. But in the Synoptic Gospels, the word appears two times and only in the Gospel of Matthew. From whatever angle you look at these two instances, you cannot ascribe their origins to Jesus. The word *ekklēsia* does not appear in the Gospel of Mark or the Gospel of Luke. Is this because the gospel redactors were not familiar with the word *ekklēsia* at the time of writing? That cannot have been the case. Luke and Mark were written twenty to thirty years and ten to twenty years after the Pauline documents, respectively. So their authors must have known the word. Perhaps they didn't use it for good reason. We can think of this in two ways. First, Jesus had no intention to start something like the church, and this is an established view in New Testament studies. So I want to deal with why Mark did not mention the church even though the church, by his time, had been built. I interpret this as evidence that there were people critical that the church was already on the path of institutionalization. We can see that the church at the time already met around a certain ideology or dogma. Another important factor might have been the intensified ritualization of the church. That is, the church was becoming a cult. Baptism and the Lord's Supper were important in the cult. Jesus himself did not give baptism or the Eucharist to the minjung. The Last Supper was not originally the Eucharist as sacrament. Also, there is no record of Jesus giving baptism. In the Gospel of John, Jesus gave baptism as if in competition with John the Baptist (3:22). There is also the record that Jesus himself gave no baptism (John 4:2). For this reason, we cannot identify the *ekklēsia* as a place of worship that includes the sacraments. Some people came to be critical of the degenerating church. These people were the minjung, who were not at the center of the institutional church. The grounds for criticism were precisely the experiences as they lived together with Jesus. Therefore, their yearning to return to earlier ways developed into an oral transmission movement that continued to remind people of the Jesus event. As a result, they could not help but become critical forces against the church institution on the way to ritualization. One of the representative issues was apostolic authority. Already in the epistles written by Paul in the 50s and 60s, we can see that the authority of the apostles figured prominently in the church. They were not merely the leaders of a group but claimed charismatic authority. This was the origin of church authority. The foundation of church authority was the sense of privilege attached to teaching.

We can see Paul's claim of apostolic authority and the tension between him and the apostles. Paul demanded that they acknowledge his own apostolic authority. This is the question of the authority of the teacher. However, in the minjung-centered Gospel of Mark, criticisms of these apostles figure prominently. The apostles in Mark appear to be people who are in the dark about what Jesus intends to communicate. Jesus's rebukes are stern. In the passion predictions, one of them is even called Satan. They are ignorant of the meaning of Jesus's suffering. They did not participate in his suffering or resurrection but fled away. These critical narrations about the disciples seem to be the minjung's resistance and accusation against apostolic authority. There is no trace of any attempt on Jesus's part to gather his followers together and create a structured institution. Here, Jesus is clearly different from the Essenes and the John the Baptist sect. But in Matthew the word *ekklēsia* appears two times (16:18; 18:17), and it is said that the foundations for this church are precisely the faith of the apostles who have confessed Jesus as Christ. However, no trace of this kind is to be found in either Mark or Luke. Luke in the Acts of Apostles narrates the birth of the church after Pentecost. From this point of view, there was a distance between the institutional church and Jesus's minjung. There is no denying the fact that the minjung felt at odds with and resisted the church. Seen from this perspective, the ecclesiology founded and developed by Paul cannot escape criticism from minjung theology. But we are required to think about the positive meaning of the church in a different respect, which is a big task.

5.1. Minjung as Leaders of the Church

The church was born in the frustration and unfulfilled expectation that the kingdom of God would come after the death of Jesus. It was inevitable and had a positive meaning. Then what characteristics should define this community?

The first thing to point out is that the church should be a community led by the minjung. According to this outlook, the true church should be sought at the intersection between Jesus and the minjung. The archetype of the church can be found in this exact moment. We must not give this up. The community is not led by a select religious group or privileged class of people. If we assume that the community where Jesus and the minjung coexist is the church, should it be no different from the community of secular social movements? With this question in mind, let's reconsider the site of Jesus's work and the original shape of the community of Jesus's minjung. That Jesus met the minjung on the open plains without restrictions means that this community was not bound to the moral or religious norms of society. It also means that it did not impose any ritualistic prerequisite. The community participated in the creation of a new world, namely, the advent of God's kingdom. Jesus calls people into this new world. Here, calling does not just mean calling the twelve disciples. It also means making people gather around Jesus. The community of Jesus is precisely the people who gathered in response to the proclamation that the kingdom of God has come near. With the advent of the kingdom of God, extraordinary things were happening in the world. The community gathered in this *eschaton* moment when the kingdom of God was arriving—this is the original manifestation of the church. When we pursue this line of thinking, we must ask whether the kingdom of God is in the future or in the present. German scholars claim it is in the future, while Anglo-Saxon scholars, including Charles Harold Dodd, claim a "realized eschatology" in the present. But what is certain is that the kingdom of God is being realized. The kingdom of God is now being fulfilled. Every value system changed in light of this development. Class divisions changed, and what is required of them also changed. The church was never supposed to be anything like the Greek *ekklēsia*, which created law and order for the *polis*. Rather, it was to bring down all of the existing orders as the final outcome. The original church refused the status quo and participated in the advent of the new kingdom. So the advent of the kingdom of God is not a vague expectation but is taking place right now. The event is happening. Shocked by this event, Jesus shouted before its presence, "The kingdom of God is arriving," "It is arriving right now," and "It is being fulfilled right now." Those who gathered in response to these words did not evaluate the kingdom of God with the value system of the past. They accepted it unconditionally. The aim of preaching is to spread the message, "You are precisely the new people of the kingdom of God." This is what preaching is all about. You cannot dare to do this without having truly felt that the kingdom of God is arriving. The Sermon on the Mount proclaims the nature of the community at the site where the kingdom of God is arriving. The message that the kingdom comes first to the poor, the weeping, and the hungry is the reality of the advent of the kingdom. Where those who are poor, those who weep, and those who suffer come running, the kingdom of God is guaranteed. This kingdom is yours. The satisfied and the powerful do not come and so are automatically excluded. They have given up the kingdom of their own accord. At the same time, I believe, healing the sick and the mentally ill and so forth are all deeds that are done under this premise. This was how the community of Jesus was formed and how the church was formed at the root. It is my belief that Mark conveyed to us this surprising picture of the original Jesus community transmitted by the minjung. This picture stands against the notion of church Paul formulated. In doing so, he no doubt attempted to deliver a picture of the church different from the church that had already become formulaic and authoritarian.

5.2. The Jesus Community Was a Meal-Sharing Community

Q: What did the very first Jesus community look like?

A: We cannot really reconstruct it as it was, for we don't have sufficient information.

Mark 16:7 deserves our first attention. The messenger who spoke of Jesus's resurrection told the disciples to go to Galilee. This suggests that the site of Jesus's epiphany was Galilee, and so I believe that most of Jesus's minjung started their community in Galilee. This tradition was reflected in the Gospel of Mark to a great extent. The Jesus event in Galilee was the foundation for the Jesus community. But what it was like specifically we can only imagine. Having said that, we can roughly imagine the following.

Some disciples, like Peter, settled down in Jerusalem. Other disciples filled leadership positions in the community. However, they claimed no charismatic privilege. This community was not a well-defined organization. Perhaps it was not led by means of established ethics or religious norms and had no sacramental elements. But they gathered, for they were waiting for the fulfillment of the great eschatological expectation in the second coming of Jesus. But they did not merely gather and wait. They went out to spread the news of his imminent arrival. We can distinguish between the *gathering community* and the *sending community*. The Galilean community was a sending community. The leadership in particular left for different places and proclaimed repentance. In the gathered community wonders and miracles occurred frequently. Casting out demons and the advent of the kingdom of God were considered the two sides of the same event. This community was also a sharing community. Here, class distinction was not relevant, which was inspired by the many episodes of Jesus sharing the same table with the minjung. In Mark, we have the stories of Jesus feeding the five thousand (Mark 6:30–44) and the four thousand

(Mark 8:1–10). In the story of feeding the five thousand, it is worth noting that Jesus "had compassion for them, because they were like sheep without a shepherd" (Mark 6:34). I understand this as meaning that the crowds did not recognize anyone other than Jesus as charismatic. At least in the earliest days, there doesn't appear to have been baptism or Eucharist as sacrament. I suppose they were the first to commemorate the day of the resurrection as it had strong eschatological expectations.

There was another tradition that ran parallel to this one. It was the tradition of the Jerusalem church. At the beginning of the Acts of the Apostles, Jesus "ordered them not to leave Jerusalem, but to wait there for the promise of the Father" as they had heard from him (1:4). The apostles were not merely the disciples of Jesus but representatives of the twelve tribes, symbolizing the people of Israel. Therefore, they elected a person to replace Judas Iscariot and complete the number twelve. This means that the church inherited the tradition of Israel. What was promised was not the second coming of Jesus but the Holy Spirit. Therefore, Acts 2 designates the descent of the Holy Spirit on Pentecost as the birth of the church. The political and regional walls broke down as the apostles spoke. What is noteworthy is the fact that the agents in this event were Galileans (Acts 2:7). That is to say, some of Jesus's disciples who had followed Jesus in Galilee went up to Jerusalem and made it the home base of the Jesus community. In this way, the minjung took root in the religious aristocracy. Put differently, they claimed to be inheritors of the privileges God granted to Israel. They emphasized that Jesus was indeed the one God had promised to Israel, and they contended that they themselves were the true Israel. Therefore, they observed the Jewish law including the Sabbath and respected the temple rituals as they were. However, they simultaneously accused the Jewish leadership of sin, including executing Jesus. For this reason, they were persecuted. While these things were happening, they gathered together to sing hymns, pray, and bear witness. They became a voluntary and autonomous community that shared meals and resources.

Following the tradition of John the Baptist, they baptized in the name of Jesus (Acts 2:38) and connected Jesus's sharing event with the Passover to sacramentalize it. Above all, it has to be pointed out that they heightened apostolic authority. This was perhaps to supplant the priestly system of Judaism. They organized their community in the same manner as Judaism.

Paul stood in the tradition of gentile Christianity but respected the tradition of the Jerusalem church. Not only did he respect it, but he apparently was the person who finally systemized it. For he was indeed, as he confessed, a Pharisee and a Hebrew of the Hebrews (Phil 3:5). Paul was willing to call the minjung of Jesus "Abraham's offspring" (Rom 4:16; Gal 3:29). Abraham was the symbol of Israel. But Paul says Abraham was the father of every person (Rom 4:12), and that Christians were his heirs (Gal 3:29). He says that the Christian community was God's temple (1 Cor 3:16). This kind of Judaism, in the end, gave rise to another Christology that links the death of Jesus to the sacrificial lamb.

5.3. The Fall from the Community of Living to the Community of Worship

This change meant that the community of living gradually changed to the community of worship. Jesus, by becoming Christ, became the object of worship rather than someone who lived with them. This is why there is little mention of the historical Jesus in Paul.

Q: How can we evaluate the existing church, which has been in place for two thousand years, with reference to the church as the Jesus community mentioned earlier? Do we have to say it departed from the essence of the original church community? Or can we use a different description?

A: That is a difficult question. An answer would only be possible after reexamining the actual development of the original church into what it is today.

As previously mentioned, the Jesus community quickly took the form of the institutional church. The institutional church included various forms of leadership and authority (apostolic authority, bishops in later times, etc.), the sacramental system, and unique rules applied to Christians. In the process of formalization, the church had to secure its own place and made compromises with worldly powers, institutions, and values. The Jerusalem church was so keenly aware of Judaism that the compromise made it legalistic. Gentile churches tried to avoid conflict with the Roman Empire and Hellenistic culture. As a result, it became depoliticized and assimilated into Hellenistic culture. These are changes that any community must go through, but it is regrettable that they lost sight of the church as a place where Jesus and the minjung come together with no need of any intermediary.

Still, some remained active holding onto the tradition of the Jesus event. But after this community movement was absorbed into the Roman Empire, the resulting state of degeneration became fixed in doctrines and institutions. The church became a friend of the government. The emphasis on church authority led to the installation of the papal system, in which popes claimed to be successors to Peter. But in reality some argued to have even more authority than was ceded to Peter from Christ, claiming the doctrine of papal infallibility. When was Peter ever infallible? Citing Matt 18:19—this material is found only in Matthew and runs counter to the original text in Mark (cf. Matt 18:13-20; Mark 8:27-30)—popes professed themselves to be the surrogate of divine authority. In this way, dogmatic foundations were laid, and the current ecclesiology was forged. The Reformation advanced the idea of universal priesthood and deprived the pope of the right to monopolize biblical interpretation. But this did not change the hegemony of institutional ecclesiology. Of course, we cannot underestimate the fact that the Bible was translated into the vernacular so that everyone might have access to it. The reason I criticize the Reformation is that even the reformers failed to break meaningfully away from medieval ecclesiology. Luther waged his campaigns with the backing of feudal chieftains, and for this reason he responded in such a brutal way to the sufferings of the peasants that Thomas Müntzer represented. John Calvin executed a great number of people on the basis that they believed in different doctrines. These examples show that it was as if these reformers were sitting on the seat of a pope. We cannot overlook the fact that they underestimated and even disregarded the gospels. This form of ecclesiology held sway and has continued as the ideology maintaining the existing church today.

In light of this history, what ecclesiological position should minjung theology take? Minjung theology has to begin by viewing the church as the site where minjung and Jesus meet each other. This does not mean that minjung theology upholds something radically new. Rather, it invites people to find the authentic manifestation of the church in the resistance against the formation of the institutional church described above.

As I have already said, the institutional church sprouted early. The Jerusalem church imitated Judaism, and gentile Christian churches were institutionalized under the influences of the Greek *ekklēsia* which, in this process, kept adding various doctrines to emphasize its distinctness. The church was confined to a particular location and started to build walls against the world. Although this was part of its defense measures for survival in the Roman Empire, nevertheless the church armed itself with ahistorical kerygma, namely, dogma, in the process.

All this time, however, the minjung of Jesus continued to transmit the event of the meeting between Jesus and the minjung. But this work inevitably took on an unofficial nature because the church leadership refused to make it official. The minjung challenged apostolic authority, which was church authority that stood between Jesus and themselves. They disregarded things such as the sacrament as the condition for entering the Jesus community. They passed on the political nature of the Jesus event. Furthermore, they emphasized the events that occurred between Jesus and the minjung, namely, the poor, the sick, the oppressed, and so on. This information was transmitted in the gospels. I believe this is the primordial resistance movement against the institutional church. Similar movements of this lineage have continued up until now. But its participants were ignored or executed as heretics by the institutional church. Therefore, they were inevitably defined as a religious sect and have maintained its existence as a small group. Minjung theology intends to stand precisely in this lineage. Then, the question will arise what meaning this movement will have for the established church in practical terms.

The life of the Jesus community is its eschatological nature. That is to say, the advent of the kingdom of God made the community of Jesus and the minjung possible. This eschatological consciousness led them to renounce the existing system. The status quo of politics, ethics, and even religion has no power in light of the coming kingdom of God. For this very reason, a minjung-oriented meeting was possible. The declaration of Jesus's public life in Luke 4 poignantly expresses the eschatological consciousness. But the eschatological consciousness is hard to maintain. For it means a continual conflict with the status quo. The church gradually absorbed eschatological elements and turned itself into a special realm. That is to say, it worked on creating a buffer zone for avoiding conflict with the existing system. Along with this, the kingdom of God lost its relevance for the world as it came to be viewed as something religious, otherworldly, and private. Together with this, ethics and doctrine gradually came to the fore, and this became the wall that blocked the minjung off.

5.4. The Church Has to Recover Its Original Shape

Here, it becomes clear what the church must do first in order to recover its original shape. It must return to its original eschatological nature. Otherwise, the church cannot be the site of meeting between Jesus and minjung.

The church is not a building. The kingdom of God does not arrive in the church alone. Then the church has to tear down the walls it has built itself. Why should the church actually shut the kingdom of God out by monopolizing it? Have we exhausted the meaning of the church by defining it as the eschatological community where Jesus and minjung meet each other? No. There is another emphasis in the Synoptic Gospels.

Jesus builds a community where he and the minjung meet unconditionally and share everything. But meanwhile he designates a group of people among the minjung as disciples and gives them a special mission. We can characterize this mission with the phrase "to send."

"To send!" The disciples were sent out just as Jesus was sent. To where? To the world. They are sent out to testify that the kingdom of God is arriving. They were told not only to bear witness in words, but to cast out demons and heal illnesses, like Jesus, as proof of the advent of the kingdom (Mark 6:12–13). So the first participants in the Jesus movement scattered in all directions. They abandoned everything and left. And this tradition of sending is inseparably tied to eschatological consciousness. But some thought the advent of the kingdom was being delayed due to the dimming of their eschatological consciousness and their misunderstanding of the representation of the kingdom. They changed the tradition of sending into that of gathering. For example, whereas sending the disciples is an important command in the Synoptic Gospels, sending and gathering go hand in hand in Paul. In Paul's later writings, the tradition of sending disappears completely; only gathering remains. Since the church eventually became a place where people gathered for worship, it became isolated from the world.

In this respect, we have discovered other elements missing in the existing church. The church defied its original purpose by becoming complacent. The church must be a moving body that empties itself in order to be sent to the world, to the minjung of Jesus, to the site of minjung's life. The church has no other choice since it belongs to the genealogy of the Jesus movement.

For this purpose, the church has to boldly do away with all the ornaments that hamper its movement of going out into the world.

Q: Is it possible to maintain the form of the church and add a strong eschatological element? Or, since content and form are inseparable from each other, would it be impossible for the existing form to bear that element?

A: The question is misleading. Didn't you say content and form are inseparable from each other? A change in content inevitably brings about a change in form. The present system or constitution of the church was formed precisely from an anti-eschatological basis.

Of course, I don't mean that we only need content and not form. If we tell these two apart, content has to come first and form can be adjusted according to content. But the established church sticks with form and adjusts content to it. It maintains conservative doctrine in order to preserve form. Some people may say that the problem is easy to reform, but there is a class of people who obstruct it—namely, the leadership of the institutional church. To put it plainly, it is the clergy. In order to strengthen their positions, they like to invest the church with a distinctive aura and claim exclusive ownership of the church. This is exactly the same phenomenon that happens at secular organizations. Rather than understanding the church as a place where Christ and minjung meet and where the calling of being sent to the real-life sites is fulfilled, they interest themselves of staying in power over those who are gathered. Theologians play a role in this, too.

5.5. The Image of the Church as Minjung Theology Envisions It

Q: What is the ideal church as envisioned by minjung theology?

A: The phrase "basic community" used in Latin America comes to mind. This refers to the church in the social reality of Latin America where lay believers gather without a priest. Perhaps we can call unorganized churches in Korea without a pastor "basic communities." At a gathering where only the laity come together to read the Bible and understand Jesus, they are likely to gain understandings that differ from received ones. Asking questions that grow out of their own lives may give birth to new understandings of the Bible. As a child, I had a lot of experiences of this nature. As a child I remember hearing ignorant deacons and elders sharing many far-fetched interpretations. I used to mock them from where I was standing, but now I come to consider what kinds of life conditions those interpretations grew out of. They read the Bible with their own eyes—without an intellectual filter—right where they were standing. But I remember that this happened only once in a while and that most of the time they faithfully repeated a handful of doctrinal premises from the church. The so-called basic community is the community (*Gemeinde*) that grows out of self-sufficiency without traditional theology or church authority. And this is exactly the condition where you can work toward the minjung church. This has involuntarily resisted the dominance of Catholicism, and I imagine it can be an indispensable model of reform.

The minjung church should begin with minjung interpretations of the Bible that has been monopolized so far by the clergy. Ministers and theologians should defer to the theological insights of the minjung and render them in a theological language. And the church leadership should institutionalize them. It is more important to find out how they read the Bible with their sorrow and *han*, and what kinds of words comfort and encourage them. Church leadership should respect the minjung and listen for insights on how they read and interpret the Bible in their worries and troubles. They should create an institutional environment where members can freely voice their own feelings and thoughts.

The current movement of the minjung church is emerging from the site of laborers. First of all, thanks to the industrial mission, laborers gather together at a designated location with many problems. They express their frustrations, complaints, and anger about the injustices of society. They share, cry, and sing together, creating a festive atmosphere in one spirit as if a new world would arrive right away. Their cries and songs sound like prayers and hymns even though they do not mention God or the name of Jesus. Clergy should not try to solve their problems with the existing doctrine but accept them as they are; they should pray and bless them in a different language. Then this should be truly a worship that offered a living sacrifice, and the very place where it is happening should be a church. During the last few years, we have seen a budding sprout of churches everywhere. The Friday prayer meeting, the Thursday prayer meeting, the Galilee church, and the rallies for local concerns—the existing church should accept the living spirit that grows out of such experiences. This requires the resolve and courage to reform the existing order and system.

Lastly, there is another model of church, and this is a form of worship that has emerged in the Korean minjung tradition.

I would like to bring up two examples. The first is a village ritual I experienced as a child in a Manchurian village of Korean expatriates. Poor folks perform this ritual once a year. Every household pitched in a certain amount of money for a few pigs to be slaughtered. Every household brought over cooked white rice.[1] The head of the village arranged all of these on the altar.

---

1. White rice was not readily available for impoverished Koreans at this time.

He recited a designated spell and did other things for the ritual event. Then the people ate food that was offered to one god as a symbol of unity. The same principle applies to the ritual for a family's ancestors. At every meal, the family offered food at the altar for their ancestors and then ate together. I remember that this moved me more than the formulaic sacrament.

Another model is the shaman's ritual. Professor Suh Nam-dong gave shamans the name "the priests of *han*." The role of shamans is to resolve the *han* of those who have been unfairly treated. The motive doesn't matter. In resolving the *han*, a shaman becomes one in spirit with the person with *han* along with his or her family, and the audience. The shaman consumes his or her whole body and spirit, liberating them from resentment, vengefulness, or sorrow. The atmosphere of a shaman ritual defies comparison to that of traditional worship of the existing church. Here again I see a model of a living church. The mask dance in our traditional folk culture carries many of the important features of the minjung church. Professor Hyeon Yeong-hak is studying this subject. The mask dance helps the oppressed class overcome their despair by means of comedy and an exciting festival, thereby sublimating their resistance against the oppressive higher classes.

5.6. Moving beyond Institutional Ecclesiology

The essential question here is whether or not this can be a church. But the premise underlying this question is that a church must meet certain conditions. Only after reflecting on where these conditions come from can we ask this question. In ecclesiology, there is a view that distinguishes between the visible church and the invisible church. Recently a distinction has been made between the sending church and the gathering church. These views emerged from the judgment that church cannot be defined in relation to external conditions. They are the result of recognizing the limitations of the institutional church. Moreover, since *missio Dei* is widely accepted, and we are currently living in a pluralistic society, the view that a church is possible only when a particular set of conditions are satisfied is nothing more than stubbornness.

In this kind of situation, church leadership has a role to play: to bear testimony to the true church free of conventional standards. For example, Jesus declared to the alienated, who were all defined as sinners by Judaism, "You are the sons and daughters of Abraham," "The kingdom of God is yours," and "I have come looking for you to serve you." A true disciple of Jesus testifies to the presence of the Lord right here. For example, the words of Hebrews, "Let us then go to him outside the camp and bear the abuse he endured" (13:13), and the story of the last judgment in Matt 25:3–46 are pioneering testimonies to a new church, namely, the minjung church beyond all institutional ecclesiologies.

Q: Rev. Suh Nam-dong briefly mentions minjung ecclesiology in his books. More specifically, he defines Catholicism as clergy-centered churches, Protestantism as Bible-centered churches, and the minjung movement as minjung-centered churches. He compares the minjung church as an organization for human rights, a litigation struggle, industrial mission, mission for farmers—whatever is taking place as part of the minjung movement. He is looking for the manifestation of the minjung church in these examples. What do you think of that? When we follow Professor Suh's line of thinking, what kinds of differences are there between the secular minjung movement and the minjung event, between the current church movement and the secular movement?

A: In the past, I used to think that Christianity contributed little to the March First Movement. For I thought the movement received no support from theology. Now, however, I look at it from a different angle. At that time, those who flocked to the church with the *han* of the minjung and the nation went out for the movement as if the floodgates had broken open. They continued in this manner no matter how much the missionaries had preached the felicity of heaven and the separation of church and state. This was an expression of the nation's *han* and simultaneously a festival of triumph. But the institutional church neither were prepared to be the priests of their *han* as minjung nor conceived of connecting their sufferings and hope to the cross and resurrection. If anything, it despised them and built the walls of religion increasingly high to block their entrance. Consequently, there were countless rules against the minjung such as "Don't perform the ancestral rites, don't drink, don't smoke!" The more rules there are, the harder it becomes to enter the church because it even forbids the minjung from some unbreakable conventions such as drinking *makkeolli*.[2] This essentially keeps them from joining the

---

2. *Makkeolli* is a rice wine that is cheap, milky in color, and low in alcohol content. It is a popular alcoholic beverage in Korea and is consumed during breaks by manual laborers.

church. What does *makkeolli* have to do with Christianity? And when forbidden even from this, could they ever do effective farming? Stop performing the ancestral rituals, stop any dealings with shamans; if not, don't come to church—what should they do, then? Nothing except what the church tells you to do. What the church tells them to do is obvious. Singing hymns, attending early morning prayer meetings, giving offerings, or obeying the pastor's words—in the end only what does not suit us remains. Meanwhile, the church cuts out Korea's rich cultural heritage as with one stroke of an axe. So they have indeed made Christians non-Korean. Therefore, what became important to the church was to exclude the minjung. The words, "Anyone is welcome," turned out to be insincere. Reviving the "just as you are" tradition of Jesus is the top priority. How might this be possible? It is only possible when those in the church with power give up their vested interests. Perhaps the most important of these are their status in the church and the church property. In the Acts of the Apostles, an ideal community embodying Jesus's ethos appears where the haves and the have-nots share meals. A community like this has a direct connection with the eschatological consciousness. The extinction of the eschatological consciousness led to the dissolution of the eschatological community. Today's church does not have the eschatological consciousness. In Korea, we see the popularity of megachurches and the competition for building a bigger church building. This reveals the absence of an eschatological consciousness.

Here we need to reflect on the difference between the existing church and the Jesus community and, further, the difference between the church and secular activism.

Eschatological consciousness gives you the power to risk your life for the sake of righteousness. But does the existing church of today have such a spirit? If not, can we still call it church? If, on the contrary, secular activists go to prison and risk their lives for the human rights of the oppressed, where could this passion come from? We need to dwell on Professor Suh's ecclesiology in light of these questions. He said that Catholicism was a clergy-centered church, that Protestantism is a Bible-centered church, and that now we should build a minjung-centered church. These distinctions are correct but may occasion a misunderstanding without proper explanation. I understand the contrast between the clergy and the minjung. But I think separating the Bible from the minjung may occasion a misunderstanding. The Bible is a text from the minjung, by the minjung, and for the minjung. But the clergy doesn't share this perspective. The past picture of the church was also presented by the clergy and theologians. They supported their view by means of the Bible. However, when we read the Bible now, it turns out that church is not what they said it was. This opening of the eyes occurred thanks to the stimulation and shock by the minjung events. But it is in the Bible, after all, that we find the criteria for the church as the true community of Jesus. One of them is what I mentioned above, namely, whether or not it has the eschatological consciousness. If it does, it is biblical and is a church. In this sense, it is not possible to tell the difference between a church and a secular activist movement. The duty of theology is to bear witness with reference to the Bible in these words: "This is the church of the Lord!"

Here I need to elaborate on the meaning of *eschatological*. It has a deep relation with the formation of the idea of the church. The advent of the kingdom of God means the end of existing systems. Therefore, it allows no room for class division. The *eschaton* means the end of history. Therefore, the kingdom of God is the reality of all historical irregularities coming to an end. But as long as history continues, there are institutions. And as long as there are institutions, there will be higher and lower positions, teachers and students, givers and receivers, and rich and poor.

The first Christians represented the kingdom of God in a similar way as apocalyptic literature. They expected the kingdom to come in a manner as described in the apocalyptic literature, but that did not happen. So they tried to find another solution to this situation, and this struggle finally gave birth to the church and church-centered theology. Even though Jesus is said to have belonged to the group that adopted the apocalyptic eschatology, he offered no objective statement about the kingdom. He simply proclaimed that it was being realized. In spite of telling many parables of the kingdom of God, Jesus did not describe what it was like. What he did was direct his hearers to make a decision before the kingdom that was being realized and to fight at the site where it was being realized. But Christians who failed to understand this fully came to think that the kingdom had not yet come or that it would not come, since the kingdom as they had represented it was not arriving. We can already see this in Paul. The kingdom of God recedes, and God's righteousness and the church become more prominent. For Paul the belief in the present kingdom of God and the future intersect with each other. In parallel, the church has two aspects: on the one hand, it is the community that realizes the kingdom; on the other hand, it is a community that is awaiting the kingdom. In the latter understanding, the church continues in history and so makes efforts to build temporal institution and order. But the Gospel of Mark, which centers around the minjung tradition, highlights the kingdom of God. The translation of the word *ēngiken* (has come near) in Mark 1:15 was a subject of great controversy. The correct understanding does not come from grammatical debates on the word but from looking at the behavior of Jesus. As already pointed out, Jesus's actions towards the minjung are incomprehensible without considering his belief that the kingdom would be realized.

But at least twenty years after Mark, in the periods of Matthew and Luke, the kingdom took a backseat in actuality. The age of the church was postulated and was considered a special period in history. This justified the institutionalization of the church, which obscured the present-ness of the kingdom. So what became of the kingdom? Here emerged the medieval view on the church, which identified the kingdom with the institutional church, even though this church had already deteriorated into an ideology for the establishment. This means that, by being assigned a place in the existing order, the institutional church inevitably caused the church to suffer class division as society in general.

5.7. Realizing the Community of Liberation

However, the early church knew what it had to overcome. Paul was angry at the discord between the rich and poor and between Jews and non-Jews in the Corinthian church. He asserted that they had to relinquish worldly values. He also criticized those in power and declared that there is in Christ neither master nor slave, Jew nor non-Jew, and male nor female (Gal 3:28). Yet, as long as the church acknowledged its location within the existing order, this kind of declaration would have little power. This established a church-centered way of thinking in Christianity, which gradually moved in the direction of dualism.

A true community has to overcome social divisions in the church. Of course, division in a given society is not directly reflected within the church because it is by nature a religious group. For this very reason, however, church authority was formed, religious aristocracy emerged, and class division was engendered between the clergy and the laity. At some point, the clergy took up the position of the ruler. This happened under the influence of the established religion of the time when Christianity was coming to be. And for this reason, in the Gospel of John, Jesus, by washing the feet of his disciples, emphasized that the role of the disciples was precisely that of serving (John 13:3–15). Also, in Matthew Jesus said that, since he was the only rabbi, there could not be a rabbi-disciple relationship between people (Matt 23:6–8).

As far as the church is in the world, it is only natural that the rich and the poor, the powerful and the obscure coexist in the church. But in the church, the rich and powerful must serve the poor and obscure and protect their rights and interests. At the same time, thanks to the poor or the obscure, they must discover and recover the humanity that they have lost by their wealth and power. More specifically, the rich and the powerful must be liberated from the bondage to their possessions and power on account of the poor and oppressed; they must also be liberated themselves by participating in the liberation of the poor and the oppressed. In this way, they form a community of liberation.

In response to my view, some people ask if I completely disregard the sacraments, ministers, and elders of the institutional church.

I admit that all institutionalized groups require internal order and division of its functions. Until the fulfillment of the kingdom of God, the institutional church and the spirit of the minjung community of Jesus will coexist. But it is not desirable to take such coexistence as conclusive and be content with doing nothing about it.

Leaders should realize the fundamental spirit of Jesus again. They have to take Jesus's parable of a lost sheep as specific guidelines for the church. The church must always stand with the alienated party—alienated because an event happened to them—between the ninety-nine good sheep and the one lost sheep, between the so-called prodigal son who left home and the exemplary elder son. Better yet, the church should mobilize its entire membership for the lost one. Ministers of the institutional church complain that minjung theology is simply partial. After all, this criticism should be leveled at Jesus, who said, "I have come to call not the righteous but sinners" (Luke 5:32) and "Come to me, all that are weary and carrying heavy burdens" (Matt 11:28). No, this is not partiality. We should not forget that, when all of the church members concentrate on the one for whom the event has happened, that is, the one who needs help, the path to salvation opens up for everyone. Salvation is not available for someone who does not share what they have with the one who needs help. For this reason, those who are alienated offer the key to salvation. The original spirit of sacrament lies in sharing. I think that Holy Communion is a precious tradition. It means sharing the blood and flesh of one body, namely, performing a ritual to become one body. But this sharing should not be done as a religious ceremony; it should be connected with real life. Why do people who are willing to share in drinking the blood of Jesus not think of sharing meals? They enjoy peace of mind because they have written sharing off as a worship ritual. For this reason, we are compelled to fight against this form of religiosity. Sharing is one of the most important things in a community, and how it is practiced determines the grounds for the church's existence.

Why is it the case that there are a great number of young people in the West who are enchanted by different Eastern mystical religions? An important reason, I believe, is because they are attracted to the life of working together and sharing together. They share not only religious experiences but their whole lives. But there arises yet another question. There are in the West many big monasteries as sharing communities, but why do they not feel attracted to them? Probably because they see something closed-minded in them, and I am still trying to work out what it is.

Q: But it seems to me that Jesus's notion of the church was very much in line with the prophetic tradition of the Old Testament. Jesus denied many of the temple rituals, including those of the Jerusalem temple. Does Jesus's view of the church trace back to the prophetic tradition?

A: If we pose a division between ritualistic and prophetic traditions, Jesus certainly belonged to the latter as does the church. But the institutional church leaned gradually and continuously toward the ritualistic tradition of the Jerusalem temple. The Roman Catholic church borrowed many of its rituals from this tradition. (By the way, you can see religious similarities in colors and ritual methods. When I participated in a Catholic mass in Europe, I was reminded of the atmosphere of Buddhist temples I visited.) Didn't Jesus confront the authorities of the Jerusalem temple in the last days of his life? The church is not a temple. But it is called a temple as the day of the Lord is called the Sabbath. The tendency of the church to find its roots in traditional religion has made the church lose its prophetic calling.

A ritualistic community is naturally exclusive and self-centered. In contrast, the prophetic tradition does not distinguish between sacred and secular, church and society. The prophets never hesitated to intervene in rotten power politics and religious order and fought against injustices.

There is another important point to mention in discussing the Jesus tradition in relation to the church. It is a new understanding of the idea that the church is a gathering place of the people of God.

Jesus treated the minjung as the people of God. This was consistent with the thinking of the Israelites as the people of God. But this thought actually went through many complications. The view that Israel as a whole was too corrupt to be called the people of God gave rise to the idea of the remnant in Isaiah—the belief that only the remnant was the genuine people of God. But at the time of Jesus, Judaism excluded sinners from the people of God. By accepting these people who had been alienated owing to their incompatibility with the Jewish system, Jesus acknowledged them as the people of God. Many parables, including those of feast invitation, reveal this point clearly. But Jesus's behaviors to this effect were not a sentimental gesture. They have roots in the formation of Israel.

Israel was formed by the Hebrews after the exodus and the Habiru (*'abiru*) in the areas of Canaan, Syria, and Palestine who escaped from monarchic oppression. Israel started as a federation of the oppressed who escaped from monarchs. (This is called a tribal alliance, and Martin Noth gives it the Greek-derived name *amphictyony*.[3]) The Yahweh faith was inseparably related to liberation from monarchic tyranny. Early on, they proclaimed mono-Yahwism, a confession directly connected to the belief that no human being was supposed to dominate or rule over them. Therefore, Israel was a minjung community. It started to degenerate when it became a monarchy during the time of David. Jesus enacted the revival of the essence of that primordial Israel precisely in Galilee. For this reason, we must not forget that a Jesus community must be rooted in this kind of origin. The moment its members forget this, they will be cut off like a branch from a tree.

Q: So what are we to do with the system and form of the existing church?

A: I have already spoken of the general direction to take. As for specifics, the existing church has to implement them through continual reform with a view to returning to the original shape of the church.

But that is not so simple a matter. The Jesus movement and its community were a minjung-centered and simultaneously heretical phenomenon. But Jesus's minjung did not think of it as a new movement severed from Judaism. So for some time they considered themselves to be a reform sect within Judaism. For this reason, they observed the Sabbath, practiced the

---

3. Martin Noth, *The History of Israel*, 2nd ed. (London: SCM, 1960).

temple precepts, and attended the synagogue. But the awareness that they were a totally new community was triggered by persecution from Judaism. At first, they kept the Sabbath but at some point replaced it with Sunday (the Lord's day), the day of the resurrection experience. They started to have their own meetings instead of going to the temple or synagogue. This was what happened with the Jerusalem sect. Gentile Christians recognized Christianity as a new movement and a new community earlier. They considered leaving Judaism and the law altogether for the beginning of a new Christian identity.

The gathered people were of marginalized social classes within Judaism, and so the changes were inevitable. For those who gathered in this community, the passion and resurrection of Jesus were essential. The gathered people newly interpreted these experiences as the foundation of the community and the source of its character to construct ecclesiology in a retrospective way. The community of Jesus's minjung entered the realm of religion in general with an intensified religious consciousness. Its reacceptance of the Jewish tradition and incorporation of Hellenistic religious thinking forged what you call Christianity. Still it retained the minjung-centered character until it totally degenerated after becoming the state religion of the Roman Empire. After the Dark Ages came the Reformation. It started with remarkable proclamations such as Luther's idea of the priesthood of all believers, taking the Bible and its interpretive right away from the church authority and giving it to the minjung. The existing moral and ethical system was rejected through an emphasis on *sola fide*. Calvin also attempted a radical reform, which included discarding all the sacraments, except for baptism and holy communion, abolishing all kinds of icons as idolatry. However, the reform suffered a counteroffensive from the Enlightenment, going back on the defensive by making itself conservative. The goal of maintaining internal order allowed church authority a gradual ascent to power.

5.8. The Ideal of the Church—the Equal Community of God's People

How the existing church should reform itself has been repeatedly discussed in church history and frequently suggested through the World Church Council in recent years. The church itself was not unaware of its own illness. But pointing out these maladies directly would bring the existing church down. This is why it was not done. Therefore, minjung theology does not have to discuss new details of the reform. I only want to emphasize that a church that cannot identify with the minjung—those who are poor, deprived of real rights, and suffering in many respects—is no more than a social club of people with a similar social status.

Another point I would like to stress is that the existing church should discard the notion that it monopolizes God and Jesus. Why should God be an instrument of the institutional church? God is free. Where God fulfills God's work in what ways is God's own concern. Therefore, the existing church would do best to hold the conviction that the *missio Dei* will take place at different locations in history. Additionally, the existing church ought to cultivate an awareness of the kingdom of God and turn this awareness into practice.

Finally, I would like to emphasize the elimination of social standings in the church. The priest-centered or pastor-centered system has gone beyond a functional distinction to become an authoritarian system that has been worsening. The church as the collective of God's people has to be an equal community. Pastors are not the descendants of priests. They are teachers by function. There is no biblical grounds requiring only pastors to administer the sacrament. The most important characteristic of the church is sharing. Why should this sharing be the exclusive privilege of the pastor?

I hope that there will arise many basic communities led by the laity. I hope that lay believers with secular jobs in their respective areas form a community. I hope that sermons consist of testimonies that those with teaching competence bear to the Bible and the reality based on the lives of the members. If every denomination opened up this path and provided an institutional apparatus for accepting this kind of a community, it would provide a great stimulus to the reform of the existing church. I neither have nor should give more specific suggestions beyond this. It is the job of church leadership.

6
Sin and the System

6.1. The Root of Sin

Q: Our topic today is sin, and I would like to start the conversation with concrete reality instead of the church or a theological theory. I am going to offer examples of the three kinds of sinners: a thief and murderer, a prostitute, and a social misfit. I suggest that we weave our conversation around these examples.

Case 1: A Thief and Murderer

A person is serving a prison term for theft and murder. He was born into a poor peasant's family that suffered constant hunger. When he was a child, his father got injured at work and became bedridden. His mother worked as a peddler for the bare subsistence of the family. Upon his father's death, his mother remarried a somewhat well-to-do apothecary in Eastern medicine. Her children stayed with her. But in the new household they were no better than servants. He didn't finish elementary school.

At age fourteen or fifteen, he went into another home to work as a servant. Since then he moved from one house to another as a servant. One day he stole a ride on a train to Seoul. The first work he did in Seoul was that of a tail pusher. He pushed the tail of the handcarts of vegetable vendors for little pay. He settled down near the Yeomcheon Bridge Market. In order to beat his competitors, he got up as soon as the curfew-lifting siren went off[1] to push the carts of the vendors going from Muak Hill to Bulgwangdong. He slept at a bunkhouse near the market, where a great

---

1. The siren sounded at 4 a.m. The nighttime curfew from midnight to 4 a.m. in Korea was canceled in 1982.

number of boys in a similar situation were packed in like sardines. When he didn't even have enough money to get into this place, he was forced to sleep on straw under the eaves of a stranger's house. Later, he worked as an *jige* carrier[2] but still didn't earn much. Unable to bear the crushing poverty, he thought not a few times that he would be better off dead. Once he jumped down into the Han River[3] in an unsuccessful attempt to commit suicide. He washed his clothes in the water of the river, dried them, and came back with a renewed resolve to carry on. But things didn't improve. He often had to skip meals. He started to steal food to quell his hunger. He was caught stealing as a repeat offender and was sent to a youth detention center. At this place, he learned the art of theft. Afterwards, he served multiple prison sentences and worked with a partner. He became a career criminal. He had no other choice because, branded as an ex-convict, he was not accepted anywhere.

At one point, he found himself missing his mother unbearably. He went back to his hometown and started to live as a servant again. One day he lost his virginity to a barmaid and fell in love for the first time. In order to help the barmaid out of her plight, he decided to steal rice. He broke into the barn of a wealthy old man. When he was leaving the barn with a big bag of rice, the old man saw him and started to scream. Not realizing what he was doing, he picked up the sickle hanging on the wall and struck the old man in the neck with it. In a snap he committed an enormous crime. He was sentenced to life in prison for the crimes of theft and murder.

When I met him, he had already served more than seventeen years. My impression was that he was good-natured and with keen literary sensibilities. Despite having a lack of provisions, he shared goods with other inmates worse off than he was. He was good-hearted and loved by many. He showed me poems he wrote, which mostly concerned longing for his mother's presence, his first love, his yearning for freedom, and lamenting his lot in life.

---

2. *Jige* literally means "a device for carrying on one's back." A Korean traditional carrier, a *jige* was made of wood and looked like an unclosed "A" when seen from the front. For this reason, it is called "A frame" in English. Nowadays *jige* is virtually out of use in Korea.

3. The Han River is the biggest river that flows through Seoul, the capital of Republic of Korea. *Han* has such meanings as "great," "at the height," and "accurate." Ever since Joseon Dynasty made Seoul its capital in 1392 (then called *Hanyang*), the Han River has served as an important lifeline for Korean civilization.

There were many prisoners like him in the penitentiary. The worst mental problem for them was a sense of sin. Christians from conservative churches evangelize in the penitentiary. A good number of inmates embrace Christianity and practice it passionately. Sometimes they kneel down in the auditorium, repent with tears, and do early morning prayers. However, they often continue to feel tormented. They envy political criminals supposing that they would not feel as tormented. They feel peace while praying or listening to the sermon of a pastor. But once it is over, they cannot get rid of the sense of sin from having killed a person.

Case 2: A Dongducheon[4] Prostitute for the US Soldiers

Dongducheon is a byword for a military-base town. There are about five thousand prostitutes who work for the clientele of the US soldiers. They have entered into this place by and large by following four routes.

The first is an illegal broker. Unlicensed brokers lure women at a park, around an industrial complex, or in the vicinity of a bus terminal or train station. The women who fall into prostitution cannot escape from the clutches of the pimp because of the ransom.

A second route is a newspaper advertisement. A daily or weekly newspaper carries an advertisement that goes, for example, "Wanted: Waitress for U.S.-soldier-only Hall. Hired on the day of application. An advance of 200,000 won guaranteed." Applicants to this kind of advertisement are sent to Dongducheon.

A third route is a pimp. In Dongducheon there are about seven hundred pimps, who go out into countryside to trick and coerce women into following them.

Lastly, some women enter into Dongducheon of their own accord after moving around in the bottom stratum of society. For example, female factory workers with a low wage are motivated to change jobs for better payment. When they are fired from a relatively well-paying company, they go into the red-light district in order to maintain their standards of living.

---

4. Dongducheon is a city in the northernmost part of Gyeonggi Province and is strategically important for the defense of the Korean capital. It is located approximately 40 kilometers (25 miles) north of Seoul and about 20 kilometers (15 miles) away from the Demilitarized Zone. The main camps of the Eighth US Army's Second Infantry Division are stationed in the city.

It is even said that there are women who work at a factory by day and prostitute by night because they cannot make ends meet.

There are a number of underage women in Dongducheon. The Minors Regulation Team finds underage women and sends them to a rehabilitation center for a six-month education before they are sent back to society. But the pattern is that about 70 percent are integrated back into society, while the remaining 30 percent return to Dongducheon. The rehabilitation center took a survey of seventy-nine women on why they went to Dongducheon. Domestic troubles account for ten persons, poverty for sixteen persons, a friend's enticement for fourteen persons, failure in marriage or romantic involvement for nine persons, and vanity for thirty persons.

Here is the daily routine of these women. They get up around 10 a.m. and do laundry, listen to music, or read comic books until around 4 p.m., when they take a bath. Their workday starts around 6 p.m., when they put on makeup and receive US soldiers. They earn $20–30 for sleeping with a US soldier for one evening and $200–300 a month for living together with a US soldier in a contractual marriage. However, they are usually hard-pressed because of their debt to the pimp. Since they entered into Dongducheon penniless, the pimp buys them clothing, cosmetics, a record player, bedding, and so forth. Since they have to pay the debt with a high interest plus rent, they cannot afford to escape from financial difficulty. Those who are lucky enough to get married to a US soldier number around 1,500 to 2,000 a year. They can marry a US soldier easily because Americans do not ask a question about their past and because they can live in America, where no one knows them. However, many of them who get married end up divorced due to language and cultural barriers.

Some women save enough money to leave Dongducheon. But most of the women are stuck where they are and go on a downward spiral.

Beauty exists even in the midst of their lives. They have created the Dandelion Society to help one another. Members pay dues of five hundred won a month, collect recyclable waste to support aged colleagues out of work, and pay funeral expenses of members who pass away.

Case 3: A Social Misfit

A person spent most of his time between his teens and forties in prison for thirteen convictions, and this seemed to have had an adverse effect on his character. His parents divorced when he was a child. He lived with his mother, who didn't lead an exemplary life. He first went to prison as a teenager, and his numerous prison terms made him unable to function normally in society. He was a person of double character who speaks like a saint and cunningly cheats people. In the penitentiary, it was in vogue to repent and embrace Christianity. A dramatic incident such as this creates a sensation not only in the prison but in society as a whole. His psychological complications in relation to his conversion experience allow us to clearly see him for who he is.

At the Seoul Detention Center, Park Cheol-wung, the convict in the famous Geumdang murder case,[5] converted to Christianity a little before his execution. The man I am talking about was in the same cell as Park and was influenced by him. Later he was transferred to the Daejeon Penitentiary, where he created a persona. He often said to others, "At the Seoul Detention Center, I became a new person by going through conversion and coming to know Jesus's love. But since I failed to become a completely new person, I relapsed into who I was in the past. So I need to have another conversion to be a new person." At the same time, he painted a very exaggerated and hideous picture of his past and glamorized people close to him, including his mother. He kept saying that someone's perfect love for him would make him a new person. For dramatic effect, he fasted for three days and avidly read the Bible, but it failed to make him a new person or to make him psychologically stable. The only thing that could comfort him was medication. Taking too much medication puts one in a hallucinatory state. When not given medication, he cut himself with a shard of glass all over his body. He cut himself so many times his body was riddled with scars.

He said in a carefree manner that he was very content with prison life and that he was not worried about his life after prison. But his complaints reveal that he suffered from a deep sense of defeat and despair of a poor, uneducated, and unskilled person who is unlikely to find acceptance anywhere in society.

Thus far I have cited three examples of sinners. Before examining these examples, please first tell us how the church commonly defines sin.

---

5. On June 20, 1979, the proprietor of Geumdang, an antique shop in Seoul, his wife, and their driver were abducted and killed. This murder case was solved one hundred days after the incident when Park Cheol-wung (thirty-two years old at the time), his girlfriend, and his brother were arrested.

6.2. The Existing Understanding of Sin Reinforces the Church Authority

Prostitutes, thieves, and murderers are typically judged and dismissed without an examination of the process that gave birth to these outcomes. On this point, both the church and society in general are identical. In fact, if anything, there is something more offensive to the way the church condemns these people. In society, sin can be relativized in view of the circumstances or psychological process leading up to criminal behaviors. But the church applies the Ten Commandments or a certain doctrine in a dogmatic way and thereby rules out the possibility of forgiveness.

Let's think about the basis for what defines a sinner according to the church. The first definition is regarding sexual desire. Paul uses the word "covetousness" (*epithymia*) for sexual desire (Rom 7:7–8; Gal 5:24). The expression "of the flesh" is often used with a sexual connotation (John 1:13). This tendency found its way into the Western church in Augustine who connected sexual desire (*concupiscentia*) with original sin. Many small sects considered sexual intercourse itself sinful. I think Freud hit the nail on the head suggesting that suppressing sexual desire as sinful creates a neurotic attachment to it.

A second definition is lack of faith. Sin is defined as not believing the doctrine set down by the church about God or Christ. According to the church, sin is departing from church-centeredness. This definition does not help people be liberated from sin through faith, but rather is a form of subjugation to the church in the name of believing.

Why is there no progress at all in the church's discussion of sin? Could it be because the church never turns its eyes beyond sin as an outcome to psychological factors and social conditions (structural evil) as the source? Is it because the church cannot? Or is it because it is unwilling? I think it's the latter. Understanding sin apart from the church-centered standpoint relativizes sin. When this happens, the claims of the church weaken as does the authority of the church. The church cannot afford to have a different understanding. This is precisely the reason Marx and Sigmund Freud advanced anti-Christian propositions. Their refusal of Christianity was legitimate, and the responsibility for this state of affairs was the church. Now Christianity is in a phase where it has no other choice but to develop a new understanding of sin.

6.3. The Definition of Sin in Judaism

Q: How is sin defined in the Old Testament?

A: The exodus was indeed the starting point of the Old Testament faith and so deserves our first attention. Beginning with the exodus, sin was not defined individually but in collective and structural terms. The Old Testament view of sin started with the reality of enslavement and exploitation by the structural evil of the monarchic system of the Egyptians. Liberation for the Hebrews was defined as being free from this sin.

Furthermore, sin in the Old Testament is based on the covenant between God and Israel. Failure to observe the covenant is sin. This covenant was condensed into the form of law with two defining characteristics. First, it was a collective covenant between God and the Israelite community. Its meaning was that the strong should not exploit or afflict the weak and that all the people should equally share what they have. Sin is defined as a violation of this fundamental principle. The Ten Commandments assume a collective framework. Here, the sins of individuals figure in a secondary way. For example, the person who has shed the blood of an innocent person or commits adultery is certainly treated as a sinner. But this kind of violation is not central. Moreover, the law provided sinners refuge. The story of Cain and Abel reflects this point. After murdering his brother, Cain was protected from vengeance and was provided a path to forgiveness. In this regard, we can say that sin in the Old Testament was mainly defined as structural forms of oppression.

However, this tradition started to change during the Davidic monarchy. Since then, the religion of Yahweh was ritualistic, and the definition of sin was determined by conformity to institutional religion. Purity laws were of utmost concern. Take Sabbath regulations, for instance. They were originally intended to give a day off to the poor, slaves, and laborers every seven days. Not giving these people a break should be a sin. However, with temple religion in place, the Sabbath itself was designated as a holy day and therefore became an objective to achieve. After all, sin now came to be defined in relation to all of the rules and institutions of the temple. As a result, the practices designed to benefit the poor became formal and indirect. Many gave offerings to the temple as their way of helping the poor, even though the exhortation to give alms to the poor stayed. Some even believed giving a small amount to the temple would increase their chances of receiving salvation.

In early Judaism there was a clear distinction between the Torah and the prophetic books, the former being acknowledged as scripture. But in later Judaism during the time of the Pharisees, both the prophetic books and interpretations of prominent rabbis were also included in the materials for everyday life regulations. The Pharisees started a movement for practicing these regulations. At first, it was a nationalistic movement to preserve the independent spirit of the people of Israel under the rule of a foreign power. But after King Jannaeus, in the time of Queen Alexandra, the ideas in question were incorporated into the national policies. In other words, since the Pharisees were incorporated into the ruling system, regulations of the national movement changed into legal regulations that were forced upon the people. Rather than leading a national movement, the Pharisees were more interested in enforcing obligatory regulations of the Pharisaic system. In other words, the ruling system defined the righteous from the sinful, and the word *sin* became a synonym for breaking the law. Under these circumstances, people in certain social classes, such as prostitutes, tax collectors, and ill persons, became paradigmatic examples of sinners who violated Sabbath and purity laws. What I have said so far by and large summarizes the understanding of sin until right before Jesus's time.

6.4. Paul's View of Sin

Q: How do these views relate to the writings of Paul?

A: In order to understand Paul's definition of sin, we first have to know how he understood the law. He sees the law in two ways. First, he says that the law is holy, righteous, and good (Rom 7:12). Here, the law refers to the spirit of the Torah, which is not prohibition of what is wrong but encouragement of love and sharing what is right. In this sense, Paul suggests that the law is originally good. Second, the law is something that binds humans (Rom 7:6). In this case, the expression *written code* is used to define the law as a system.

These two characteristics are not unrelated. For example, the command "Do not divorce" conforms to the spirit of the law when interpreted as the command "Love." But only the literal meaning of prohibiting divorce was emphasized, and the law was understood as a condemnation of sin. That was what the Pharisaic system was about. Paul rejected a view of salvation by observing the legal system, and in this respect he opposed the legal system. Since the system determined what sin was, Paul's rejection of sin meant resistance against the system. Paul concurs with Jesus in this respect.

Now let's examine in detail what Paul thinks of sin. He uses the word *sin* no fewer than sixty-four times. It can refer to one of two things. The first is the Pharisaic system. The second is the substance of sin that exists within every human being. In Rom 5:10, Paul says that we are in the condition of being God's enemies. He believes that sin is the destruction of the relationship between God and us.

Then, what does it mean to be at enmity with God? How was it possible for humans to become God's enemies? Could it be because humans could not ever know God's will? I have to point one thing out before answering this question directly. Barth presupposed that humans can never know God. He interpreted the clause, "What can be known about God is plain to them" (Rom 1:19) as "What can be known about 'the fact that we cannot know God' is plain to us." This is a far-fetched interpretation. Paul clearly states that for Jews the law becomes the grounds for knowing God. For gentiles who do not know the law, their conscience (*suneidēsis*) is the grounds for knowing God's will (Rom 2:12). Therefore, humans did not become God's enemies because they were unable to know God's will. God's will, as demonstrated in the Torah, is "Love" and "Share." Paul believed that there is something inherent in human nature that opposes God's will—original sin. In today's language, original sin is a self-centered desire or a desire for exclusive possession. This is the fundamental sin of which Paul speaks; it breaks down one's relationship with neighbor and ultimately destroys one's relationship with God. Bultmann believed that sin was relying on one's own self for self-preservation.

In Paul's understanding of sin thus construed, we see three implications. First, sin is not something abstract or individual but is defined in systemic terms. That is, Paul espouses a structural understanding of sin. Paul views sin in relation to legal structures. Second, Paul emphasizes the associated nature of sin. Paul implicates all of humanity. All have sinned through Adam's sin, and every person is liberated from sin through Jesus's death. For example, if a person has committed theft, it is not just the fault of this one person, but the responsibility of the whole society that made the person steal. In this sense, every person is sinful. Third, Paul speaks of overcoming sin through Christ. It is important to note that Paul's hamartiology and Christology are intimately connected. We are liberated through Christ from the state of original sin and from the state of condemnation by the law as the system and have entered the reality of grace and freedom.

6.5. John and Luke's View of Sin

Next, let me examine John and Luke's understandings of sin. John's understanding is similar to Paul's. First, there is a similarity in the language of sin. Paul uses the word *sinner* (*hamartolos*) eight times and John four times. Paul uses the word *sin* (*hamartia*) sixty-four times and John seventeen times. Considering the quantity of Paul's epistles and the Johannine documents, Paul and John used the two words with a similar frequency. John's basic premise is that human beings originally dwell in sin. That is, every person is found in sin. It seems to me that this shows that John was greatly influenced by gnostic thinking. In line with the gnostic belief that the spirit is imprisoned in the flesh, John believes that the spirit's residence in the flesh is part of humanity's cursed condition. Put differently, the reality of a certain individual committing sin is secondary. Human existence itself is sin. Therefore, John says that if we say that we have no sin, we are deceiving ourselves (1 John 1:8).

Luke uses the word *sinner* more frequently. He uses the word eighteen times in comparison to Mark who uses it six times and Matthew five times. In Luke's usage, the sinner is defined by the established system. Luke does not say that every person is a sinner but refers to certain individuals as sinners. He believes that God rejoices over repented sinners more than the righteous. Whereas Paul and John stress the universality of sin, Luke focuses on the sinners as those who are alienated by the system.

6.6. Satan Is a Structural Evil

Next, let's discuss Jesus's understanding of sin in the Gospel of Mark. First of all, Jesus didn't take interest in sin but made an issue of Satan. Jesus's basic premise was the kingdom of God, which was the antithesis of the world that Satan ruled. What was the true identity of this Satan? Satan's true identity is structural evil. Defeating Satan means liberating the minjung who have been oppressed by structural evil. Jesus fought to bring an end to Satan and bring liberation for the minjung, the offspring of Abraham, who were being treated as sinners. Jesus believed that overcoming structural evil would ultimately lead to the elimination of sin and bring about the fulfillment of the kingdom of God. In this respect, Jesus resembles Marx, who believed that the advent of the true communist world would eliminate selfish desire and inequality.

To continue our examination of Jesus's understanding of sin, we need to look into the six antitheses that appear in the Gospel of Matthew. They concern murder, adultery, divorce, swearing, vengeance, and loving the enemy. In those days, Judaism took murder to be the most serious of sins. But Jesus defined hating a person as a kind of murder and thereby heightened the demand of the law. Similarly, Jesus said concerning adultery that lusting after a woman is already adultery. As for the issue of divorce, too, he denied divorce and advocated for women. In addition, Jesus forbade swearing an oath over and against the current religious system. Jesus also forbade taking vengeance. Lastly, the issue of loving one's enemy is linked to Jewish nationalism. By saying, "Love your enemies" (Matt 5:44), Jesus abolished the antagonistic relationship with gentiles set down by the purity laws of Judaism.

These six antitheses reveal that Jesus denies sin as defined by the system. Identifying anger with murder or lust with adultery goes beyond the scope of legal regulations. In other words, it denies the legitimacy of the very existence of the law. From these antitheses, we can clearly see that Jesus is redefining law-defined sins.

Then what is the active meaning of these antitheses? The clue to their interpretation is found in the golden rule of Matt 7:12, which concludes the Sermon on the Mount: "Do to others as you would have them do to you." Sin is defined as the opposite of love. Let's consider a story about the Sabbath laws. Jesus took pity on a person with a withered hand and healed the hand on the Sabbath. The Pharisees in bondage to legalism tried to kill Jesus for violating the Sabbath laws. But from Jesus's standpoint, it was natural to have pity on the hungry and the sick, and it was sin to block his deed by the Pharisaic legalism.

When Jesus was interacting with someone, he didn't make an issue of their sin. What concerned him can be known when we look at some expressions in the New Testament. First of all, let's consider the words *kakos* and *poneros*. In the Korean translations, they are mostly rendered "to be evil." A more accurate translation is "the state of being unhappy from being sick, poor, or banished." Another important word is *skandalizō*. Korean Bibles have translated "to cause someone to sin," but this is a little different from the original meaning. A better translation is "to cause someone to fall down, to bring someone into a trap, to anger someone, or to make someone miserable." *Skandalizō* refers to an action that brings someone into an unhappy state or forces someone to do something against their will. These words are rarely used to refer to evil and sin. Here, sin is not conceptualized as an independent substance, but as a reality that makes love impossible. The word *Satan*, too, originally meant not an independent reality but a relative reality as "the opponent with a different standpoint" or "the accuser." We can conclude that the words, Satan, *kakos*, *poneros*, and *skandalizō*, indicate the reality of structural evil.

Let me sum up what I have said so far. It is our reality that this world ruled by Satan is falling ever deeper into sin by structural evil. The first task is to eliminate the ruling power in order to be liberated from sin.

6.7. The Root of Sin—Privatizing the Public

Q: What you are saying is understandable under the premise of minjung theology. But those who identify with traditional hamartiology may wonder if your treatment of original sin is not serious or rigorous enough. What would you say to the claim that structural evil is the result of sin?

A: In traditional hamartiology, sin first existed and then entered the world, making the world miserable. But what we have to clarify here first is that the world mentioned in the Bible is not the world in the sense of cosmos. It refers to the world of humans and social relations. With this in mind, let's think about traditional hamartiology.

The story of the fall of humanity appears in Genesis. People have been debating what the forbidden fruit represents, but there is no agreement. Some say that it is sexuality, and others that it is human limitations. Whatever it is, we could say that it is something that is not supposed to be privatized—"the things that are God's" (Luke 20:25), to use the expression in the Bible, or the public, to use a sociological term. What is public cannot and must not be privatized since God is the creator. Therefore, everything belongs to God. The earth, the sky, the sea, and everything that is in them are all God's—that is, the public. Therefore, no one can privatize them. And privatizing or monopolizing what is God's is precisely sin because it invades the realm of God and destroys the public. This is what Adam violated. At that moment, paradise disappeared. Adam's sin resulted in the private possession of products and competition for monopoly, which, in turn, caused murder and war. The story of Cain and Abel can be understood along these lines. The fight about what is yours and mine created boundaries and divisions for your land and my land. This gradually developed into the extreme of dividing the sky and the sea. We vividly remember the incident of a Korean Airline plane shot down in Soviet airspace.[6] The Soviets say that they have the right to kill by shooting because their realm has been intruded.

This kind of privatization, when applied to sex, is lust (*epithymia*; Rom 1:24) and envy (Mark 4:19) when applied to material possessions. This desire brought about exactly the result Paul described, "for though they knew God, they did not honor him as God or give thanks to him, but they became futile in their thinking, and their senseless minds were darkened" (Rom 1:21). That is, they have fallen into the state of being unable to differentiate the public and the private.

The desire for private possession is not confined to material things alone. It also applies to power. The Bible designates God as king because kings in ancient times were sovereign. The earth belonged to the king, and this was the symbol of his authority. But the privatization of this power resulted in the monopoly of property which gave birth to social classes, including slavery, the ultimate example of privatizing human beings. The evil of the world derives from abuses of power and is expressed in the privatization of public power.

According to Paul, all rights (*exousia*) belong to God, and God has entrusted these rights to humans. But the desire for exclusive possession systematically perpetrates greed for greater individual possession. So people are divided, fight one another and start war. Criticizing war is taboo. Why is there no theological discourse on war? Is it because theologians do not know the evil nature of war? No. It is because they are dependent on and afraid of those who have the sword.

Within this structure, minjung are not innocent, either. For since the minjung are living in a society based on possession as its first principle,

---

6. On September 1, 1983, Korean Airlines (KAL) flight 007 was en route from New York to Seoul, with a stop in Anchorage, Alaska. Nearing its final destination, the plane veered off its regular course. It soon entered into Russian airspace and flew over the Kamchatka Peninsula, where top-secret Soviet military facilities were located. The Soviets dispatched two fighters to intercept the passenger jet. It is alleged that, after locating the KAL flight, the fighters tried in vain to establish communication. One of the fighters shot a heat-seeking missile and a radioactive missile. KAL 007 was hit and fell into the East Sea (also known as the Sea of Japan). All of the 269 persons on board were killed.

they are in pursuit of the same things as those in power. They envy the powerful. In this sense, we can say every human being is under sin.

The capitalist system is based on this desire for private possession. Therefore, no one can live without private possession, and so everyone becomes a slave to this desire. In this sense, the proposition is still valid that everyone stands under sin.

Is it possible to overcome this reality of sin? As I said earlier, Marx asserted that transforming the social structure was the answer, and Jesus focused on eradicating Satan's rule, namely, structural evil under the Judaic system. But the ultimate overcoming of such a reality is only possible by God's sovereignty. But the notion that only God can overcome the reality of sin could lead us back to a dualistic way of thinking. So we need to put this notion in different language. The words "by God only" we can change into "empty ourselves." We must remain vigilant against the concrete reality of sin. We should not think that our human efforts are ultimate. We must stay open to the possibility of a new reality.

Let's look at the three cases from the beginning of our conversation. In the third case, the person under discussion was a social misfit. This description can apply to all three people. The prostitute took that path because she had no other option. Statistics show vanity as a motive, but this statistic is unreliable. It is not clear how the respondents who chose vanity as their answer understood the word. It is possible they tried to escape from their despair over their former life. It is possible they had no other choice in terms of finance or class mobility. It is also possible they were disillusioned with their home environment. The person in the first case is as incompetent a person as the person of the third case. From the beginning of his life, he was under pressure in every way. He wanted to escape but had no way out other than stealing a ride to Seoul. He could be no more than a tail pusher, *jige* carrier, and servant. What despair he must have felt to attempt suicide! But what does the phrase "social misfit" mean? Doesn't it mean the inability to adapt to the existing order? Should we not first criticize the social structure that has forced them to be social misfits before calling them social misfits? The saying "Might is truth" is a principle that is alive and active even now. The existing system by nature favors the powerful and wealthy. It values possession but does not ask about the process by which one's possession has been acquired. The race is to maximize one's possessions. The person who falls behind in this race is branded as a misfit, an incompetent person. After having become an incompetent person, he or she will be trampled upon. They will have no other choice except for prostitution or theft in order to survive. We define these things as unethical, but if we view it from a little different angle, we will understand them as going against the system. Isn't ethics a fence that protects the existing system? For example, someone is caught stealing and goes to prison. But let's suppose that this person was stealing something small from a bigger thief. Can we still say this person is a sinner?

Mr. Ham Seok-heon saw Rodin's sculpture *The Old Courtesan*. He condemned the woman on ethical and biblical grounds. A prodigal woman who seduced men with the beauty of her body! But the old courtesan would not let him go when he turned around with this conclusion in his mind. Who has made this woman like this? The men who made this woman like this are exemplary persons in all levels and areas of society. Seen in this way, the old courtesan becomes not a symbol of condemnation but an accusation of the existing order.

There is another thing the three cases have in common. The Dandelion Society formed by the women of the military-base town is a concrete expression of generosity. I suppose this is not the only example. I have heard of many women in prostitution who support their family with the money they earn. Sometimes we hear wealthy people say "I have worked hard to earn this money!" as their reason for refusing to give to a charitable cause. But these women in prostitution have an even stronger claim. What kind of money is theirs? Isn't the money from selling their bodies? With this money they are helping their family or other people. This can be "presenting the body as a living sacrifice" (Rom 12:1), which is qualitatively different from almsgiving by the wealthy. In the man serving a life sentence for murder, too, we can see this kind of goodness. As a condemned murderer, he still retains an open heart and gives what he has freely to others. His motive of murder is noteworthy. He fell in love with a barmaid. He stole in order to help this woman. We don't know what specifically this meant. The woman might have lured him into it, or he might have resolved to pull her out of where she was. He was motivated by love. This love was serious enough to make him risk stealing. He went so far as to murder, but it was never his intention.

The third person was characterized as duplicitous. But is that really the case? Shouldn't we rather think that he is oscillating between good and evil, between love and hate? What use could this person have for hypocrisy, who kept fasting, trying to forget by self-medicating, and cutting himself with a shard of glass? I don't view his behavior as deceptive. Nor do I perceive his conversion experience as hypocritical. If he were granted the conditions enjoyed by those who define him as hypocritical, I believe he would be able to change drastically.

If we took these three persons to the court of the Pharisees and to Jesus, we would have two clearly different judgments. Jesus would not call them sinners; instead, he would censure those who falsely accused them as sinners. He would identify himself with them and say to them, "You who are weary and carrying heavy burdens" (Matt 11:28). Before they went wrong, the existing system went wrong. If they committed a crime, it was because the existing system created the conditions for them to do so. When I was with people like them in prison, I realized how many privileges I enjoyed in the existing system. I was able to experience firsthand the realities of the minjung from variety of perspectives. We know the legendary stories about the good work women prostitutes engaged in during the Gwangju Democratization Movement.[7]

Professor Suh Nam-dong said, "Sin is the rulers' language; *han* is the minjung's language." This is a perceptive observation. The lives of people labeled as sinners are filled with *han*. Labeling their *han* as sin adds to their *han*. They are weak, alienated, and silently carry burdens on their back. They accept society's labels and suffer affliction as prostitutes, ex-convicts, and murderers. Their disorder even drives them to despair. They live in the shadows and on the margins. Unable to escape the world's con-

---

7. Gwangju is a city located about 270 kilometers (about 170 miles) south of Seoul. The Gwangju Democratization Movement took place between May 18 and 27, 1980, in the city of Gwangju and Jeollanam Province. After the assassination of Park Jeong-hui on October 26, 1979, a group of army generals called "the new military group" led by major general Jeon Du-hwan rose to power. On May 17, 1980, the new military group extended the martial law to the whole nation, took political figures including Kim Dae-jung to the police station, and arrested democratic activists. On May 18, there was a student rally making such demands as the lifting of the martial law, the withdrawal of the new military group, and the release of Kim Dae-jung. The airborne troops dispatched to the city for martial law brutally suppressed the demonstration. The angered citizens joined the students to fight back the soldiers. At noon on May 21, the soldiers began to fire at the citizens. This led some of the citizens to arm themselves, and there were gunfights between the two parties. In the evening of May 21, the army troops retreated into the outskirts of Gwangju, and the city entered into a period of self-rule by the citizens. In the early morning of May 27, the army troops of over 25,000 advanced into the city and succeeded in defeating the armed citizen. In 1995, the government put the death toll of the Gwangju Democratization Movement at 193, including 166 civilian deaths, and the number of injured persons at 852.

demnation, they fall deeper and deeper into despair. For them, a sermon that censures their sin keeps them trapped in the quagmire. The way of salvation is not by liberating them from sin but from the complex of sin. This is the first rope to throw to them in order to rescue them. At the same time, if we help them clearly identify the structures that have made them sinners and resolve to transform the system itself, they will experience true liberation and join the ranks of the minjung as agents for the salvation of the world.

7
Minjung Liberation and the Event of the Holy Spirit

Q: In church history, the fourth century witnessed a full-blown development of the doctrine of pneumatology. On the one hand, orthodox pneumatology was formulated along the lines of Trinitarianism. On the other hand, numerous other movements departed from traditional forms of pneumatology, including Montanism, the Mendicant Movement in the Middle Ages, Joachim's historical theology, and the peasant movement by Thomas Müntzer in the Reformation period. Can you tell us more about your views on pneumatology?

A: Human beings have two contradictory desires. One is for stability, which demands a certain guarantee. This guarantee is order, which becomes system. For this reason, the desire for stability results in being settled in a system. The other desire is for freedom. Human beings constantly try to break free from bondage. This desire for freedom manifests itself as resistance against the existing order or system of one's bondage. Although the body is rooted in the ground, the spirit is free and flies up to infinity. Similarly, history shows that when there is demand for stability in society, other forces come together until a reform movement or revolutionary movement breaks out. This principle, I believe, is faithfully reflected in church history also. You offered a few examples in your question, and every one of them was a Holy Spirit movement that took place in reaction against the ossification of the church. Montanus appeared after the mid-second century, and his movement was significant enough to influence Tertullian. This is evidence that Christianity had already adopted the canon and institutionalized church authority. This is to say, Christianity had settled down into a system for self-preservation. It is no accident that Montanus rose up against this with a new understanding of the Holy Spirit and eschatology. He contended that the movement of the Holy Spirit had been suppressed by the institutional church. The Holy Spirit should be an experience of the present and cannot be something of the past. Whereas the institutional church suppressed the Holy Spirit, Montanus argued that the Holy Spirit makes the experience of the earliest Christians possible today. With this claim, he challenged the church's canonization and resisted the class structure of the church. He believed that these things blocked the possibility of the present revelation of God.

Joachim of Flora appeared after the status of the church had been firmly established by Augustine. Augustine thought of the age of the church as the age of the millennium. He held that Christ reigns in the present through the sacraments and church order. When this was the received wisdom, Joachim stood up against it. He divided history into the ages of God, Son, and Holy Spirit. This division demonstrates his unique philosophy of history. He defines the age of the Father as the feudal age that restrained human free will and "especially forced labor upon the people." He considered this period to be the age of law in religious history. The second age is the age of class when the church-ruling priestly class constituted the superstructure that defined society. He characterizes this age as one of faith that rejects legalism. It is the age of heteronomous existence. This means that participating in God's grace is possible not through any accomplishment but through participating in the sacrament provided by the priests. The third age is the age of the Holy Spirit, the age of freedom and autonomy. The meaning of autonomy is having order within itself. At the site where autonomy is realized, no external authority is necessary, and all mediating roles are rejected. Since the age of the Holy Spirit emphasizes the present, it relativizes state power, church order, even the tradition and authority of the Christian canon. Joachim was of the opinion that truth is dynamic, not static, and that it changes according to the situation. He worked out a strategy for criticizing the institutional church. Like Montanus, he advanced an eschatology in support of his pneumatology. He tied his eschatology with the third age, and specifically with the age of monastery. This means that the radicalization of monastic life will terminate human history. His claims were nullified by the Orthodox Church. Yet his influence was undeniable. His work impacted the Franciscan Order, provided theological grounds to many sects, and served as a motivating force for socialist movements.

7. Minjung Liberation and the Event of the Holy Spirit

7.1. The Holy Spirit Movement Persecuted as Heresy

Another noteworthy movement is by Thomas Müntzer. Luther calls the members of this sect "enthusiasts" (*Schwärmer*), but considering what they claimed, it is more accurate to call them spiritists. Already since the Middle Ages, there were such spiritist movements. But the Catholic church rejected them as heretical. But Luther's Reformation cleared them of the heretical charge and liberated their participants, and so these people ardently welcomed the Reformation. However, they radicalized the spirit of the Reformation and criticized and opposed Luther. They had a different understanding of the Holy Spirit. Above all, they were critical of Luther's interpretation of the Bible. In their eyes, Luther was a biblicist who failed to fully recognize God's mode of presence.

First, they contended that God reveals God's self not only through the Bible but also continues to speak to people in the present time. This is the activity of the Holy Spirit, which they believed Luther overlooked. Second, they criticized that Luther only spoke of the sweet Christ (*der süße Christus*), not speaking of the strict Christ (*der bittere Christus*). The point of this criticism was that Luther placed too much emphasis on grace and neglected the Christ who commanded people to bear the cross and follow him. Third, they emphasized the collective consciousness of calling. That was nothing other than the conviction that they were the chosen people of God. While holding that each person can receive the Holy Spirit, they were convinced that the Holy Spirit was not something to be possessed by individuals but was always the work as God's spirit. Fourth, they denied sacrament and priesthood, namely, the privileges of the institutional church. The reason was that they believed that every person was inwardly receiving the Holy Spirit as the great commission. Finally, they developed a practice of social engagement. Luther arrived at the famous doctrine of the two kingdoms through using the power of the feudal chieftains. As a result he worked out the grounds for indifference to social issues and, furthermore, the demand of blind obedience to the state power. On the contrary, Müntzer had a strong awareness of the chosen ones that it is the social calling to demolish social evils and reform society.

Müntzer's struggles for social reform were understood and practiced in two ways. The first reform was accomplished through voluntary suffering. It is the citizen's exercise of the right to resist. The second reform was using the sword to change society that obstructs the work of the chosen ones. What is noteworthy is the motivation to take up this kind of radicalism. Social reform was not part of their initial goal. Müntzer did not talk about the transformation of society itself. He thought that the poor peasants were so overwhelmed with work that they were unable to read the Bible or experience the Holy Spirit. He witnessed the lives of the laborers in the region of Saxony, where industrialization was underway. There he had a firsthand look at the realities of the laborers. They were so overworked and therefore unable to have education or practice religion. This was the motive that drove their movement into the peasant war. In the ensuing eras, Holy Spirit movements of a similar nature continued to be launched by small groups, but every one of them was persecuted by the establishment.

What is noteworthy is that the conviction about the Holy Spirit did not result in mysticism or escape to an otherworldly realm but served as a force for the change of the institutional church and society in general.

7.2. Traditional Understandings of the Holy Spirit Trapped in Dualism

Next, the traditional understanding of the Holy Spirit has undergone complications due to the apologetic need. Christianity interacted with Greek philosophy in formulating its theology and doctrine, particularly the concept of personality (*persona*). By understanding God as a person, Christian theology portrayed God as different from Greek conceptions as the first principle of the world's existence. Similarly, the Holy Spirit was understood as a person to differentiate it from *pneuma* as the core of all Greek idealistic norms. Since this apologetic effort was in conflict with Christianity's monotheism, the discussion continued in a state of confusion until after the Reformation. The doctrine of the Trinity appeared in the fourth century, which went through considerable complications and drew public criticism precisely because it wanted to hold onto the persona concept. Therefore, even up to the present day, the understanding of the Holy Spirit is unresolved. Understanding the Holy Spirit as a persona imparts independence to the Holy Spirit, and this comes close to polytheism. So the role of the Holy Spirit between God and Christ has been explained in various ambiguous ways. In addition, this understanding limited the scope of the Holy Spirit's activity. This was done to overcome pantheism or animism. But it came to cut the work of the Holy Spirit off from all of the natural phenomena. Furthermore, this understanding is problematic because grasping the Holy Spirit's movement in history as a persona limits the scope of the movement. As a matter of fact, doctrinal history does not provide an adequate explanation of the relationship between the Holy Spirit and nature or the Holy Spirit and history. As a consequence, pneumatology finally settled in a dualistic thinking. The Holy Spirit's role in connecting God and Christ, the Holy Spirit as the power by which God realizes the Word revealed through Christ—this kind of dynamic thinking was diminished by the institutional church. The scope of the Holy Spirit's activities became limited to the functions of conveying the Bible as God's Word and changing bread and wine into Jesus's flesh and blood. In a word, down to this day, the Holy Spirit's persona nature as its independent status has failed to be fully established.

By understanding the Holy Spirit as a person, the institutional church came to accept Trinitarianism. But Trinitarianism was not a solution that offered a clear solution. They understood person as *individium*. God, the Holy Spirit, and the Son are all *individium*. This posed the danger of falling into polytheism. In order to overcome this, they advanced Trinitarianism. But this only brought about confusion.

Another fact to point out is that orthodox pneumatology was marked by dualism: flesh/spirit, material/spirit, devil-dominated world/spirit-dominated world. The result was that the spirit was imprisoned by the church.

Q: Do you think that the pneumatology of the institutional church is not based on the Bible?

A: The Greek word *pneuma*, which is translated into "spirit" or "the Holy Spirit" in the Korean Bibles, was first used in the New Testament by Paul. The first question to ask is what he meant by it. Did he translate *ruakh* or *nephesh* of the Old Testament into *pneuma*? Or was *pneuma* used as an antonym of *sarx* in the Hellenistic world? For the sake of argument, I assume that Paul had both of these traditions in mind. In the Septuagint *ruakh* was translated into *pneuma*. Therefore, it is highly probable that Paul, who was well versed in the Septuagint, was thinking of *ruakh* when using *pneuma*. However, since he lived in the Hellenistic world, took the Greco-Roman world for his field of evangelism, and made the apologetics of Christianity his life goal, he surely would not have ignored the Hellenistic understanding of *pneuma*. What is important here is that *ruakh* or *nephesh* of the Old Testament does not have the idea of personality as *individium* at all. *Ruakh* or *pneuma* in the sense of *ruakh* means the realization of a certain concrete power. To translate it into an Eastern concept, *chi* is better than spirit. The Korean translation of spirit seems to presuppose *pneuma* as opposite to material or flesh. But chi is not a dualistic concept. Nor can it be understood as personality. The original meaning of *pneuma*, like that of *ruakh*, was "power," "breath," or "wind." But a more accurate understanding is *chi*. In the Pauline writing, along with "God's *pneuma*" and "Christ's *pneuma*," the expression "human *pneuma*" appears, too. (Often the Korean translation puts the character for "holy" before "spirit," which does not exist in the Greek original.) Therefore, God's power and human power means *kiun* (the power of a living being) in the Korean language. Just as the *ruakh* of God's energy is the impetus for the creation and direction of the world, *pneuma* is not something confined to a certain place like the church. It is a power working in the whole world and in all of human history. Therefore, it is impossible to understand *pneuma* in dualistic terms. It is meaningless to understand it as a personality independent of God.

Q: Your pneumatology makes it much easier to understand the relation between the Holy Spirit, nature, history, and humanity. Can you say more about pneumatology in the Bible?

A: God's *pneuma* reaches out to everything: nature, history, and all situations where individuals find themselves. There is no limit to the sphere of God's activity. When we confess God as the creator of the world or say that we are filled with the Holy Spirit, we cannot or should not delimit God. Westerners tend to guard against pantheistic thinking in order to preserve the uniqueness of Christianity vis-à-vis other religions. But this is a closed-minded way of thinking that hampers our understanding. The Bible has no such closed-mindedness.

7.3. The Nature of the Pneumatology of the Bible

In the Bible, there is no specific place or form that God requires for God's revelation. God is not limited by the temple or church, a certain person of special designation, or a certain time. God reveals God's self in a manner that defies prediction. This means that God's *kiun* also stretches out into nature and history. We see the trace of this in Paul, too. A good example is found in Rom 8. Paul says that humans, nature, and the spirit as an interconnected whole are running a cosmic race towards the ultimate goal of history.

Once we are freed from the stereotype that the Holy Spirit is personality as *individium*, we are able to witness and testify to the activities of the

Holy Spirit in all events in history. We will gain a correct understanding if we embrace the thought that the Holy Spirit is an event—not a personality. History is a series of events. The church is also a part of that history and therefore part of the chain of events. We confess the activities of the Holy Spirit taking place in history. But here we run into a question: Is all history the history of the Holy Spirit? The answer, in principle, is yes. However, there is an issue of perception here. That is to say, as limited beings, human beings are capable of perception when boundaries are drawn. Differences are shown in contrast with something else when certain criteria are provided. God of the Old Testament, despite being the creator of this world, confines God's work to Israel and furthermore shows God's self as a representative figure like a tribal chief working for a particular social class. Thus, God was called God of the Hebrews, of Israel, and of Abraham. In the New Testament, the Christ event serves as the criterion. Of course, this does not limit the scope of God's *kiun*. When our norm is God's *kiun* that extends towards history in general or the Christ event, the Holy Spirit enters the sphere of human perception. For this reason, the spirit of Christ is understood as the Holy Spirit in the New Testament. That is to say, in the New Testament, Christ replaces Israel, and through him God reveals God's self. But since the historical Jesus is not present, the way in which Jesus is present as Christ is understood precisely as the work of the Holy Spirit. The church emerges as God's collective people. Paul speaks of the Holy Spirit in a different respect. We generally say that the theme of Paul's theology is the law and the gospel. From this point of view, 2 Cor 3:3, for example, raises an important point. Here Paul contrasts *pneuma* with *gramma* (letter) to say that salvation is achieved not by the letter but by the Holy Spirit. Here the letter refers to the law—or, to broaden its meaning, the existing system. The letter of the law and the existing system cannot save people. Rather, people are saved when they are liberated from these. This liberating *kiun* is none other than the Holy Spirit.

Like the Hellenists, Paul often contrasted spirit and flesh. But his purpose in doing so was not to develop a dualism, but to elucidate the eschatological nature of the new event. He frequently identifies *sarx* with the law in order to make it clear that *pneuma* is a liberating *kiun*, signifying the end of all things. For this reason, *pneuma* is deeply related to the concept of freedom. It is the *kiun* of God that frees humans from all things that already exist. In this respect, I believe that Bultmann's understanding of the spirit is correct. In his understanding, Paul's basic intention was not to hold onto the dualism that separates flesh and spirit from each other, but to speak of how to set the goal of life. Certainly, Paul debated how to deal with these two concepts. He spoke of the body (*sōma*) in order to overcome the dualism. While affirming that the flesh cannot inherit the kingdom of God, he speaks of the spiritual body and the resurrection of the body. By using the concept of the body, he attempted to speak of a whole being in whom there is no separation between spirit and body.

Another thing to point out about Paul is the relationship between his pneumatology and eschatology. There are two aspects to Paul's eschatology: present and future eschatology. A different pneumatology implies a different eschatology. The future eschatology goes hand in hand with understanding the Holy Spirit as a religious phenomenon, while the present eschatology fits with the understanding of the Holy Spirit as an event of liberation. In the gospels, the Holy Spirit is directly related to the *eschaton*. The present nature of the *eschaton* is stressed in Mark. That the kingdom of God is being realized now is inseparably related to the event of Jesus's exorcism. What deserves our attention is the fact that the Holy Spirit does not appear in Mark except in the mention of Jesus receiving the spirit. This means that Jesus and the Holy Spirit are united. The same is true of Matthew. He believed that the Holy Spirit would not arrive until the death of Jesus. Jesus promises his disciples the descent of the Holy Spirit only after his resurrection. Luke is basically no different from the other gospels but is more specific in his pneumatology. The time and role of Jesus differ from the Holy Spirit. The Holy Spirit is not mentioned with regard to Jesus's death and his postresurrection days. The time of the Holy Spirit does not start until the Pentecost.

7.4. The Holy Spirit Is a Minjung Event

Luke identifies the descent of the Holy Spirit as the precise moment of the church's birth. Pentecost is a minjung event. Like the Passover, Pentecost is a festival that celebrates liberation. During the festival, the Jews in the diaspora all over the world came together in Jerusalem. Many of them have forgotten their mother tongue and spoke the languages of where they lived. At this very juncture, in the middle of Jerusalem, the people of Jesus received the Holy Spirit and witnessed to the Christ event. Their words were understood by all of those present there. All of the hearers are surprised by this mysterious event, being reminded of their own region of residence. The difference in language is a barrier between people. The Jews must have been familiar with the legend of the Tower of Babel. This tower was being built by collective power. God, however, wanted to weaken the power of human beings in order to strike against their arrogance. For this purpose, God caused discrepancy in language. But at Pentecost, people divided by linguistic barriers experienced unity. Luke clearly marks the main actors of this event with the expression, "Are not all these who are speaking Galileans?" (Acts 2:7) Luke was a Jerusalem-centralist. Therefore, he assumes that the epiphany of the resurrected Jesus would occur in Jerusalem (Luke 24:47) and in fact passes on the only tradition of the Jerusalem epiphany. Instead of simply calling the main actors of the Pentecost Jesus's disciples, however, he makes it clear that they were Galileans, whom the people of Jerusalem held in great contempt and whose designation (Galileans) was a byword for the minjung of the time. He did so for the sake of historical accuracy, which is highly significant. The descent of the Holy Spirit is an eschatological and revolutionary event from the standpoint of the current system. We can say that the Holy Spirit event is a revolutionary event by the minjung. As a matter of fact, this event led the Galilean minjung to begin to form communities in Jerusalem, the place of Jesus's execution. Jesus was executed in Jerusalem. And the powerless minjung following Jesus was empowered by him, who had entered in the present as *pneuma* (*kiun*) and was working in their midst and started to revolutionize the world. This is precisely the descent of the Holy Spirit and the start of Christianity. This movement enabled the minjung, who were fettered by the Jewish tradition, to escape the temple. The minjung organized new communities and abolished the Sabbath, which had lost its original meaning and degenerated into an ideology of domination. This movement went over the walls of Judaism to advance out into the world, and finally broke down the empire of Rome.

Q: We tend to think of the Holy Spirit as something that should fit our subjective needs. What do you think of this point?

A: Your question presupposes the subject-object dichotomy, but we must be liberated from this framework. Bultmann said, "*Pneuma* is the self-transcending consciousness." I define the minjung as a group capable of self-transcendence—a notion that inadvertently agrees with Bultmann's pneumatology. To develop this thought a little further, we could say that the Holy Spirit does not have a separate and objective existence, but that the minjung movement itself is the Holy Spirit movement. But then what makes self-transcendence possible? This kind of question imposes the subject-object frame on the given event and objectifies and alienates part of it. It fails to obtain the right answer. The longing for the Holy Spirit is the yearning for freedom. In this sense, one aspect of the Holy Spirit is the reflection of subjective needs. However, this differs from saying that the minjung movement itself is the reality of the Holy Spirit as the presence of Christ. I believe that the notion of event can and must be analyzed in social scientific terms. But at the same time I think this method is limited in clarifying the ultimate reality of event. Self-transcendence is an event and simultaneously transcends the limitations of perception.

Q: For this very reason, we should not talk about the Holy Spirit in an abstract way but use a reference.

A: That's right. I make the Jesus event the reference for everything. Many events are taking place in history, and even now the minjung movement is taking place in our society. Events of self-transcendence are certainly taking place. Nevertheless, we cannot stop in saying that the minjung movement is the Holy Spirit movement. We need to sort out the movement of the Holy Spirit among the minjung movements and testify to them. For example, Luke 4 is a good example. Here, Jesus, in Isaiah's words, announces, "the Spirit of the Lord is upon me" and says that he will liberate the poor, the captives, the blind, and the oppressed and proclaim the year of the Lord's favor (Luke 4:18).

Q: If we make Jesus's minjung event the criterion, can we stipulate that the Holy Spirit is also active in the events of minjung liberation that take place in the general history?

A: How we define the minjung event of Jesus will determine the scope for acknowledging secular movements as Holy Spirit movements. For example, can we understand the bourgeois revolution, which happened during the transition from the feudal to bourgeois society, as a Holy Spirit movement? Considering that the bourgeois were liberated from class bondage, it is consistent with the liberation by the Holy Spirit. But as far as they were those in power and used the weapons of their possessions, it is far from the Holy Spirit movement that appeared in the minjung event of Jesus. On the contrary, the Donghak minjung uprising (the Donghak Peasant Revolution), the March First Movement, and the minjung movements in the 1970s and 1980s sufficiently qualify as Holy Spirit movements. This begs the question: by what criterion can this kind of distinction be made? At the risk of oversimplification, let me mention two things. The first is self-transcendence, which involves transcending your own interests and abilities. This is the ultimate state of liberation. It is the exercise of power free from all that already exists. The second is the *eschaton*-like nature, which correlates to self-transcendence. The *eschaton*-like nature means having the belief that every existing value should be subverted and that everything should end. In everything here, your fate is included, too. Here, there is no I or you, but only a third thing. This can be called revolution, but it is not an attempt for me to replace you. It is the conviction that, even if I perish along with everything else, the right should win and the right world should come.

7.5. Are the Holy Spirit Movements of the Korean Church Biblical?

Q: Up to this point you offered a general discussion of the Holy Spirit. In Korea, the Holy Spirit movement has been on the rise since the 1970s, particularly with Full Gospel Church playing a leading role. But this movement seems to be based pretty much on prosperity, rather than biblical faith. So people are assured of having received the Holy Spirit when they speak in tongues, are healed of an illness, and things like that. What do you think about the Holy Spirit movement of the Korean church? Do you see any problems or merits with the movement?

A: The Holy Spirit movement of the Korean church can be seen in the early church. A big commotion occurred in the Corinthian church because of receiving the gifts, especially those of tongues and prophecy. Paul does not deny that these gifts come from the Holy Spirit. But he says in several places: "I would like all of you to speak in tongues, but even better I would like you to deliver God's words";[1] "If I come to you speaking in tongues, how will I benefit you unless I speak to you in some revelation or knowledge or prophecy or teaching?" (1 Cor 14:6); and "In church I would rather speak five words with my mind, in order to instruct others also, than ten thousand words in a tongue" (1 Cor 14:19). Remarks like these show that Paul knows the meaninglessness of such

---

1. Of the two clauses in this particular quote, the first one ("I would like all of you to speak in tongues") appears in 1 Cor 14:5, and the second one ("but even better I would like you to deliver God's words") is of Ahn's own creating.

phenomena. But he does not deny them and instead exhorts a change in direction out of a minister's thoughtfulness. Healing illnesses or falling in ecstasy through speaking in tongues is not unique to Christianity. These activities take place under the name of religion and can be found in many world religions of all ages. I believe that we have to analyze this kind of phenomenon in terms of Korean social pathology. The remarkable quantitative growth of the Korean church did not happen in rural areas but in big cities in urban areas. New members of the urban churches are mostly from rural areas. They have crowded into cities for a living, leaving behind their hometowns and home villages. The empty feeling after leaving one's home gave rise to the desire for belonging. The church became, first of all, a place that satisfied this desire. Ministers of urban churches intuitively grasp this social phenomenon and take advantage of it in the name of the Holy Spirit. City dwellers are plagued by the stress deriving from many causes. The church, we can say, provides a place for stress relief in the name of the Holy Spirit. In traditional churches such as the conservative Presbyterian church, the Holy Spirit phenomenon does not take place in the form of a movement. On the contrary, in churches of small denominations, a kind of liberation event is taking place. They are liberated in the name of the Holy Spirit from discouragement, anxiety, and even illnesses. I believe this is a reaction against conservative churches, where doctrine has become like the law. But I do not see this as the event of the Holy Spirit. In this phenomenon, all the way through, selfishness is satisfied in the name of the Holy Spirit. The Holy Spirit movement in Korea is of a much lower class compared even to the revivalist movement begun by such figures as Mr. Lee Yong-do.[2] Thomas Müntzer blamed Luther for preaching only the sweet Christ, not the bitter Christ, and the same criticism hits the mark with the Holy Spirit movements of today's Korean church. Figures like Mr. Lee Yong-do did not preach the sweet Christ alone. That is to say, they emphasized following Jesus's life and demanded their audience to overcome and transcend self. The Korean church heals illnesses in the name of the Holy Spirit. We have no record of Jesus speak-

---

2. Lee Yong-do (1901–1933) was a Methodist minister who exerted a nationwide influence as a mystical revivalist preacher. The essence of his theology was based on the mystical sense of unity between Christ and him, and therefore he rejected church tradition, the clergy, doctrine, and the sacrament as useless. Advocating an indiscriminate love, Lee was open even to socialism, Buddhism, Daoism, and the nonchurch movement. He was accused of heresy by the established church.

ing in tongues but many records of him healing illnesses. However, his healing and exorcism are eschatological. That is to say, the acts of healing illnesses and casting out demons served as concrete signs of the advent of the kingdom of God.

Q: There is another group in the Korean church that emphasizes the Holy Spirit. They stress human limitations, believe that the Holy Spirit can be experienced in a certain profound religious dimension beyond the problems of human life, and oppose Christians who participate in social movements. How do you view these tendencies?

A: That is also a fallacy that stems from confining the Holy Spirit event to a particular sphere. Earlier we talked about the claim that we can experience the Holy Spirit in the church, namely in worship, sermon, or sacrament. This position is similar to the one under discussion. Mysticism is caught up in a delusion that we, despite living in this world, can transcend it. It considers the work of the Holy Spirit as transcending this world, as something otherworldly. But transcending history and transcending the self are fundamentally two different things. The former attempts to break out of history, but the latter attempts to transcend the self in order to throw oneself into history and change it. The work of the Holy Spirit that has left the site of history is not biblical.

Q: It is a fact that a majority of church members in Korea are minjung, and they have the need to be freed from problems like illnesses or poverty. Can the wish to satisfy this need through faith itself be disregarded? If there is a problem with it, it should be that their need is limited to the personal dimension. Then could there not be ways that do not disregard such primary needs of the minjung and still satisfy them in the collective dimension?

A: As I said earlier, Jesus met such primary needs of the minjung. He gave food to the hungry and healed the sick. But the ultimate purpose of Jesus's movement was the advent of the kingdom of God. The kingdom of God is not a personal event. Therefore, it is the nature of Jesus's movement that those who were caught up in personal needs were liberated through self-transcendence in order to become active participants in realizing the kingdom of God. For this reason, we come to see not only a sweet-talking Jesus, so to speak, but a Jesus who makes radical demands. Therefore, Jesus's minjung abandoned what they had, including their home, possessions, even family. They followed Jesus up to Jerusalem to oppose and challenge the stronghold of the existing system. But the Holy Spirit movement of today's Korean church does not make people followers of Jesus in this way. To the contrary, it provokes them to be selfish and complacent.

By contrast, in the basic communities of Latin America, the outcome of their Holy Spirit experience is both peace of mind and the full awakening of their political consciousness. They clearly recognize the structure of the system that is oppressing them and fight for liberation from the political and economic structures of their country. It is precisely when this kind of phenomenon takes place that the Holy Spirit movement—or, the Holy Spirit-caused event, in the true sense of the term—takes place. In the minjung movement of today's Korea, this kind of Holy Spirit event is taking place.

8
The Kingdom of God Is the Kingdom of Minjung

Q: The topic for today is the kingdom of God. I remember you once said the kingdom of God was a concept formed in the lives of those who were oppressed and deprived and suffered sorrows in history. I suppose that ideas about the kingdom of God did not only appear in the ancient Palestine but appeared throughout history. What kind of social context was the concept of the kingdom of God generated?

A: The kingdom of God is one of the most important topics in the Synoptic Gospels and in Western theology. Western scholars have continually said, "The kingdom of God is impossible to know. It cannot be expressed in human language." I also once supported this position with these words, "If the kingdom of God is knowable and can be expressed in the words of the present day, it is already something old and not new." This was another way I was contaminated by Western theology.

Western theology placed apocalyptic literature and representations of the kingdom of God in the same interpretive plane. Aside from whether such an approach is correct, since Western theology reduced the weight of apocalyptic thought in theology, it ended up lessening the importance of the kingdom of God in theology. For example, Albert Schweitzer, who had joined the eschaton school, understood Jesus from the standpoint of apocalyptic thought and so said, "Jesus failed. He believed in the advent of the kingdom of God, but this kingdom didn't come." He thus diminished the weight of Jesus's position on the kingdom of God or eschatology.

Furthermore, even though there are many parables of Jesus about the kingdom of God in the Bible, Western theology has said almost nothing to "Just what is this kingdom of God?" Jesus talked about the kingdom of God through the parables of yeast, planting a mustard seed, and so on. Concerning these parables, Western theologians said that they are not so much descriptions of the kingdom of God itself as revelation of its existence. But I think Jesus meant the parables to indicate the hidden and invisible development of the kingdom of God like the growth in yeast or a mustard seed. The question remains with what we would identify the kingdom of God that is growing in this world like yeast or a mustard seed. At any rate, I think we can be confident that history is advancing toward the kingdom of God.

The most realistic of Jesus's parables about the kingdom of God is the Parable of the Wedding Feast. Those with vested interests did not accept the invitation to the feast. In the end, the poor who were loitering in the streets looking for a job were invited. The feast became theirs, and the world became theirs—a reality where the establishment had no place. The words that the rich cannot enter the kingdom of God, that blessed are the poor and the mourning, mean that a new history is opening up. These words of Jesus themselves challenge us and destroys our stable life.

Q: Western theology did not make the kingdom of God its central theme. The history of theology reveals a clear division between the human and divine realm. Western theology claims that humans cannot participate in God's realm, and that the kingdom of God belongs less to the human realm than to the realm of God's absolute sovereignty. Does this help explain why it has limited human participation in the kingdom of God?

A: That's right. Western theologians have made an effort to downplay the kingdom of God. Just like the historical Jesus, they find the topic of the kingdom of God frightening, for it ruthlessly criticizes and exposes their comfortable life. They draw a line and say, "This is the realm where God's absolute sovereignty rules. So let's not interfere with it." This is how they can feel safe.

Q: If Jesus had given specific descriptions about the kingdom of God, this kind of problem would not have come up. Why did he not do so?

A: I suppose it was self-evident to the people of his time. In the same way, no one needed to clarify what independence would look like in the years following Japanese colonization. Although the expression "kingdom of God" is strange to us, it was not to the Palestinian minjung of Jesus's time. Its strangeness is only linguistic, but what it refers to is nothing new. It is obvious to the minjung. However, the more intellectual you are, the more secure position you have in this land and therefore the more uncomfortable the kingdom of God becomes to you.

What is also very important is that Jesus made the first utterance about the kingdom of God in Galilee right after hearing of the arrest of John the Baptist. Western theologians take Mark 1:14 lightly as a work of redaction. But this proclamation of Jesus hits the nail on the head given the political situation of the time. In those days Galilee was a region that had an order of life that opposed the religious aristocracy of Jerusalem. Galilee was fervently expecting the kingdom of God.

The Zealots, the Essenes, and the sect of John the Baptist are anti-Jerusalem sects and were all full of enthusiasm for the kingdom of God. Jesus's group was also an anti-Jerusalem sect. Galilee was the home of the so-called *am ha'aretz*, who formed guerilla bands. First and foremost, however, it was the home of the Zealots. It was a place where groups like the Yim Kkeok-jeong and Jang Gil-san parties[1] in Korean history were based. Among them were probably bandits, thieves, and people who escaped into the mountains because they had gone broke or had nowhere to go. However, Galilee was swarming with people who were awaiting the kingdom and willing to sacrifice themselves in the struggle against the Roman Empire. In those days, the governor stationed in Syria personally led his troops to the Galilean region to sweep out these groups. But he was unable to clear all of the guerilla bands that were in the caves perhaps because the resistance was fierce and the terrain was treacherous.

Next, theology has so far exhausted itself with the question of whether the kingdom of God is present or future. This discussion is possible for someone in the position of an intellectual. But what use is this question for someone who is standing at the crossroads of life and death? In the same way, the question of whether or not to use violence is only for onlookers who are far from reality. When the sword is thrust upon your neck, you

---

1. Yim Kkeok-jeong (d. 1562) was the head of the bandits that operated in the Hwanghae Province (the middle-western part of the Korean peninsula) between 1559 and 1562 during the Joseon Dynasty. He is considered a righteous thief who stole from the corrupt wealthy and helped the poor lower class people suffering from epidemic, famine, and the exploitation by the upper class. Jang Gil-san (dates unknown) was the head of the bandits that were active in the Hwanghae Province for over ten years in the late-seventeenth century during the Joseon Dynasty. By some account, he even planned to overthrow the monarchy in collusion with some aristocrats and Buddhist monks. Jang was never captured and is considered one of the most noteworthy thieves of Joseon Dynasty.

cannot discuss violence or nonviolence or whether the kingdom of God is present or future. These discussions are only for those who have the leisure to contemplate the kingdom in the abstract. We should think that the Galilean minjung had no such leisure. Theirs was such a pressing reality. For them, immediate actions were necessary for the advent of the kingdom of God. They did not tell the kingdom of God apart from themselves who were fighting for it.

8.1. The Kingdom of God—The Yearnings and *Han* of Minjung

Q: What do you think of the connection between the Palestinian minjung's thought of the kingdom of God and apocalyptic literature?

A: We would be wrong to suppose that the Palestinian minjung acquired an understanding of the kingdom of God from apocalyptic literature. The kingdom is not a thought. It is a yearning in the bosom of the minjung who have suffered in the history of the Israelites. To use a Korean expression, it was the *han* of the minjung. It is impossible to separate Israel's history of suffering from the hope of the Palestinian minjung for the kingdom of God. Both forces persisted and came together until they finally exploded into action in the Galilee of Jesus's time. The apocalyptic literature might have provoked them and expanded the horizon of their thinking. But the fight of the Palestinian minjung was, I think, too urgent to allow them to think about the end of the cosmos in the apocalyptic literature.

Q: So the specific situation of the Galilean minjung in those days was a direct influence on their expectations of the kingdom of God?

A: Yes. The Palestinian minjung at the time were exploited in three ways: first, by the Jerusalem temple in the form of tithes; second, in the form of a feudal rent imposed by Herod; and third, by the Roman tax-collecting agency. To put this into perspective, Herod Antipas collected two hundred talents in Galilee every year in the time of Jesus, and Rome collected six hundred talents of tax per year in Judea alone. The minjung of that time swarmed to Galilee because they could not live in their homeland any longer. Therefore, Galilee was the region of the highest population density of the time. Even though the soil of Galilee was fertile, the land was possessed by absentee landlords, and residents were mostly managers or tenant farmers.

Politically, Herod used Galilee as a buffer zone to avoid a direct conflict with Arab forces—just like the United Shilla in Korean history using its northern regions to avoid conflict with China. In Galilee, there were many gentiles and Jews. So it obtained the name the land of gentiles, but this carried a political meaning too. It was a region that had no political protection from Rome or Judah. It was a region that was governed but enjoyed no rights. Rome despised Galilee and had its own ways with it.

Another point is that Hellenization started during the reign of Antiochus III. Cities were built in different places under Roman colonization. In the Galilean region, several cities, including Sepphoris, were constructed and served as a bridge for Hellenization. The urban and rural areas were in a seriously oppositional relation, which was not only a superior-inferior relation but an almost antagonistic or enemy-like relation. City dwellers were Hellenized in their administrative operations and their everyday culture. Jews in rural areas grew in antagonism towards urban Jews regarding their Jewish identity. Galilee was despised as unclean on account of its ethnic diversity. Yet this diversity encouraged Galilean Jews to maintain their national identity. They gathered that the Hellenization, Romanization, and modernization of the cities were going against the order of God. From here arose the prayer "Your kingdom come" (Matt 6:10; Luke 11:2).

Q: Was the Galilean hope for the kingdom of God linked to the traditions of ancient Israel?

A: We are unable to know precisely to what extent the Galilean minjung considered themselves the offspring of Israel. However, between Judah and Israel, they certainly lean toward Israel. For example, Saul, the king of Israel, fought the Philistines in Galilee and then was attacked by David and his ally in Galilee. His son took refuge in Galilee after his death. Taking this into account, it would be closer to the truth to say that Galileans were the descendants of ancient Israel. When it comes to drawing a contrast between Jerusalem and Galilee, we have to go back to the era of David and Solomon. David pursued an eclectic policy of appointing half of his ministers from the kingdom of Israel and the other half from the kingdom of Judah. Solomon, however, favored Judah over and against Israel. Solomon was a committed Judaist and opposed Israel. Of course, because the kingdom of Israel perished first, and the kingdom of Judah survived until much later, policies that favored Judah continued down to the time of Jesus. The thought of a new kingdom was not entirely absent in Judah.

The new kingdom it dreamed of was a restoration of the Davidic monarchy based in Jerusalem. However, this was not true of Galileans as the descendants of the kingdom of Israel. The archetype of the kingdom of God was the system of ancient Israel before the David monarchy. The serfs of Canaan united and formed an alliance in the faith of Yahweh as the liberator God. They went on to defeat the feudal chieftains and create a new community of equality, where they lived in an atmosphere of liberation for nearly two hundred years. Galileans longed for this ancient Israelite society as the model of the kingdom of God. It was just as Chinese people longed for the ancient Yao and Shun age, which they regarded to be the ideal representation of the new age.

The following cry came out of their history of being afflicted by the monarchy and one foreign power after another: "There is no person over another person. Our one and only master is Yahweh!" It conveyed a message of resistance that rejected any social or political structure controlled by humans—the message that no one other than God was supposed to rule over them. For them, longing for liberation from political oppression and economic exploitation and their deep desire for the kingdom of God were inseparably intertwined. But it was actually the former that was given emphasis and urgency. The desire was expressed by "Your kingdom has to come," which was manifested in their resolve to fulfill the kingdom of God. For this reason, they believed that the kingdom of God was present in their fight.

Q: Do you mean that the wish for the kingdom of God and the concept of the kingdom of God itself were formed in the midst of the historical sufferings of the minjung? Is there anything particular to Israel's representation of the kingdom of God?

A: Wouldn't the uniqueness of Israel appear through a comparison with China? Confucius put forward the Yao Shun age as the ideal. Yao and Shun governed as if they were not governing, but the current feudal lords wielded their power and oppress people. This kind of critical consciousness and disdain for power were probably present in Confucius. Ancient Israel, however, was different from the Yao and Shun age idealized by Confucius. Social tensions did not magically disappear following the fights and struggles against the monarchs.

While criticizing Confucius, Laotze and Juantze criticized Yao and Shun. In an apparently nongoverning form, Yao and Shun did govern.

Doing nothing at all is better. Stop governing is best. Therefore, Laotze and Juantze dreamt of a future society that has a small population and is so small that the barking of a dog on the one end can be heard on the other. Since a big population gives birth to the ruler-ruled relation, various institutions, and structural evil, they held that scattering people into small villages would be best. Laotze's *Daodejing* does nothing more than giving a vague and fantastical description of the future utopia in this way. This and the Galilean ideal share the same criticism of centralizing power. But the model of Laotzu and Juantze differs greatly from Israel. The ideal of Laotze and Juantze was created by those who enjoy great leisure and are given to contemplation. But it is a totally different story with Israel, especially Galilee in Jesus's time. The Israelite thought reveals in a really faithful manner the standpoint of the oppressed at the site of life-or-death struggles. In this respect, we can rather say the Israelite thought resonates more sympathetically with the attempts made since the beginning of the modern era by the Korean minjung who became bandits in the mountains to do away with the rotten government and build up a new country. Therefore, we cannot say that the wish for the kingdom of God was only held by the Israelites alone. Of course, there should be a difference in how deep a religious thinking it generated. Additionally, since every people depicts the kingdom of God through their own historical and cultural tradition, we could speak of the particularity of Israel.

8.2. Jesus Did Not Have to Define the Kingdom of God

Q: Jesus went to Galilee and proclaimed to the suffering minjung there: "The time is fulfilled, and the kingdom of God has come near" (Mark 1:15). What kind of proclamation was this?

A: Jesus's words "The time is fulfilled" can be paraphrased in the following way: "The atmosphere is ripe for the social transformation; the time has come for you to arise." In those days, all of the anti-Jerusalem sects, including the Jesus group, were critical of the Jerusalem temple system. In this regard, we can say they shared a similar line of engagement. Jesus didn't just criticize the Zealots and the sect of John the Baptist but even the Essenes. I imagine he had good reason. For example, he may have wanted to protect their secrets. At any rate, we find in Jesus's words no criticism of them at all. Because they all stood under the broad umbrella of the kingdom of God movement for the messiah. But it was unique of Jesus to create a new organization for his kingdom of God movement, instead of joining an existing movement. Making people disciples means the same as rounding up comrades. With a little imagination, it is not difficult to picture Jesus meeting the young men of Galilee and bringing them together as his comrades. How was it possible that they followed Jesus after meeting with him for the first time? How could such a thing have happened without any previous contact? The Gospel of John gives a clear picture of the contacts Jesus makes with young men such as Peter and Andrew. Doesn't it describe them as belonging to a group with strong inner ties? These young men were having secret meetings in their efforts to realize the kingdom. Young men such as Philip and Nathaniel appear. The thought keeps crossing my mind that this record is not necessarily unhistorical. I believe that we can imagine that patriotic people gathered here and there, worried about the state of affairs of the day, and concerned themselves with the things of the kingdom of God. At the right moment, Jesus found them and said, "The time is finally fulfilled. Come together!" So some of the Zealots joined, and some members of the John the Baptist sect joined.

From a movement-oriented perspective, it is striking that Jesus, despite telling many parables about the kingdom, gives very little detail of the kingdom itself. How do we understand this? I am of the opinion that Jesus did not need to define the kingdom of God. He accepted the notion entertained by those who were already in the movement for the kingdom of God. Also, Jesus's acts during his short stay in Galilee were not disconnected from the kingdom of God movement. In my view, the kingdom of God movement and the kingdom of God did not exist in separation, and the whole of Jesus's words and acts were fully in line with the reality of the kingdom of God. In this regard, I concur with the Western theologian Dodd's "realized eschatology"—particularly, his claim that the kingdom of God has already come in Jesus's life and community.

It seems to me that the Lord's Prayer best reveals what the kingdom of God is like. A careful look at this prayer reveals it is a testimony to and confession of the kingdom of God. It begins, "Hallowed be your name" (Luke 11:2), which confesses God's sovereignty. It says, "Only Your sovereignty is acknowledged." This can be summed up into "You only." Because God's sovereignty is the only true sovereignty, we cannot help but say next, "Your kingdom come" (Luke 11:2). It is not right to say that the word "come" signifies fulfillment in the future. The imperative "come" refers to the present fulfillment of the kingdom. What follows is the request for daily food. Daily food refers to the material world. But this does not imply greed but only what is sufficient for today. Giving to everyone just enough for daily consumption means an even distribution, doesn't it? The kingdom of God is precisely this kind of order of sharing. For Jesus, eating is so important! Jesus regularly eats with the minjung. Eating is a symbolic representation of the thought and standpoint of Jesus. In his final meeting, Jesus ate with his disciples and said, "Until that day when I eat it new in the kingdom of God."[2] He was even thinking of eating in the kingdom of God. A real kingdom of God cannot ever be conceived without eating together. The consistent attitude of Jesus in undertaking the kingdom of God movement was eating together! For poor people, nothing is more pleasurable than eating. Eating together is the ultimate expression of life's pleasure. What matters is daily food. Daily food!

Jesus healing illnesses can be understood in a different way, too, if we take it to be the curing of *sarx*. It is the concern with material. This is a very realistic understanding.

After dealing with material relations, the Lord's Prayer goes on to deal with social relations—namely, the forgiveness of sins. The term *opheilēmata* refers to debt, which came to be understood in religious terms as sin (*hamartia*). The advent of the kingdom of God is deeply related to the liberation from material bondage. Heard in this way, the Lord's Prayer sounds to me like a song of confession sung by those who are marching for the construction of the kingdom of God.

The Jesus group marched toward Jerusalem singing this kind of minjung song. As Bornkamm says, "Jesus worked as if he were the commander on the war front for the kingdom of God." But Western biblical scholars consider it doubtful that Jesus intentionally went to Jerusalem. We have to pay attention to the atmosphere of the movement back then. Considering that many of the anti-Jerusalem groups were determined to purge Jerusalem, it becomes evident that Jesus set his sights on Jerusalem. Attacking the Jerusalem temple entailed putting his life on the line. It is unthinkable that, contemplating such an important task, he made no plans in advance. Jesus was not alone in considering purging the Jerusalem temple. In those days, the Zealots fought also against the Jerusalem forces, and all the other groups attached great importance to purging the Jerusalem temple. For in Palestine during those days, the Jerusalem temple was the headquarters of

---

2. This quote is based on the following phrase in Mark 14:25: "until that day when I drink it new in the kingdom of God." Ahn replaces "drink" in this phrase with "eat" for his quotation.

Rome's and Herod's exploitation. In other words, the temple functioned as the vehicle through which political oppression, economic plunder, and ideological domination took effect. Therefore, attacking the Jerusalem temple was the action that concretely expressed both Jesus's recognition of the kingdom of God, as shown in the Lord's Prayer, and his plan for fulfilling the kingdom. We cannot help but admit that Jesus's comprehensive understanding of Palestinian society was the foundation for his risky behavior. For without an understanding of the given society, it is not possible to make a moral decision. To use the language of our time, Jesus correctly understood the contradictory structure of his time and society that bred injustice, oppression, and exploitation. He set out with specific practices to transform this structure. And his selection of the timing was perfect, too. For he chose the Passover, or the festival of the liberation of the Jewish people, when the Jewish minjung flocked to the Jerusalem temple from all regions.

8.3. The New Kingdom Whose Owner Is Minjung

Q: What do you think Jesus was planning to establish after attacking the temple? Could it have been the restoration of ancient Israel?

A: That is a question to examine from different angles, and we need first to consider Jesus's behavior. First of all, it is certain that Jesus was socially aware of class differences at the time. He was aware of the relation between the religious aristocracy of Jerusalem and other groups of people, as well as the relation between the haves and the have-nots. The main actors of the kingdom of God movement—those on the frontlines—were the poor and oppressed, namely, the minjung. This idea is clearly expressed in Jesus's parables and the Sermon on the Mount. In the Beatitudes, Jesus says, "Blessed are the poor, for theirs is the kingdom of God."[3] Those with vested interests are left out, and the neglected class of people in society are brought to the fore. Their starting point was Galilee. All of the gospels highlight the people and place of Galilee. This fact carries extraordinary significance. For the people of Galilee in themselves are the object of contempt in Jewish society. At the gathering on Pentecost, the question was

---

3. This quote is based on Luke 6:20: "Blessed are you who are poor, for yours is the kingdom of God."

raised, "Are not all these Galileans?"[4] and Peter was asked, "Aren't you a Galilean?"[5] The deeds of women were recorded along with a clear identification of their origin by the phrase, "women from Galilee."[6] From a perspective based on class, there is a total subversion of the identity of the main actors in building the new order of the kingdom. Jesus's conception of transforming reality used oppositional social forces symbolized by Jerusalem versus Galilee. The Galilean minjung would take the lead in advancing toward and destroying Jerusalem and become masters of history. I don't think this imaginative understanding is an exaggeration. What was the transformed reality like? It was a new world by the minjung that turns upside down the status quo—this much we can say easily. The preconditions for establishing a new order were the rejection of Jerusalem and the resulting removal of the forces that helped Rome set a foothold in Palestine. A world where God's sovereignty alone rules, and a kingdom of God for the minjung that brings an end to temple religion.

8.4. John's Resistance—God Who Became Material

Q: You have often said that the Gospel of John 1:14 is a text that sheds new light on the question of material. Can you say more about how this question relates to the kingdom of God?

A: The Gospel of John is said to have been written around 100 CE, a watershed point when Christianity was becoming catholicized and church authority was becoming established. The Johannine community was deeply troubled and resisted the intensification of church authority. Catholicization dehistoricized the tradition of Jesus the Nazarene, made Jesus an object of doctrine, and obscured the dynamic picture of Jesus. Then an individual or group called John stood up against it, objected to the tendency, and brought it to a halt. At the juncture where the Jesus age was giving way to the church age, and the gospels were being canonized,

---

4. This quote is based on Acts 2:7: "Are not all these who are speaking Galileans?"
5. This question is Ahn's adaptation of the sentence in Matt 26:69: "You also were with Jesus the Galilean."
6. This quote seems to be based on Mark 15:40–41, "There were also women looking on from a distance.... These used to follow him and provided for him when he was in Galilee," and Luke 23:55, "The women who had come with him from Galilee followed."

the Johannine community did not want to repeat the gospels as they were. For repeating them reinforces the legitimacy of the canon. Therefore, they felt the need to use new resources to think up alternative interpretations, which gave birth to the Gospel of John. This is how I view it.

In the record of the temple purge in the Gospel of John, we read, "Destroy this temple, and in three days I will raise it up" (John 2:19). These words can be interpreted as a declaration of starting a new gospel. In another story, the Samaritan woman asks, "Is the place to worship God Mount Gerizim or Jerusalem?" Jesus responds, "It is neither Mount Gerizim nor Jerusalem. It is right here now!"[7] This is the site where a new history is beginning after the wall between Samaritans and Jews or Galileans is torn down. But no longer able to bear Jesus becoming increasingly abstract, doctrinized, and dehistoricized, John drops a bombshell, "The Word became flesh (*sarx*)!" (John 1:14)

From the time of ancient Greece down to the writing of the Septuagint, the referent of the word *sarx* was always taken to be among the basest and dirtiest. It reminds us of *ochlos* and Galilee. It is certain that John was in so critical a circumstance that he must use a radical word like this to explain the gospel. Here, John has two clear presuppositions. The days of Judaism are over. For this reason, the purge of the temple was done first and foremost. The story of the Wedding at Cana, where new wine was served after old wine had run out, was none other than the declaration, "The age of Judah has passed. Now a new age is here!" Furthermore, Jesus says in his conversation with Nicodemus, "Are you a rabbi of Israel, and yet you do not understand these things? You must be born again!"[8] This expression "must be born again" is a fierce challenge to the view that salvation comes through the torah of Judaism or the law of Moses. It was the rejection of the entirety of Judaism. Each and every action of Jesus's was a rejection of Judaism. John was the person who undertook this rejection in the most thorough way. It is as if Jesus says, "Your days are over. You are all finished!" This is a frightening declaration.

When did the writer of the Gospel of John make this declaration? When the Pharisees were at the height of their power. In the age when the temple had collapsed, Judaism as a temple religion was turning into a doctrinal religion, and the Jesus event was already being dehistoricized

---

7. The two direct quotes Ahn gives here are not literal quotations but adaptations based on John 4:20–21, 23.

8. This quote is an amalgam of John 3:10 and 3:3.

and mystified in its early stage of catholicization, John revolted against this by writing the Gospel of John: "Jesus is the bread of life. Jesus is the light of the world. Jesus is the water of life. Jesus is the resurrection and the life." He brings together all of the most beautiful symbols in describing Jesus. But before saying, "Jesus is the bread of life," John first tells the story of Jesus feeding the five thousand. Before saying, "Jesus is the living water," he presents the story in which Jesus met the Samaritan woman and said, "I am thirsty. Give me some water." Prior to saying, "Jesus is light," he narrates the event of Jesus opening the eyes of a blind man. He connects "Jesus is life" with the story of Jesus bringing Lazarus back to life. His reason for doing so is obvious. He wants to vividly testify that Jesus's words are not abstractions; they are events taking place here and now. Jesus is bread, light, life, and so forth not merely in words but in tangible reality. Jesus says, "Eat my flesh," not abstractly but after actually feeding hungry crowd. By doing so, John conveys the meaning of *incarnation* more fully than anyone else. Therefore, saying that the Word became flesh is saying that God became material, and this brings God down to earth, to the world of material. Whereas Catholicism speaks of a God that has gone up to the heaven, John sets forth a God that became material in order to resist being an abstract ideal that is dehistoricized. In this respect, we cannot emphasize enough the importance of the Gospel of John. John stresses the realized *eschaton*, that is, God's presence here and now.

Q: Your interpretation of the Gospel of John is striking. The conventional view is that John provides a rich spirituality that the Synoptic Gospels lack. In the circle of the New Testament studies, are there other scholars who have the same view as you? Perhaps in the recent development?

A: Not that I know of. Some time ago Professor Arai of Tokyo University sent me a book, saying it was world-class work. It was a study on the Gospel of John, entitled, *The Light of the World*, written by a student of his, a young scholar named Onuki Takashi.[9] I read it and found out his interpretation was the direct opposite from my interpretation. He depicted Jesus as the highest divine being. Despite claiming to take a sociological approach, the author offered a spiritual conclusion. This reflects the theological climate of Japanese scholarship.

---

9. Takashi Onuki, *The Light of the World* [Japanese].

Q: The main category by which you reinterpret the Gospel of John is material (*Materie*), right?

A: Yes. John testified to an extremely practical God who performed concrete actions of healing illnesses, feeding the hungry, and bringing the dead back to life. God works. I am not sure if we can use the word "labor"—actually, I believe we can. The creating God is the laboring God. You labor with your body. You labor not high above in the sky but on earth at the site of minjung's life, down at the bottom of the world. To paraphrase Jesus, "Look at what is happening now. The blind are gaining sight. The lame are walking. The hungry are eating their fill. That is, material events are taking place. Here, in these events, we see the reality of the kingdom of God."

As I have often said, there is no report of the Eucharist in the Gospel of John. Instead, there is a story where Jesus is portrayed as a servant and washed the feet of his disciples. This looks to me like a challenge to the church that was being institutionalized through the Eucharist. It is a resistance against the Eucharist receiving only a christological interpretation and so being dematerialized. Although there is no report of the Eucharist, there is a moment where Jesus says, "I am the bread of life, and so take and eat it."[10] But it does not appear at the end of the gospel but right after the narrative about feeding five thousand people. In order to resist against the Eucharist that had degenerated into a religious ritual, John located the saying into the site of the minjung's life in chapter 6. By this move, he lodged a specific protest that the essence of the Eucharist lies in sharing and not in christological salvation. This is how I view it at least. In fact, the spirit of the Eucharist in the Synoptic Gospels is nothing other than sharing in a community. Eating together with his disciples, Jesus said, "This bread and this wine are my flesh and blood. Share these among yourselves." Here, a path was created for the meal of love and the Eucharist to be combined as a sacrament. But the Synoptic Gospels also retain an emphasis on sharing as the essence of the meal. By connecting this immediately with the story of the five thousand sharing a meal, John reinterpreted the Eucharist and restored it back to its essence. This is how I view it. After all, wasn't Jesus's life characterized by sharing? We have to ask again what the kingdom of God is from the perspective of *sharing*. To the question, "What is the kingdom of God actually?" Luke answers that it is restoring what belongs in

---

10. This quote is based on John 6:35 and 6:48–51.

the public realm. In everything, including politics and economics, we have to return what is divided and torn by privatization to the public. Minjung has no need of a kingdom of God that is idealized, over-spiritualized, and otherworldly. "Return the public to the public" means returning what is God's to God. To translate this message into the language of minjung, it is returning to those who have been deprived what is theirs, returning to laborers and farmers a fair share of their production. The best way to help people become conscious of the kingdom of God is to recover their lost share. At any rate, the fulfillment of the kingdom of God is inextricably intertwined with returning the public to the public, that is, returning what is privately owned to the true owners.

Q: In Rev 21:3–4 we read, "See, the home of God is among mortals. He will dwell with them; they will be his peoples, and God himself will be with them; he will wipe every tear from their eyes. Death will be no more; mourning and crying and pain will be no more, for the first things have passed away." The first part concerns God's direct rule, namely, the new order that includes God's being with us; the second part depicts the concrete condition of this new order by means of very material expressions. What do you think of this passage in Revelation that seems to describe the kingdom of God?

A: In this case, we don't really have to use the word "material." But this passage in Revelation has something in common with the Gospel of John. First, the disciples in this gospel refer to John's community; the "mortals" in the Revelation passage refers to the same. These mortals are not individuals but a community. And the new order where there is no tear, mourning, or death is the very opposite of the present reality. Now we are suffering, now we are oppressed, now we are crying, now we are being killed—this is the reality reflected there in reverse. These pains are of the flesh and material. In other words, pain is not imagined in the abstract, but refers to the real, concrete pains of flesh being cut, hearts being rent, and people being killed. The Revelation to John was written in the time of Domitian, right? In the 90s, Domitian deified himself, forced emperor worship, and intensified persecution. Those who suffered pains in the flesh at the time must have desired the kingdom of God where they would be set free from pains, tears, and death. They did not merely crave but assumed a fighting attitude to bring about the kingdom. They understood this world as the battlefield between the sovereignty of God and the devil. The kingdom of

God in their understanding was always a material world, a world realized on this earth, not an ideal world realized in some other realm beyond this one. Wiping tears from everyone's eyes was not meant to take place across the Jordan River. They were rejecting and resisting this kind of thinking from the beginning: "Unless we drove out Domitian now, unless we were liberated from his grip, the day would never come when we stopped crying tears." They must have thought of the movement replacing unjust forces with the forces of God. We must not reduce this kind of record of political reality to something merely religious and otherworldly.

8.5. The Lord's Prayer as the Song of the Kingdom of God Movement

Q: Could not the advent of the kingdom of God be in some sense an expression of the idea of incarnation? In Jesus Christ God became flesh. In the midst of the people earnestly expecting the kingdom of God, this God as flesh is present for the fulfillment of the kingdom. Therefore, God who became flesh is constantly confessed in the form of the kingdom of God movement. What do you think?

A: Indeed such an interpretation is possible. In fact, that is precisely the cry of the Lord's Prayer, "Your kingdom come!" That's why I referred to the Lord's Prayer as a song. It is a marching song for the kingdom of God movement. If "Your will be done, on earth as it is in heaven" (Matt 6:10) was the comment of the Matthean school, our interpretation could be: "God who became flesh! You are incarnate today in our kingdom of God movement." We are so accustomed to thinking of God strictly as a spiritual being. But God continues to incarnate God's self and to represent God's self in material form in the minjung event that is taking place throughout history. Using the word "material" has the drawback of not sounding real. But it is the reality of today's Christianity that we have no other choice but to use this word in order to resist idealizing God, Jesus Christ, and the kingdom of God. We must return to their original meanings in the gospels.

Q: We have reinterpreted the incarnation of God in the language of a new kingdom without tear, pain, or killing. I do not believe that the fulfillment of this new kingdom can ever be separated from an analysis of our society. I would like you to respond to a passage from Pixley's book, *God's Kingdom*:

Jesus and the Zealots formulated different strategies of liberation because they understood the conjuncture of first-century Palestine differently. We cannot know whether Jesus's strategy had more possibility of success than that of the Zealots. That is not what is important. Neither the one nor the other can be applied to our dependent capitalism. We must make an analysis of our situation in order to formulate relevant strategies of liberation. In doing so, we can count on a significant liberating tradition within our sacred texts. But the Bible will do neither our analyzing nor our strategizing. This is the task of Christian groups in their particular places.[11]

A: That has been my usual point of emphasis. Jesus did not start programs or provide a blueprint. It is wrong to seek a certain model of action from Jesus in the spirit of following his example (*Imitatio Christi*). It makes no sense because the life settings are different. Our lives are our own, and so it is unrealistic to expect to find strategies in the Bible for our movement.

8.6. The Kingdom of God Faith Should Be Incarnate in Minjung Liberation Movement

Q: The movements of young people contend that the Christian faith should be incarnate in the fight on behalf of the minjung. Minjung liberation is the only viable expression of faith. What do you think of this claim?

A: I agree. Earlier I said that the discussion whether the kingdom of God is present or future sounds like idle speculation. For those who are fully engaged in fighting for the cause, there is no distinction. Faith in the kingdom and the present manifestation of the movement is not easy to distinguish. In this sense, I believe that we are right to construe the movement as the incarnation of faith. The reality of the kingdom of God is dynamic and never static. When we understand it as dynamic, we have no room to question whether the kingdom is present or future. The Jesus movement and the advent of the kingdom are not different from each other. The kingdom of God cannot be identified with anything that already exists such as the church or a certain social system. But the minjung feel that it is experienced in the middle of the fight that is going on in the present; the kingdom of God is being fulfilled in this fight. The kingdom of God becomes a vivid reality in the practices of the minjung.

---

11. Pixley, *God's Kingdom*, 103–4.

But here we must not forget one thing—the fact that human beings are not satisfied with the dynamic alone but want some image, that is, a *status*. Therefore, it is necessary to show them a concrete image.

So far I have postponed discussing Luke's interpretation of Jesus's proclamation of the kingdom of God. Mark suggests that Jesus's preaching is summed up in the advent of the kingdom of God (Mark 1:15). But Luke cites Isa 61:1–2, a reference to Jubilee, at the beginning of Jesus's public life: "to proclaim the year of the Lord's favor" (Luke 4:19). Luke found himself in a stage where he had to answer how the kingdom of God would be fulfilled. He believed that the institution of Jubilee was in the process of fulfilling the kingdom of God. Liberation is the essence of Jubilee. We find expressions, "to proclaim release to the captives" and "to let the oppressed go free" (Luke 4:18). The word translated into "release" and "let go free" is *aphesis*, which means "to set a slave free" and "to free from debt." This is what Jubilee is all about. Since the institution of the sabbatical year every seven years was poorly observed, the forty-ninth year (at the end of seven cycles of sabbatical years) was designated as a year of great social reform. In this year, monopoly was cancelled through practices such as exemption from debt and releasing slaves. Luke seems to have interpreted "the time is fulfilled" as meaning the coming of the Jubilee. Therefore, the advent of the kingdom of God for Luke consists primarily in liberation from debt and bondage. This proclamation of Jubilee is indeed good news (gospel) of "blessed are the poor" for the poor and bad news for the rich who monopolize, privatize, and find security in their possessions. The content of Luke 4:18–19 is virtually identical with Matt 11:4–5, where Jesus responds to the question of John the Baptist. This material comes from the Q source, so we cannot say this was Luke's invention. Liberation in the Jubilee institution is one of the most important elements of the advent of the kingdom of God.

But the Christian kingdom of God became increasingly otherworldly and spiritualized. It is the weakening of an eschatological consciousness that is responsible for that. So the kingdom of God was pushed outside the sphere of life. As a result, it lost its political and economic power. At this point, another concrete image appeared in the form of the millennium found in the apocalyptic literature. In place of the kingdom of God that was being spiritualized, a belief emerged that the messiah would eradicate all the forces of evil to establish the messianic kingdom. This belief was the will to fight and the belief that the kingdom of God will erupt as an active volcano in history.

What we need to learn here is that a concrete picture should be presented on the journey to the kingdom of God. The minjung need it. But this image should not be set up as something ultimate. That is why the millennium leaves its ultimate ending open.

The specific first-stage embodiment of Jesus's kingdom of God, I believe, can be the Jubilee. Jesus's behaviors suggest this. However, Jesus does not stay with that. His kingdom of God is an ultimate reality that goes beyond the Jubilee.

Part 3

9
The Transmission of the Jesus Event by the Minjung

Today I am going to issue a bold challenge to form criticism and redaction criticism, two important methods in Western biblical scholarship. As minjung theologians repeatedly say, this kind of challenge arises not out of armchair studies but the process of asking the Bible the questions shaped by our political reality and receiving the answers from the Bible.

My lecture today is going to deal with the matrix of transmission of the Jesus event from the standpoint of biblical studies. Bultmann's *The History of the Synoptic Tradition* addresses the same topic.[1] It is a famous book that analyzes the Bible using the form-critical method and serves as an important background for my remarks.

9.1. The Starting Point of Minjung Theology

First of all, let me tell you where these thoughts originated. It was 1970, a tumultuous year, when the birth of minjung theology was inevitable. Specifically, it was November 13, 1970. Jeon Tae-il, a young Christian man, then aged twenty-two, did not have much of a formal education; he only finished elementary school. He was a machine operator in a factory at the well-known Pyeonghwa Market in Seoul. The laborers of the Pyeonghwa Market consisted mostly of female factory workers aged between fifteen and twenty years old. They worked fifteen hours a day in very poor working conditions. Jeon Tae-il employed every means available to communicate with the outside world about the miserable conditions. He wrote a letter to the Labor Administration, submitted a petition to the president of Korea,

---

1. Rudolf Bultmann, *The History of the Synoptic Tradition*, trans. John Marsh (Oxford: Blackwell, 1963); translation of *Die Geschichte der synoptischen Tradition* (Göttingen: Vandenhoeck & Ruprecht, 1931).

and paid a visit to the mayor of Seoul. When these measures didn't work, he met with prominent Christian ministers to let the world know about this situation to no avail. In the end, Jeon sacrificed his own body to draw attention to the reality of laborers to the world. He presented his body as a living sacrifice, as Paul said, by pouring gasoline on his body, setting it on fire, and dying. This happened on November 13, 1970.

In a sense, minjung theology came into being provoked by this Jeon Tae-il event. The sacrifice of this one person served as a rude awakening—through body, through death—to the world about the true state of the Pyeonghwa Market and the painful realities of its laborers. It awakened students and laborers in many places from a long hibernation and encouraged them to cry out. The government was afraid of this and forbade people from speaking or writing about Jeon Tae-il. Furthermore, it prohibited people from writing about issues of labor or human rights.

However, this event woke up the church, which had been in deep sleep up to that point. Many Christians opened their eyes, and so Urban Industrial Mission, with Seoul as its axis, came into being in 1971. Also, the Human Rights Committee, an organization affiliated with the National Church Council of Korea, was founded in 1973. Thanks to this committee, pastors, students, and laborers organized a series of events for human rights during the 1970s until the Park Jeong-hui government fell.

Following the death of Jeon Tae-il, it was nearly impossible to speak or write about issues of labor and human rights. However, the story of Jeon Tae-il spread through rumor. It was forbidden to talk to the press about these issues. Furthermore, in those days, the possession of a mimeograph had to be reported to the police, and so even printing with a mimeograph was not freely to be done. For this reason, the only available form of communication was by word of mouth.

Even now, we do not have legitimate forms of communication. We are not in a position to convey the reality as it is. The poet Kim Ji-ha[2]

---

2. Kim Ji-ha (b. 1941), whose real name is Kim Yeong-il and who intended *jiha* to mean "operating underground," was one of the most prominent dissident literary figures during the Park Jeong-hui dictatorship in the 1960s and 1970s. As a student of Seoul National University, Kim participated in the April 19 Revolution against the Lee Seung-man dictatorship in 1960. He was one of the leaders of the student-led movement for the Korean reunification. He was first published as a poet in 1963 and wrote for the May 1970 issue of *Sasanggye* a poem titled "Five Thieves," a poignant accusation of the most powerful of the ruling class. This poem led to his imprisonment. Kim

wrote a poem titled "Rumor" and was sentenced to death for this act.³ In Korea, even rumors are subject to legal punishment. Students who speak and write about the truth could go to prison according to the rumor crime law. Rumors, as the means of conveying the truth, have become something very precious and indispensable in our lives. Rumors pose such a threat that the government considers them as its first enemy. But for us, they are like oxygen, something we cannot live without.

For the minjung living under the dictatorship, rumors are not made-up stories. They are the means of giving and sharing life. They are a method of the minjung's own invention. In a sense, they are the same as the mouth-to-mouth method ants use in order to communicate about places to find food. I would like to emphasize that rumors, which were the most effective means for conveying the truth in a time when the Bible came to be, are still vitally important.

For the past twenty years or so, we have experienced the power of rumors at political sites. We witnessed how they differ from public institutionalized forms of communication. The government as well as institutional churches with a strong public presence speak in a very different way than the minjung. The minjung can convey the truth in the form of rumor; what is said is not necessarily logical or rhetorically elegant. They are simply an accurate rendering of the way things are. There is no fixed form that rumors are supposed to use. They convey a message truthfully and vividly. On the contrary, when institutionalized churches gather together and issue an official statement or express their position publicly

---

served multiple prison terms under Park Jeong-hui's rule, which amounted to a total of eight years. Since the mid-1980s, Kim worked as an intellectual on the themes of life, inclusion, reconciliation, love, and peace. He was awarded the Lotus Prize for Literature by the Afro-Asian Writers' Association in 1975 and the Grand Poet Prize by the International Poets' Conference in 1981.

3. This statement of Ahn's is not quite true. Kim Ji-ha's poem "Rumor" was published in the April 1972 issue of a Catholic monthly named *Changjo* (creation). It was in July 1974 in connection with the incident of the General League of Democratic Students of Korea that Kim was sentenced to death (see 233 n. 14, below). His sentence was commuted to life one week later, and he was released in February 1975 thanks to the domestic and international movement for his release. By the way, in Kim's poem "Rumor" appears as a figure who utters a complaint and is sentenced to death on the charge of spreading a rumor. The Korean word for the poem's title is *bieo* and means literally "flying language."

over an issue, the event often becomes formal. They do not convey the event as it is but make it abstract. In other words, they dehistoricize it.

For example, when speaking of a sin, they do not mention specifics on what kind of sin it is. When exhorting people to repent, they only mention the need to repent without specifying what people need to do and how. The same is true of judgment. Likewise, when commenting on politics, the message is framed in a way in order to avoid a clash with the government. In so doing, they make things nonhistorical and abstract. I have realized with the most poignant clarity that they have no other choice but to use this method. Their primary concern is to preserve themselves in this world. There is a stark difference in how they communicate. So I have come to read the Bible anew with the minjung's mode of expression in mind.

Although I am called an expert in the New Testament, I was expelled from the university twice. During the last ten years, I worked in the field rather than in the ivory tower. So I am no longer a scholar in the traditional sense of the word. Perhaps I am a biblical scholar in the streets? I have neither the stamina nor the time to study everything rigorously and precisely. But I am reading the Bible in my own way, from the standpoint that you must eat when hungry and drink when thirsty.

It is generally known that Japanese theologians and Christians read much more than their Korean counterparts. This means that they have more theological knowledge. Therefore, I suppose that, despite being numerically smaller, you feel proud of being qualitatively superior to them. Therefore, I will start my discussion with the assumption that you already have a certain level of theological understanding.

9.2. The Historical Jesus and the Kerygmatic Christ

Thus far biblical theology has remained within the confines of what is called the theology of kerygma. I myself stayed for a long time under Bultmann's strong influences and so was unable to think independently. It was Bultmann himself who said that directing inquiries behind kerygma is unbelief. This means that inquiring into the historical facts behind kerygma does not qualify as a question in the first place and is unbelief. So he ended up rejecting asking about the historical Jesus. It was in the 1920s that he wrote a book on the kerygmatic Jesus. For the following thirty years or so, no one ever thought of inquiring into or writing about the historical Jesus. This shows the enormity of Bultmann's influences.

It was not until 1954 that there was a break: Käsemann, one of Bultmann's former pupils, gave a lecture entitled "The Question of the Historical Jesus" at a Bultmann conference. The year 1956 saw the publication of the book, *Jesus of Nazareth*, by Bornkamm. This happened after thirty years, so these scholars are post-Bultmannians but never overstep the bounds set by Bultmann. I think they only made some revisions to the theology of kerygma but did not issue a direct challenge.

Rather than discuss kerygma in an abstract way, I would like to examine a few passages from the Bible. First, let me read a passage that I am sure is familiar to you, part of the famous *kerygma of resurrection* in 1 Corinthians, namely, the credo:

> For I handed on to you as of first importance what I in turn had received: that Christ died for our sins in accordance with the scriptures, and that he was buried, and that he was raised on the third day in accordance with the scriptures, and that he appeared to Cephas, then to the twelve. Then he appeared to more than five hundred brothers and sisters at one time, most of whom are still alive, though some have died. Then he appeared to James, then to all the apostles. (1 Cor 15:3–7)

As you know, these are not Paul's own words but what had been transmitted to him. If we postulate that 1 Corinthians was written in the 60s, the kerygmatic message had already been solidified in this form by 40 or 50 CE. Here a problem is identified. In speaking of the death and resurrection of Jesus, the passage twice uses the expression "in accordance with the scriptures." It says that Jesus died for our sin "in accordance with the scriptures" and came back to life "in accordance with the scriptures." But it says nothing at all about where in the scriptures you can find these points. This means that the words, "in accordance with the scriptures," cover up the historical events. Specifically who killed Jesus, where, why, and when are not spelled out. These details are concealed or rather are dehistoricized. This is what a public announcement is like.

Let's read another passage. The Christ Hymn appears in Philippians and is considered as some of the earliest existing material:

> who, though he was in the form of God, did not regard equality with God as something to be exploited, but emptied himself, taking the form of a slave, being born in human likeness. And being found in human form, he humbled himself and became obedient to the point of death— even death on a cross. Therefore God also highly exalted him and gave

him the name that is above every name, so that at the name of Jesus every knee should bend, in heaven and on earth and under the earth, and every tongue should confess that Jesus Christ is Lord, to the glory of God the Father. (Phil 2:6–11)

This passage was transmitted to Paul and is the archetype of the Christ kerygma. The passage takes the form of a poetic song that breaks down into three parts. The first part expresses a theory that Christ existed before the beginning of history. The middle part concerns Jesus's incarnation. The last part deals with the Christ who was resurrected and ascended to the heaven.

Of these three parts, what is most interesting is the second one where the word *cross* appears. He became obedient to the point of death on a cross. However, it is not mentioned who it was that became obedient to the point of death on a cross. Moreover, it is the generally accepted view that the clause about the death on a cross was added later. If we accept this view, the expression "death on a cross" did not exist in the original song. Even if the phrase was added later, it was placed between two important presuppositions: the preexistence of Christ and Christ being lifted up to the heaven and ruling over the world. For this reason, the event of Jesus's incarnation and death on the cross merely played a role of bridging these two important ideas. This is a significant weakening of the cross event.

Who killed Jesus, when, why, or how is never mentioned. This is precisely the nature of kerygma. The expression "becoming obedient" is generally understood as a religious expression. However, we cannot help but ask about the social background of this expression. But we can hardly find an answer from this passage. We can only find a dehistoricizing process—a change that had taken place to a significant degree already by 40 CE.

First Corinthians 15:5 reports that the resurrected Jesus first appeared to Cephas, that is, Peter. This is, of course, not a historical fact. It was Peter as the representative of the church of that time, not Peter as a historical figure. In the same way, the twelve apostles that show up next were a symbol. Therefore, there is no denying that this passage was the confession of the already institutionalized church. There is a lively debate on where the Christ Hymn was composed. Ernst Lohmeyer contends that a confession like this hymn was made during the sacrament. Another scholar maintains that the confession was made during worship. Whichever is right, the two views agree that the place for this confession was neither under Roman rule nor where persecutors of the Jews were present. The confession was made in the religious atmosphere of worship.

In the Acts of the Apostles we find the oldest archetype of preaching. Dodd offers a good analysis of the archetypes of preaching in *The Apostolic Preaching and Its Development*.[4] What surprised me about what he said was that the preaching to the public made the facts about Jesus abstract and nonhistorical.

In general, what is most surprising about the epistles, including those by Paul, is that they make almost no mention of the historical Jesus. The general tendency is to conclude that not the historical Jesus but the kerygmatic Christ is what matters. We do not understand this. We want to know. Why could Jesus not help but die? Who and for what reason could not help but kill him? This we want to know. We want to know because we are living in the site of life where a diabolic power is violating human rights beyond count. We want to know the facts about Jesus as a human rights concern. We will not be satisfied with abstraction. We just cannot tolerate our ignorance of the truth.

Why was Paul, who said he was willing to die for Christ, virtually silent about the Historical Jesus? A single exception is Gal 4:4, where he says that Jesus was born of a woman under the law. But this one instance is far from sufficient. Why does Paul, who asserted he knows nothing but the cross, hide facts about the cross from us? If we only had Paul's epistles, the cross would have carried no more significance than as a symbol of docetism. Moreover, Paul even declares in 2 Cor 5:16, "From now on, I will not know the Lord from a human point of view."[5] This means that he would not try to know history. Still, I don't think Paul means by this declaration that the historical Jesus was meaningless.

So was Paul compelled to make such a declaration? Is it possible that there is evidence of this in the words themselves? "Why do you only speak of an abstract Christ?" "Why do you not explicitly say that Jesus was killed?" I am sure that criticisms like these made Paul say the words in question. In response, he says, "I intentionally do not say" and "*Sarks* doesn't interest me. Only the *pneuma*-like Christ interests me." The pas-

---

4. C. H. Dodd, *The Apostolic Preaching and Its Development: Three Lectures* (New York: Harper & Row, 1964).

5. The way the verse in question is actually worded is: "From now on, therefore, we regard no one from a human point of view; even though we once knew Christ from a human point of view, we know him no longer in that way" (2 Cor 5:16).

sages he quotes as the words of the Lord for this point are not words of the historical Jesus but kerygma.

Concerning the important subject of the law, the historical Jesus has some good suggestions to offer. But Paul never resorts to Jesus. What could have constrained Paul to keep silent about the historical Jesus? Strangely, the same attitude appears in the pseudo-Pauline epistles composed later. For this reason, we have fallen in a peculiar position where we have few materials to tell us about the historical Jesus.

9.3. Criticisms of the Disciples in the Gospel of Mark

Thus far, Christianity has continued to reinforce a dehistoricizing tendency in the name of theology. Theology has placed more stress on ontology than on movement. Events were philosophized, and as a result the historical Jesus gradually disappeared. The only thing that grew larger was the church on earth. Jesus vanished forever, and the Roman church, which ruled from the earth as his surrogate, put forward its foot and made people kiss it. Dostoevsky describes this foolish act ironically in the episode of "The Grand Inquisitor."[6]

The Grand Inquisitor of the world says that, if Jesus appeared now, he would banish him mercilessly in the name of the church. In all actuality, Jesus is being banished from the institutional church. Nietzsche said to this effect: "There has been only one true Christian in history. It was Jesus himself." This is true.

I came to feel deeply discontent with kerygmatic theology. First and foremost, looking at our site of life in light of kerygma makes everything abstract. This may be a strange figure of speech, but I came to wonder if the events taking place in Korea are being reported in a kerygmatic way. They are being reported in a logical, systematic, and analytical way. In this way, the events cannot be conveyed as they really are. In the same vein, I have come here to Sapporo not with the view to reading a written script and developing a logical explication. I have come here with the wish to transmit something by talking face-to-face with you. I have come here in earnest to convey something. The victory of kerygma was defeating the historical Jesus and establishing church authority as the main pillar of the-

---

6. This story appears in Fyodor Dostoyevsky, *The Brothers Karamazov*, book 5, chapter 5.

ology. I myself am one of the theologians, but I admit that I have been committing this error up to now.

In the age of the New Testament, however, there were people who were dissatisfied. As you know, the first written gospel is the Gospel of Mark. It was written around 64 at the earliest. In all likelihood it was written between the end of the Jewish War and the fall of Jerusalem in 70, or perhaps a little past this point. I myself hypothesize that it was after the year 70.

The behaviors of Jesus, as the Gospel of Mark transmits them, were simply unimaginable from a kerygmatic standpoint. At one point, it was claimed that Paul's epistles and kerygma were produced based on the historical Jesus. But this is false. The transmission of the Jesus event through the gospels was possible due to a matrix of transmission different from kerygma. Therefore, I have gradually come to believe that one group of people formulated and transmitted kerygma and another group, standing on a clearly different premise, transmitted the Jesus event. The Gospel of Mark reflects the latter.

Last night I read the Gospel of Mark again. I read it not as a biblical scholar but as a lay believer. And its meaning was something that is evident to anyone. In narrating the Jesus event, Mark begins with his public life. It does not speak of the birth of Jesus. As soon as Jesus's public life starts, a number of people, mostly whose names are not given, gather around him. In Mark 1:35, Simon (Peter, i.e., Cephas) and his companions come running to Jesus and say, "Teacher, people are looking for you. Let's go." To this, Jesus says, "I have not come to work here only. Let's visit the neighboring towns, so that I may proclaim the message there also."[7] Already here, Jesus exposes the ignorance of Simon and his group.

In Mark 3:13 we encounter the scene where Jesus calls his disciples to him. As you know well, however, the names of the twelve disciples are not consistent across the gospels. Luke and Matthew give different sets of names that differ from Mark. However, it is not possible to ascertain whether the original number of disciples was twelve. Three disciples make a repeated appearance: Peter, John, and James. Of the other nine, one sold Jesus, and another said he could not be sure of Jesus's resurrection without

---

7. What the last two sentences say is based on Mark 1:36–38: "And Simon and his companions hunted for him. When they found him, they said to him, 'Everyone is searching for you.' He answered, 'Let us go on to the neighboring towns, so that I may proclaim the message there also; for that is what I came out to do.'"

touching him. These nine were, to use the language of theater, nothing more than extras. They were insignificant. For this reason, Bultmann says that the number twelve is symbolic, not historical; yet, his former pupil Bornkamm argues that there were actually twelve disciples. But neither has the last word here. At any rate, the fact that even the names of the chosen twelve are not definitive proves that the twelve disciples were not treated properly from a historical standpoint—and this is what matters.

In Mark 4:11, Jesus says to his disciples that, even though he tells them the secret of the kingdom of God, he speaks to other people only in parables. But this is strange and defies explanation. For he says that, while explaining the kingdom of God to the disciples, he only gives parables to others, who are less capable of understanding him. Here, we get to surmise that the disciples know better. A little later, however, we hear Jesus strongly criticize, "Do you not understand this parable? Then how will you understand all the parables?" (Mark 4:13) Parables are used because the literal telling of the secret of the kingdom of God is difficult to digest. But the disciples do not even understand them. Here, there is an implicit critique of the qualifications of the disciples.

In Mark 4:35, we hear another criticism of the disciples. I would like to mention to you an instance of Jesus complimenting his disciples, but surprisingly he only criticizes them. In verse 35 and following, Jesus commands his disciples to go to the hill on the other side of the Galilee Lake. Jesus gets in the boat along with them and falls asleep there. Then the waves arise, and the disciples are at a loss in what to do. Jesus rebukes them. In chapter 5, when the child of the leader of the synagogue is dead, Jesus goes to his home with the three disciples whose names are consistent across the gospels. But they do not play any role there. Jesus also goes to his home region together with his disciples. Again, they play no role at all there.

Mark 6:7 presents the famous scene of Jesus sending the disciples. Here, Jesus is giving the disciples specific instructions of what to prepare, what to carry, what to say, and so forth. This is the first place where the essential mission of the disciples receives specific description. But why such a detailed description? In my opinion, this reflects the sharp contrast between Jesus's commands at the time of his sending his disciples out and the disciples who were alive at the time of writing the Gospel of Mark.

I am doing minjung theology, but I am afraid that you should find out how I live. "You say, 'Minjung, minjung,' but what kind of life are you leading?" I fear you might find that out. For this reason, this report of sending out the disciples is one of the passages that pastors dislike the worst. When someone asserts their authority saying, "I am a disciple of Jesus," if they are married, have a family, can do whatever they want to do, and live in Japan, a nation with the world's second largest GNP, what could they say about themselves? This is the problem. It would be no exaggeration to say this is what Mark is pointing out. If a lay believer were to press this point quoting the words of Jesus, it would be a criticism of the pastor. Those who transmitted this passage were leveling criticism at those who were asserting their authority and charisma and protesting that their ways of living differed from their claims. I can find no other understanding for this passage.

Mark 6 narrates the famous event of Jesus feeding the five thousand. Here, again, the ignorance of the disciples is expressed. This chapter also contains the miracle of Jesus walking on the water, which signifies Peter's unbelief. Chapter 8 narrates the event of Jesus feeding the four thousand. Here, once again, the disciples' unbelief is portrayed. Later, the disciples are described as misunderstanding what Jesus said. Here we read severe words of criticism:

> And becoming aware of it, Jesus said to them, "Why are talking about having no bread? Do you still not perceive or understand? Are your hearts hardened? Do you have eyes, and fail to see? Do you have ears, and fail to hear?" (Mark 8:17–18)

Jesus scolds the disciples. In effect, he says they are utter fools who have no ears, eyes, or reason. They don't know anything. That is how Jesus rebukes his disciples.

Mark 9 tells the story of Jesus's transfiguration. There is an underlying assumption that the disciples were receiving special treatment. Nonetheless, when the transmitted material in question was being redacted, a critical emphasis was placed. Jesus takes three disciples up to the mountain where the transfiguration took place. But here, too, Jesus finds fault with Peter, who failed to grasp what was going on.[8] As soon as they came down the mountain, he again attacks the disciples for their ignorance and unbelief. "In this faithless generation, how much longer must I be among you? How much longer must I put up with you?"[9]

---

8. There is no explicit criticism on Jesus's part to be found in the given narrative.
9. These words of scolding by Jesus appear in 9:19 in the context of healing a boy

Among passages of this nature, the most important is Mark 8:27, which Schweitzer called "the watershed in the Gospel of Mark." Jesus repeatedly asks, "Who do you say that I am? Who do people say that I am?" Peter confesses, "You are Christ." In response, Jesus orders the disciples not to tell anyone about this confession. In the past, this passage was understood as the "secret of the messiah." Jesus was understood as saying, "Do not tell anyone what you have said. I am Christ. But be silent about it." However, here I agree with Bultmann, who understood that Jesus did not mean "Do not tell anyone what Peter has said," but "Do not tell anyone what I am going to say from now on." That is why Jesus does not say "Yes" or "No" to the statement, but says, "Listen carefully to what I am going to say from now on. But don't tell anyone. Now I am going to go to Jerusalem and will be killed. After three days I will resurrect." He says these things for the first time. At this moment Peter objects by saying, "No way!" And now we hear the famous rebuke of Jesus's: "Get behind me, Satan! For you are setting your mind not on divine things but on human things" (Mark 8:33). He rebukes Peter with these harsh words.

Later, after the second prediction of Jesus's passion, there is a scene of the disciples arguing about who is the greatest. In Mark 10:13, people bring children to Jesus so that he may touch them, but the disciples scold the mothers of the children. Jesus is indignant and says, "Whoever does not receive the kingdom of God as a little child will never enter it" (Mark 10:15). In my opinion, these words do not merely address the relation between the kingdom of God and children. Here, he is saying specifically to the disciples, who have already fallen into the snare of authoritarianism, that they must become like children. He is calling into question the way the disciples are—they have become poles apart from children.

In Mark 10 we find the widely known story of the rich young man. Jesus makes the famous remark, "It is easier for a camel to go through the eye of a needle than for someone who is rich to enter the kingdom of God" (Mark 10:25). These words mean that it is almost impossible for rich people to enter the heaven. Representing the disciples, Peter says, "We

---

seized by a spirit. Therefore, they do not occur right after Jesus's and the three disciples' descent from the mountain. Furthermore, these words are not addressed to the disciples alone but to the crowd that has gathered to watch the interaction between the disciples and the possessed boy's father. In this connection, the phrase Ahn renders as "in this faithless generation" is, in the Markan text, "You faithless generation [*Ō genea apistos*]," which is Jesus's designation for all the people who were present on the scene.

will leave everything and follow you."[10] Jesus responds with the following words, which also appear in other contexts: "Be careful. Never forget that many who are first will be last, and that the last will be first."[11] To paraphrase, Jesus says, "You think that you, as the chosen ones, are the leaders of the church. But you may become the last." Afterward, in Mark 10:32, Jesus advances towards Jerusalem. Here, we see a very serious Jesus who makes an important decision. In going up to Jerusalem, Jesus was so serious as to create a solemn atmosphere that forbade anyone from saying anything to him. Jesus is now going up to Jerusalem toward his death. On the contrary, the disciples are arguing with one another about who ranks higher. When Jesus comes to the seat of glory, who will sit at his right hand, and who at his left hand? Their debate is exposed to us. After verse 41 come two well-known statements, "The current government is a dictatorship that rules coercively, but you must not be in that way," and "Whoever wishes to be first among you must be slave of all."[12]

Mark 11 gives us the scene of Jesus entering Jerusalem. In the same chapter, we also read the stories of Gethsemane, the Last Supper, Peter's denial of Jesus, the fleeing of all the disciples, and so forth. None of the disciples remained with Jesus during his passion. It is not probable that those who were not present at the scene of the passion were present at the resurrection. The implication is that none of the disciples witnessed the resurrected Jesus.

9.4. *Ochlos* and *Mathētai*

When we adopt this perspective, we realize that there is a great tension between the disciples and others who are not named. Who are they? Mark 2 repeatedly says in verses 1–6 that many people were around Jesus, and the word used for them is *ochlos*. The Greek word has a derogatory

---

10. This quote is based on Mark 10:28: "Peter began to say to him, 'Look, we have left everything and followed you.'"

11. This quote is based on Mark 10:31: "But many who are first will be last, and the last will be first."

12. These two quotes are based on Jesus's remark in Mark 10:42–43: "You know that among the Gentiles those whom they recognize as their rulers lord it over them, and their great ones are tyrants over them. But it is not so among you; but whoever wishes to become great among you must be your servant, and whoever wishes to be first among you must be slave of all."

connotation. The word *laos* can be rendered into "nation" or "people," but *ochlos* refers to those who are despised. Most of those around Jesus were *ochlos*. In the Gospel of Mark, the word *ochlos* appears no fewer than thirty-six times. The two instances of *laos* are to be found only in the quotes from the Old Testament. The *ochlos* are opposite of the *mathētai* (disciples).

Let me give you two examples of this point. In Mark 3:31 when Jesus is with the *ochlos*, he is told that his mother and brothers are on the way to see him. Looking at the *ochlos*, Jesus says, "Who are my mother and my brothers?" (Mark 3:33) "They are no one other than this *ochlos*."[13] "Not *mathētai* but *ochlos*," he means.

Another example is found in Mark 14:3 and following. An unnamed woman anoints Jesus. Here we hear Jesus saying the kind of words of praise that he never said about anyone else: "Truly I tell you, wherever the good news is proclaimed in the whole world, what she has done will be told in remembrance of her" (Mark 14:9). Jesus only praises the woman, not Peter or the other disciples. Furthermore, it was only women who were present at the final scene of Jesus's passion, the central event of his kerygma. The men, namely, the disciples, all fled; no one remained. For this reason, the prerogative of finding the empty tomb was given to the women. The disciples were not entitled to that. Here, it comes to light that the nameless women were in tension with the disciples. That I am not alone in thinking this way can be seen by comparing Mark to Matthew and Luke.

9.5. Institutionalization of the Church and the Prevailing of the Priestly Class

A representative example is that Matthew changed the words of Jesus's in Mark 8, "Get behind me, Satan!" (Mark 8:33) into "Blessed are you, Simon son of Jonah! For flesh and blood has not revealed this to you, but my Father in heaven. And I tell you, you are Peter, and on this rock I will build my church, and the gates of Hades will not prevail against it" (Matt 16:17–18). Matthew excised almost all of Jesus's criticisms of his disciples. So did Luke. In Matthew, Jesus has a final meeting with his disciples in Galilee and gives them a command. Luke records Peter as an eyewitness to the

---

13. This quote is based on Mark 3:34: "And looking at those who sat around him, he said, 'Here are my mother and my brothers!'"

empty tomb. In addition, while not giving the names of the two persons on the way to Emmaus, he writes what the disciples did. He also writes that Jesus appeared to the twelve disciples. All these details are absent in Mark. So in Matthew and Luke, both written about twenty years after Mark, the apostolic class of the church prevails in this way. The disciples are being increasingly glorified.

From this we can draw an obvious conclusion. In 1 Cor 15:3 and following, surprisingly, the event of Jesus's cross is described in an abstract way. What's more, among the witnesses to the resurrected Jesus, the women are not even named. In contrast, Mark only gives women witnesses. This makes me wonder if there were not two distinct matrices of transmission. One was a group who thought that they must preserve the church. The other was the passionate minjung who didn't care about preserving the church, but were determined to testify to the vibrant Jesus event no matter what. In other words, there were the minjung who were unrealistic, naïve, irrational, and uncalculating. They did not have the concept of a leader. They were just the minjung who had no other choice but to testify to the Jesus event, and could not stand not witnessing accurately to what they saw and heard. Although not being able to predict what kinds of influences or outcomes they would have, they simply could not remain silent or stop witnessing.

9.6. Advocates of Institutional Church Authority

Here is the bottom line. From the beginning, form critics held that the church is the very site (*Sitz im Leben*) where the Bible is formed and never attempted to go beyond the church. The words, "it is the church that ..." are abstract and insufficient. They do not account for the whole. It is evident that there were in the church two clearly distinct matrices of transmission. There were two groups of people standing for two different interests and concerns. One of them consisted of advocates of institutional church authority who would eventually prevail. The passage representative of their position is found in Matt 18:

> If another member of the church sins against you, go and point out the fault when the two of you are alone. If the member listens to you, you have regained that one. But if you are not listened to, take one or two others along with you, so that every word may be confirmed by the evidence of two or three witnesses. If the member refuses to listen to

them, tell it to the church; and if the offender refuses to listen even to the church, let such a one be to you as a Gentile and a tax collector. (Matt 18:15–17)

These words are typical for advocates of church authority. If what this passage says comes true, all of what Jesus has said so far comes to naught. This is how important they considered order. Now this passage gave the church the right to banish a member. The church came to banish those who didn't obey, treated them like gentiles, and even gave the right to execute heretics. There is no reason Jesus himself could have said the words in question. For he has nothing to do with the church. The word *ekklēsia* (church) shows up, as you know, only in the Gospel of Matthew.

The language of institutional church leadership conveys abstract kerygma. Rome was wielding unflappable power, the Jewish forces were far from negligible, and Christianity merely existed as part of Judaism. Therefore, the church leaders avoided as much as possible provoking any of them with direct criticism. In consequence, they spoke in such a way that was sufficiently abstract to conceal the facts so that no one could be blamed. "For proselytism there is no other choice. Political conflicts must be avoided; human rights can take a backseat; mission work comes first; the church cannot evangelize in any other way"—this was how they thought.

Around 1940, the leaders of Korea employed a similar strategy. "We must preserve ourselves; we must survive; let's make a compromise for now"—this is the thinking that prevailed in the end. They all became pro-Japanese. They compromised and so survived. But what became of them afterward? Twenty-five years later, they do not have any qualification or position before the minjung. All of the prominent Christian leaders survived through compromise. "We must survive; Shinto worship[14] is inevitable," they thought. The same goes for the present.

---

14. The state religion of Japan until 1945, Shinto incorporated the worship of ancestors and nature spirits and a belief in *kami* (sacred power) in animate and inanimate things. Through Shinto Japan deified the emperor and took advantage of this for ruling its own people and its militaristic invasions and colonial rules. The Japanese colonists started in 1932 to demand that the Korean Christians perform the Shinto worship. Many of the Korean churches succumbed to the pressure, a most significant occasion being the resolution by the Presbyterian General Assembly in September 1938 to practice the Shinto worship.

Paul had a clear goal: "It is my goal to evangelize to the ends of the earth." He thought that the end of the earth was Spain. For he lived before Copernicus. So he was determined to go as far as Spain by all means. However, since Spain was also under the reign of Rome, it was a source of clash with the empire to worship someone it executed as a political criminal. In order to prevent this serious problem, Paul hid this fact. Instead of the abstract phrase, "the death of Jesus," he used the word "cross." By using this word, Paul conveys the fact that Jesus did not die but was killed. The cross was the mechanism for killing a political criminal under the Roman rule. It is possible that someone who was familiar with the circumstances of the time detected an anti-Roman message hidden in the words of Paul, "I decided to know nothing except the cross."[15] Therefore, the words *death* and *cross* mean two totally different things. The word "death" has no difference between Buddhism and Christianity. But cross is different. Paul used this word, and said nothing more.

9.7. Minjung and Their Use of Language

One of the two matrices of transmission mentioned earlier was those who were not named, the minjung. This minjung use their own language. The language of those who dominated the church was abstract and, as demonstrated by Paul's epistles, was a proclamatory language. But the language of the minjung is story. This is the language of the minjung. The minjung say what they have seen accurately. Even if it is not clear what they mean, this is not a problem of primary importance. "It was like this and that," "I saw it," they say. They describe what they actually saw and heard.

The theologians of kerygma, however, treat the words that the minjung used in this way as if they were a text in a unified Hellenistic style. That is, they analyze these words with the same method that is used for texts of the Hellenistic culture. They make a hasty conclusion, "This is most important, and the remainder functions as nothing more than a frame." Consequently, they render the gospels as nothing more than a compilation of Jesus's sayings.

Yet, what matters the most is not the words of Jesus but the events. Stories of Jesus casting out Satan, healing the sick, meeting the minjung,

---

15. This quote is based on 1 Cor 2:2: "For I decided to know nothing among you except Jesus Christ and him crucified."

and so forth—the whole of these, with nothing missing, is the Gospel for Mark. At the very beginning, Mark says, "This is the beginning of the good news." The good news is not Paul's conceptual gospel. It is not merely the death on the cross and the resurrection but the entirety of what is written in the gospels. That is the gospel. Everything—including Jesus's behaviors that are far too crude and nonreligious in the eyes of the Jewish religious authorities, such as his *koinōnia* (fellowship) with sinners—is the gospel.

Telling stories is the language of the minjung. Witness is only possible through death. The English word *martyr* means both witness and martyrdom, namely, death—the kind of death you must die when you open your mouth and speak. The minjung were powerless and could not speak directly to the powerful. Nevertheless, their message was conveyed by word of mouth. Church leadership found it dangerous and so refused to commit it to official documentation. For this reason, their stories were transmitted orally down to around the year 70. Kerygma had already been formulated. Mark knew both the kerygma and the stories of the minjung and wove them together in composing the Gospel of Mark.

Lastly, I would like to mention that Mark makes a degree of compromise. A compromise does not occur between two parties in actual opposition to each other. Church leadership did not omit the stories of the minjung out of spite, but because they focused on what they deemed to be more important. In other words, the leaders didn't explore the Jesus event not because it wasn't a fact, but because the survival of the church was hanging in the balance. Mark understood this.

Why did the leadership not trust the minjung's stories of the Jesus event, whose main actors were women? Why did they say that the resurrected Jesus was first seen by Cephas and then by the disciples, but say nothing at all about the women having seen him? Mark 16:8 provides an answer. I wonder if we could refer to this as Mark's compromise. Mark 16:8 says, "The women said nothing to anyone, for they were afraid." This is a hypothesis, but Mark concludes his narrative in this way in order to suggest that, since the women were afraid to say anything, the leaders didn't know that they were the first ones to see the resurrected Lord. The original Gospel of Mark, I think, ended at verse 8.

9.8. The Question and Answer Session

Q: Would you please give us a more detailed discussion of Paul's use of the word *cross*?

A: Paul says that Jesus was killed by the hands of sinners. But their identity is not specified. Still, Paul deserves credit for the cross becoming the symbol of Christianity. Around the tenth century, there was a movement for adopting, instead of the cross, the image of the resurrected Jesus holding a banner as the symbol of Christianity. But the symbol of the cross endured. Only in reading the gospels did I come to understand the meaning and the profound significance of the word cross.

This is how I imagine it. I suppose that it was after some inner struggles that Paul used the word cross rather than simply saying death. The word cross, despite not explicitly indicating by whom Jesus was killed, has a hidden meaning in it. Nowhere in the Pauline epistles is the identity of the killer of Jesus mentioned. Pilate's name does not show up. Neither does the idea of "by Rome" appear. It is surprising that Rome is not mentioned even in the Apostles' Creed. This creed is extremely abstract. The only improvement is that it mentions the name of Pilate, but this is not sufficient. For example, if Hitler's name were mentioned only once in a text about the Holocaust, it would not be sufficient. In this regard, the Apostles' Creed comes up short. This is tantamount to disregarding the great life and death of Jesus. This is the way a public confession always goes.

We need to exercise caution not to be caught up in church-ism, which makes us take the Apostles' Creed literally and focus only on protecting the church. But, concerning this tendency, I am not in a position to blame others. I myself am to blame. I am a theologian, not a pastor. Still, I call forth a church-defending mentality. This is dangerous. Oftentimes the intention to protect the church does the truth in. This is indeed frightening. We must be warned of this over and over again.

Q: Please tell us about the relation between Luke and *ochlos*.

A: It is Luke who specified *ochlos*. I never evaluate Luke in a negative way. I do not say that Luke was wrong for using the word *laos* instead of *ochlos*. More than anyone else, Luke emphasized the poor. There is a lot of stress on the poor in Luke's special material. I think this amounts to a little more specific characterization of *ochlos*, I think. I am currently preparing a thesis on Luke's view of the minjung.

Q: Would you please share with us about minjung theology?

A: In the beginning was the *event*. I wrote an essay titled "The Theology of Event," and it is the event that is important.[16] Some Westerners develop the theology of the Word based on the view that in the beginning was the Word, but this is Greek thinking. As far as the Bible goes, in the beginning was the event.

Let me illustrate with an example. If asked what was more important, ninety-nine sheep or one sheep, most people would answer, "ninety-nine sheep." But it is problematic to listen to the stories of the Bible in this kind of paradigm. The event happened to the one sheep. The event of "being lost" happened. The problem begins here. In this manner, a different question leads to a different answer. If the parents love one of their four children, it is partiality on their part. This is not the right way to ask a question. The event has happened to the one child. Both the question and the answer should start with this. This is not a matter to deal with in a legal and level-headed way.

The *ochlos* were called sinners and despised by the world. But they were not sinners to Jesus. They were just the same human beings as others. But the event of them being negated as sinners, namely, the event of their humanity being negated, was happening. And those who were at the site of this event were fighting without even the leisure to plan for the future. The story of Jesus started here.

Theology developed in the West. As the church acquired great power, theologians and clergy came to take no note of the event. In the West particularly, since university professors in theology are all state-employed officials,[17] the event has stopped being a concern for them. Because strengthening their scholarship argumentatively and going ahead in the disciplinary competition with good achievements became their top priorities, their sense of calling as the torchbearers gradually dimmed. The clergy, too, only focus on how to govern the church. Certainly, this is an inevitable problem in a sense.

At any rate, we must do away with the myth that only pastors and theologians can properly read and understand the Bible. If anything, there are aspects to the Bible that are invisible to them. For knowledge has blinded their eyes. But those who read the Bible at the site of their own lives find out surprisingly new messages in it. Theologians and biblical scholars sub-

---

16. Ahn Byung-Mu, "The Theology of the Event" [Korean].

17. By *the West* here, Ahn seems to indicate not the Western world in general but Germany at the time of his speaking.

ject each and every word of the Bible to a grammatical analysis and argue as if a single subtle grammatical analysis determined everything. By doing so, they make the Bible feel increasingly difficult. As a result, they say, "I am an expert. You humble laity don't have a say here." By the way, there are in Korea many people who have been fired from a job. Young people who have barely finished the elementary school, laborers and young girls who are accepted by no one—these people we bring together to read the Bible. And they are given the chance to share how the Bible speaks to them. Again, we have an amazing outcome. Therefore, we learn from them. The theologian becomes not the teacher but the student. She or he translates the words of these people into language that is accessible to intellectuals, who study the Bible intellectually. This is the only role for a minjung theologian to play. We should have this kind of humility. This is the conclusion I have reached.

We already belong to a certain class and are standing in a certain position. University professors don't have to worry about food, clothing, and shelter. They stand far away from those who suffer and have trouble earning their daily bread. For this reason, I try to go to their site of life to listen to them. I aim to be in solidarity with them. As a result, both Professor Suh Nam-dong and I went to prison for a while. I consider it a great privilege to experience the life of those who are killed or deprived of their rights as a human being. We have come to grow out of the arrogant notion that we are raising the consciousness of the minjung. I feel that there is something pure within the minjung. Jesus talked with minjung of this nature, but there was a long history of changing the story into a really difficult language. Perhaps Paul's position was inevitable. For he used certain language to introduce the gospel of Jesus to the world of Hellenism. But this does not mean that we have to use the same kind of language.

Q: You said that the meaning of the crucifixion was lost due to the symbol of the cross. Please expand on that.

A: The word *cross* used by Paul, of course, refers to the crucifixion. In Paul's day, the cross was not abstract. Later on, both the Eastern Church and the Western Church made a symbol of the cross. It became decoration, especially in the Eastern Church.

When I went to Europe, I was surprised at what a mockery the cross had become. At a carnival, scantily clad dancers were wearing something sparkling on their chest, and it was a cross. Why should the cross be found at a place like that? Why is it mocked that way? I could not shake off these kinds of questions.

There is another thing I cannot forget. In many Catholic regions, there stood a cross at every crossroad. When I came up close to the spot, I saw red blood running down the body of Jesus on the white-painted cross. It truly looked like drops of blood were falling down. But right underneath a young man and woman were undressing and kissing. What could the cross mean to them? Could they be saying, "In order for us to enjoy ourselves here, someone has to toil. You toil over there. We will have fun here." It is evident that the cross meant nothing to them. Our sensibilities have been numbed to such a degree. The cross has become a mockery in the same way that the historical Jesus was mocked.

The event of the cross did not happen once two thousand years ago; it is taking place now again and again. I myself am a witness to that. You are, too. It is sin to make this event of the cross abstract. We cannot say that the slave-like people in Japan and the slave-like people in Korea are the same. However, the basic event common to both groups started with the cross of Jesus. Or perhaps I should say that the event of the cross is an event of culmination. The Jesus event took place and is taking place in the Philippines in a Filipino way; in Latin America in a Latin American way; in Africa in an African way, and so on.

Q: Who are minjung?

A: The question of who minjung are repeatedly comes up. However, those who do minjung theology have decided not to answer this question for the time being. Giving a proper definition to a term is thoroughly Western, and doing so may even lead to forgetting the minjung. Because defining minjung may become so big a concern as to subject the minjung to the realm of scholarship, we have decided not to define it for now.

Whether or not I belong to the minjung is a foolish question to ask. It's not the kind of thing someone can tell you. Someone who confesses, "I am the minjung," of their own accord is not true minjung. To quote Bultmann, "The person who asks what love is either already knows love or would never know no matter how much explanation she or he might hear." The same principle is at work here. The one who asks, "Who are minjung?" either already knows the answer but still asks to find some kind of escape route, or may be the kind of person who would never understand however much instruction she or he might receive. Minjung can only be experienced and is not an object of intellectual understanding. We have clearly seen. We have experienced. We are witnessing to the minjung event just as we have seen it. Asking, "Are you participating in the minjung event?" is the same as asking, "Have you witnessed the resurrection?" or "Have you seen Jesus who was killed on the cross?"

Although I have no intention to define minjung, I have two ways to understand them. One is the understanding that they are the people who are poor and powerless due to oppression and economic exploitation by the powerful intelligentsia. Another understanding is that they are the object of everyday exploitation. At the real site of the minjung's life, there is an experience of colonialism. The site of everyday exploitation is a colony and, in today's parlance, it is the Third World. It is a fact that the minjung event is taking place there, not anywhere else.

When I was giving a lecture in Germany, someone asked, "Who are minjung in Germany?" In Germany there is no slum, and laborers there have strong labor unions. At that moment the laborers from foreign countries crossed my mind. In particular, there are many laborers from Turkey in Germany. So I asked, "What about the laborers from foreign countries? I am responding with another question rather than an answer." Then the person who asked the question blushed, for he himself already knew. Germany once invited more than a million foreign laborers for their need to run the factories. But now that they have outlived their use, Germany is treating them as a nuisance. For the Turkish people have been the enemy of Germans from the olden days. Now Germans harbor a serious hostility toward the Turks. The person who asked the question blushed perhaps because he himself disliked the Turks.

10
The Minjung Biography of Jesus

Today I am going to talk about Jesus as minjung with a focus on how to read the Gospel of Mark. Last night I told you about my conversation with Moltmann about the proposition "Jesus is minjung." And since one of you asked, "In what sense is Jesus minjung?" I will keep that in mind as I address how the Gospel of Mark has led me to such a conclusion.

10.1. Mark and Jesus

In attempting to paint a picture of Jesus according to the Gospel of Mark (and also according to the other Synoptic Gospels), we can overall point out the following: according to Mark, Jesus is not a descendant of David. Luke and Matthew presuppose him as an offspring of David with far-fetched genealogies, but they are unreliable.

Mark has no prehistory and shows no interest at all in Jesus's social station or family. Only twice does the phrase "son of David" show up, which is not uttered by Jesus's disciples or Jesus himself but by someone else. Mark does not adopt the assumption that Jesus was a descendant of David. If anything, although I merely pointed it out yesterday without any explanation, I think Mark 12:35–37 is an important passage. As far as I see, Western theologians are missing the point of this passage. What Jesus says is daring and seemingly out of the context: "David himself calls him (the Messiah) Lord; so how can he be his son?"[1] This was the response to his own question during his teaching in the temple, "How can the scribes say that the Messiah is the son of David?" (Mark 12:35). Here, he is giving a clear-cut answer, "That can't be the case!" It is significant that Jesus said this when it was generally believed that the Messiah was the son of David.

---

1. This remark appears in Mark 12:37. The parenthetical addition was made by Ahn.

Indeed, the Gospel of Mark makes no mention at all of Bethlehem or Jerusalem concerning the birth of Jesus. He emphasizes that Jesus was born in Galilee, and that his public life started in Galilee. In light of this, we can see that Jesus does not come from a royal lineage.

Next, a theory of Jesus's preexistence does not appear in Mark. There is actually no need to mention it again at this point. Bultmann said something similar, but Catholic New Testament scholar Joachim Gnilka, in his extensive commentary on the Gospel of Mark (*Evangelisch-Katholischer Kommentar zum Neuen Testament*), affirms that the notion of preexistence is not attested in the Gospel of Mark.[2] In fact, Mark does not accept the idea that Jesus was a divine being. For he thought of him as a regular human being. It is noteworthy that he ignored it in an age when the belief already existed, as is shown by Philippians, among other New Testament texts.

Third, Jesus lived in a rural area in the region of Galilee. We find no record of him visiting a city. This is consistent with the fact that his language in Mark is the language of a rural society. There is virtually no Hellenistic influence in Jesus. He roamed from one rural area to another. It is only Mark who says over and over that Jesus is from Galilee and that he is a Galilean. Mark says "Galilee, Galilee" nineteen times when he does not really have to. The rural areas of Galilee were the site of Jesus's work, and the cities at the time were already Hellenized. Hellenistic culture dominated the cities as footholds of Roman colonization. Jesus was never interested in the cities, where even the lifestyle was different. Only Galilee was an important place for Jesus. He started his public life there and undertook all of his important works there. In Mark 14:28 (cf. 16:7), we read the famous words, "Let's meet in Galilee."[3] Although the place where Jesus was killed was Jerusalem, the place where he lived and was gathering his disciples anew was Galilee. Jesus was born in Nazareth, a small and obscure village in Galilee.

To the question, "Where is the Galilee of Korea?," we answer, "It is Gwangju," although some people say, "It is Jeju Island."[4] I grew up in Jiandao

---

2. Joachim Gnilka, *Evangelisch-Katholischer Kommentar zum Neuen Testament* (Neukirchen-Vluyn: Benziger, 1970).

3. This sentence does not literally occur in, but merely bases itself on, the two verses mentioned: "But after I am raised up, I will go before you to Galilee" (Mark 14:28) and "But go, tell his disciples and Peter that he is going ahead of you to Galilee; there you will see him, just as he told you" (Mark 16:7).

4. Jeju Island is the largest island annexed to the Korean peninsula and is located in the southernmost area of Korea. With a beautiful volcanic topography, the island

of Manchuria. Koreans who were driven out from their homelands were leading a miserable life there. So we say that Jiandao is the Galilee of Korea. Where is the Galilee of Japan? Could it be Sapporo? Galilee is neither Tokyo nor Seoul.

The fourth question to deal with is: With whom did Jesus have fellowship? On this subject, I have written several theses. The people Jesus communicated with were those who were alienated in his day, social outcasts, and those who were called sinners. It was just like these words of Jesus's: "I have come to call not the righteous but those who you call sinners."[5]

10.2. Liberation from *Han*

Yesterday I received a book of Mr. Suh Nam-dong's lectures and read a little of it at night. In this book, Mr. Suh says that *han* is related to sin. He notes that the word *sin* is a word that those in high places impose on those who are down below. Yet the same idea can also be expressed by the word *han* on the part of those who are down below—those who are cornered, the crushed, and the afflicted. In a sense, *han* expresses an aspect of social psychology and defies simple explanation. The Chinese character for *han*, 恨, represents the state of the heart being closed.[6] It indicates a state of

---

is recognized as a renowned international tourist destination. Jeju Volcanic Island and Lava Tubes were inscribed on the World Natural Heritage by the World Heritage Committee in 2007. It is likely that the view that Jeju Island is the Galilee of Korea originates from the tragic history called the Jeju April 3 Incident. This incident is officially defined as having lasted from March 1, 1947 to September 21, 1954, and its main phase started on April 3, 1948, when an armed group of communist sympathizers attacked police stations and government offices in resistance against the suppression of communist sympathizers by the police and the Northwest Youth League, a rightist group made up of North Korean refugees, and in opposition to the establishment of a single government in South Korea. The ensuing armed conflicts between the punitive expeditions and communist sympathizers involved tortures and killings of many of the island residents. According to the estimation made by the government in the early 2000s, at least 14,028 persons were killed during the incident. On October 31, 2003, the then president Roh Moo-hyun made an official apology to the families of the victims and the people of Jeju Island for the large-scale violence by the national power.

5. This quote is based on "I have come to call not the righteous but sinners," which appears in both Matt 9:13 and Mark 2:17.

6. The left part of the given Chinese character means "heart" and serves as the basis of the meaning of the whole character. The right part, by itself, means "limitation" or "to stop," but in the character as a whole, it functions as the basis of its pronunciation.

deep dissatisfaction in your heart, a state where your bosom is full of sadness, anger, afflictions, and humiliations that you are unable to express in words. If this condition persists and breaks out in an illness, it becomes *hwabyeong*.[7] Women in particular suffer this illness often. When a violent husband abuses his wife and only asserts his rights, *han* builds up in his wife's heart and becomes an illness in the end. She goes insane or develops a psychological disease. Its specified form is *hwa* (火)[8] and is related to *han* (恨). This carries a different meaning than the German *Klage* (uttering anguish). *Klage* is voluntarily expressing in words what is possible to express, a complaint. However, the state of being unable to express what must be expressed is *han*.

If we try to express *han* as a Western concept, we can perhaps equate it to the overwhelming emotions a person experiences in a tragedy as an example. Kierkegaard classifies tragedy into two types. In the first type, the protagonist knows the precise cause of the tragedy but perishes in amazement at the tragedy. The second type is a tragedy in which the protagonist, without knowing the reason at all, experiences anguish and eventually perishes. *Han* belongs to the second category. It is a state in which your heart is filled up with suppressed sadness and anger that escape clear expression.

I am digressing a little bit, but we Koreans have a lot of stories about *han*. Well into the night, a ghost shows up with her hair let down, bleeding and biting a knife. Most of the ghosts in these stories are female. A woman who died an undeserved *han*-filled death appears as a resentful ghost to plead for the resolution of her *han*. For this reason, there is a close affinity between *han* and the shaman. The shaman liberates ghosts and people from this *han*. In this sense, the shaman fills a similar role as Christ. This is a very important fact. The church has ignored this up to now, but it must change. Isn't Jesus Christ like a priest of *han* who relieves suffering? If shamans serve in the role of liberating *han*-afflicted people, could we not in this sense call Jesus a shaman? A shaman exists in the world of fantasy. But eventually she or he is liberated from it. The ghost of the dead person is swallowed by the shaman and expresses everything they were unable to say while alive. As a consequence, the disease is cured. It is crucial to resolve *han*. In the event that *han* breaks out into an illness like a blaze, it destroys everything of the existing order. Before things come to this, liber-

---

7. *Hwabyeong* literally means "fire disease" and refers to stress-caused emotional disorder.

8. The Chinese character in the parenthesis represents "fire."

ation from *han* must occur. This is why *han* makes a frequent appearance in minjung theology. The clergy must become priests of *han*. No matter how you understand it, the rich and the poor alike are *han*-stricken in spite of themselves. No matter how cheerful a person may appear, there is pain and sorrow beneath the surface indicative of the human condition.

The most important thing Jesus did in his relation with the alienated minjung was to liberate them from their *han*. This includes people whose life is *han*-stricken due to illness; people who receive no care from anyone and whose illness has deprived them of even the life of a believer; people who have developed illnesses such as Hansen's disease and are cast out from the human society. Jesus even accepted tax collectors, who are unacceptable from the standpoint of minjung theology, because they were alienated in their society and *han*-stricken.

10.3. Jesus's Words and Behaviors

The fifth point worthy of our attention are the words of Jesus and the minjung. I have already told you that Jesus's language was the language of rural society. It was simultaneously the language of the minjung. The language of the minjung is story. It does not develop a thesis logically but tells facts in a straightforward manner. Pay attention to the way Jesus speaks, especially in his parables. They are stories. They are words that anyone can comprehend that come from the real life and are not difficult. The closer words get to real life, the easier and the more story-like they become. The more distant from real life, the more abstract your words become.

The Japanese church has a reputation for its well-organized and well-structured sermons. People listening to this kind of sermon would think, "What a well-organized and well-structured delivery!" "How smart!" "It's full of good sense!" But there is something wrong here. For that is not why we go to church. Such things we can read in books, newspapers, and magazines all we want, which would be better than listening to the pastor's sermon.

The same tendency is also found in Korea. My own denomination in particular takes an open-minded position in theology, and so it preaches intellectual and logical sermons in cultured language to introduce new ideas and concepts. However, although this kind of sermon may sound nice, its impact does not go beyond the church door. They make no appeal to your heart. I can't stand sermons that make sense to my head but have nothing to do with me and so don't stay with me. We must, I think, go back to the stories that came out of Jesus's life.

The sixth topic to consider is Jesus's behavior. "Behavior" is *hurumai* in Japanese. This word sounds a little frivolous, but I don't have a better translation. Jesus never tried to go above the minjung of his time. Far from disliking things of the minjung, he did whatever was necessary to communicate with them.

For example, comparing between Mark and Matthew or Luke shows us an interesting discrepancy. In many cases, Jesus, when healing a sick person, does not merely say, "Be healed (of the illness)!" For a blind man, he also applies his saliva (Mark 7:33; 8:23) and asks for his reaction by saying, "Do you see anything?" (Mark 8:23) Or he mixes mud with his saliva and applies this mixture to the person.[9] These details appear in Mark but are deleted in Matthew and Luke. Could this have happened because Matthew and Luke were worried that intellectual readers would find these things too primitive? Could Mark's accounts not have been the real and original stories? It is more important to actually touch than say, "Be healed!" I suppose people of Jesus's time thought so, too.

Holding someone's hand or touching them is a minjung-like deed. The body-to-body communication is very important. Jesus didn't treat people of his time in a mechanical fashion but did just what they really wanted him to do for them in their heart. I think that was the single most original behavior of Jesus. It is imperative not to distant yourself from the minjung thinking, "I am an intellectual" or "I am a modern person." It is the duty of theologians to convey the demands, possibilities, and messages of the minjung. Jesus himself did that. We can say that in a sense Jesus did not take the initiative but acted passively in dealing with the minjung. He first asked, "What do you want?," and then acted according to the answer. This is something we need to give more thought to.

Seventh, Jesus might have had the ability to read, but he did not study. That is to say, he had no formal schooling. This is suggested by both the Synoptic Gospels and the Gospel of John. Although we read that people called Jesus "rabbi," there is not even a hint of his having had a rabbi's training. Jesus had no education and therefore had no credentials. He didn't have a bachelor's degree or pass qualifying exams for a pastor. Of course, it is absolutely unthinkable that he had such a thing as a doctorate. For this reason, people asked him for the proof of his authority by saying, "Where did you get the authority from? You don't have the qualifications

---

9. This act of healing by Jesus occurs not, as Ahn claims, in Mark but in John 9:6.

for a rabbi, do you? We will stop doubting you if heaven sends a miracle as evidence. But you are a nobody and dare to talk nonsense!" However, he had no proof at all to show to them. He indicated the only thing he had to show with the words, "Wait. I will show you my death." Dying was his only possession. He had neither money nor a wife nor children. I don't think he was married. Of course, there is no record that says he was not married. I hear that there was an American author who wrote a book titled *Was Jesus Married?* that became a bestseller.[10]

We do not know whether or not the disciples were married. But considering the mention that Peter's mother-in-law was ill with a fever (Mark 1:30; Luke 4:38), Peter seems to have been married. Other than this, no mention is made of the other disciples being married. Jesus, as I imagine him, is the kind of person who cannot get married. I don't mean that Jesus was not a man, but that someone that lives as seriously as he did could not marry. The same is true of a person like myself. Having only average talents, I cannot do two things at the same time. As a young man, I thought that I would not be able to successfully pursue both Jesus and marriage and so I decided to give up marriage. Able people can do two things at the same time. I myself can do only one thing. So I lived with no intention to marry. But when my mother woke up from her cancer operation, she immediately said to me, "Son, I have one last wish before death. Please get married before I breathe my last." I was forty-seven at that time. "Yes, I will," I said and got married on December 29 of the same year and presented my wife to my mother. Considering I got married for such a reason, you can tell I am such a mediocre person.

The Synoptic Gospels suggest that Jesus's public life spanned a little over a year. The view that his public ministry lasted for three years is based on the Gospel of John. Which is closer to the truth? I think the Synoptic Gospels. The reason is because Jesus's kind of life would not last you for more than a year even now. It is hard to imagine that Jesus would have had a family while leading such a radical lifestyle. Therefore, I believe that Jesus was not married.

Did Jesus have a home? Since Jesus spent most of his time at a certain place in Capernaum and made it the base of his work, some wonder if it was not his house. But we have no conclusive evidence. Jesus himself said,

---

10. Ahn seems to be referring to William E. Phipps, *Was Jesus Married? The Distortion of Sexuality in the Christian Tradition* (New York: Harper & Row, 1970).

"Foxes have holes, and birds of the air have nests; but the Son of Man has nowhere to lay his head" (Luke 9:58). This is an autobiographical description. He was indeed a penniless wanderer. Jesus was a laborer, too. He likely labored until age thirty. Of course, we cannot be sure. But I imagine so based on the words, "Jesus was about thirty years old when he began his work," in the Gospel of Luke (3:23).

After this, Jesus of course performed miracles like a superman. There was certainly such an aspect to him. But Mark is not reluctant to express that Jesus's power was limited. Jesus says that he cannot work miracles in his hometown owing to the unbelief there (Mark 6:4). The Gospel of Matthew does not specify whether or not he could but uses the revised wording, "did not do" (Matt 13:58).

The gospels reveal various aspects of Jesus's incompetence. He is shown as thoroughly incompetent in the passion narrative. Jesus as portrayed in this narrative is powerless with no other capabilities than an ordinary person. He looks just the same as the general minjung of his day and has no ability to perform a miracle or call down help from heaven. He is depicted as a person who is simply weak having no means to counter the false accusations and mistreatment.

In sum, Jesus was an obscure and penniless young man in a colony of the Roman Empire. To make things worse, he became the target of a murderous plot by the Jerusalem sect, the empire's pawn and collaborators. This is the Jesus the Gospel of Mark presents to us.

The cross event of Jesus is only given in general outlines. But what is interesting is that, whereas the Roman Empire preserved many records of crucifixions around Jesus's time, the case of Jesus escaped notice. It is as if his crucifixion was so trivial that no such record was made of it. Even the Jewish historian Josephus does not say anything about Jesus. There was an addition made to his writings in later years, but it was not original.

10.4. The Tasks of the Gospel of Mark

Let me change the subject and talk about Mark's *Sitz im Leben*. As I briefly mentioned yesterday, while writing about the Gospel of Mark in *An Introduction to the New Testament* back in 1968 or 1969, I dated the writing of this gospel to 64 CE.[11] However, now I think it was after 70, the year when

---

11. Ahn Byung-Mu, *An Introduction to the New Testament*.

Jerusalem was destroyed. Catholic biblical scholar Joachim Gnilka postulates the date around 73, and I suppose this is right.

What a bloodshed the Jewish War at this time was, as you all are well aware. It was a horror of exceptional proportions. For example, the number of the people who were put to death through deception reached eight thousand. Rome's attacks focused on Galilee first, moving down until they reached Jerusalem. Fierce battles raged on for five months in the area surrounding Jerusalem. A ferocious battle at a small city for five months is something serious. According to the records, a certain day during the war saw the deaths of five hundred people. Those who rebelled against Rome were crucified. To crucify that many people at the same time required a great deal of wood. Josephus records that, after the simultaneous execution of five hundred people, the shortage of wood made it no longer possible to crucify every single rebel. The Jews were responsible for the war, but the major atrocities were perpetuated by Rome. Eventually, Jerusalem fell, and the temple was destroyed. Thereafter, the Roman authorities called Jerusalem the name of *Aelia Capitolina*, which means the same as Jupiter.

The name Palestine, which we use now, comes from *Pleshet*. Pleshet was an old foe of Israel, Israel's eternal enemy. *Palestine* is an exceedingly cruel and concrete designation. It meant that the land belonged to Pleshet, and so all of the native Jews were driven out from there. As soon as war broke out, Christians left their home regions to go out of harm's way. This may be regarded as nothing serious these days, but back in those days being cast out of your hometown meant death. For back then life in the town community was the sole guarantee of survival. Wandering around in foreign regions meant death. Food acquisition was certainly a challenge, and grave dangers threatened life in general. Therefore, most of the Jews driven out of Palestine, including Christians, could not help but live for each day's survival during their wandering. The regions surrounding Palestine swarmed with countless wanderers who had been banished out of their hometown by the war. In this kind of life setting, Mark (or the Markan sect or community) had a few crucial tasks to accomplish.

One of them was to find out what to do with the traditions of Judaism and how to connect Greek and Jewish traditions in light of the destruction of the temple. The second task was to determine what to do with the people who had lost their homeland—those who had lost their homes like birds having lost their nests and being scattered around with no assurance of survival.

The third task was how to deal with the controversy over church authority, which was, surprisingly, already beginning to take place at this time—in the midst of the war. Paul's famous words in Gal 1:8–9, "Let the person be accursed who proclaim a gospel different from what I have proclaimed,"[12] reflect this situation and can be construed as already declaring a doctrinal war. According to studies on the epistles to the Corinthians, various doctrinal sects had emerged at the time of their writing, which created serious problems. How to address these problems was a challenge for Mark.

Additionally, the question of apostolic authority was a serious issue. The apostles credited themselves with the right to teach and, based on this, told people to follow their teachings. The apostles were a symbolic entity, and so the Acts of the Apostles even contains the passage about there having to be twelve apostles and casting lots in order to replace the twelfth one. The task was how to cope with the assertion by the twelve—a symbolic number—apostles of their authority as apostle. This was an issue related to the doctrine of church authority.

The fourth task, which is related to the second one, was how to explain Jesus's suffering and cross to the suffering minjung, who faced danger, death, and uncertainty of survival.

Lastly, Mark was interested in the question of Jesus's resurrection and the kingdom of God. The expectation was frustrated that the kingdom of God would arrive shortly after Jesus's resurrection. Against their expectation that Jesus's resurrection would mean the end of all the problems, wasn't just the opposite the case? Then what was the meaning of the resurrection? How should they explain it? Should they deny the resurrection? Mark had to address these challenging questions.

There is one presupposition underlying these tasks. As mentioned earlier, I have been developing my discussion under the assumption that Mark was written after the start of the Jewish War, namely, after 70 CE. I have two reasons for this view. It is the general view that the Little Apocalypse in Mark 13 reflects the Jewish War prior to the writing of the gospel. Additionally, Jesus's prophecy about the destruction of the Jerusalem temple is said to reflect what already happened. But my thinking does not stop here.

---

12. This quote is a summary of the two verses in question: "But even if we or an angel from heaven should proclaim to you a gospel contrary to what we proclaimed to you, let that one be accursed! As we have said before, so now I repeat, if anyone proclaims to you a gospel contrary to what you received, let that one be accursed!"

The second reason is the existence of two narratives of a large hungry crowd following Jesus. I am of the opinion that the presence of two miraculous feedings of the five thousand and four thousand in such a small gospel goes against common sense. What Jesus said about the crowd that had been following him with no food for three days is important: "We have to give something to eat to the group of sheep that have lost their shepherd. We must give something to eat to the people who have been scattered without even a leader and so decentered."[13] Apart from whether or not these events took place historically in the time of Jesus, I think they do reflect the situation of the Jews and Christians at the time when Mark was written. That is, I think they reflect the situation of the minjung after the year 70.

10.5. The Image of Jesus as Seen in Minjung Life

What did Jesus do at the site of the minjung's suffering? I have been asking myself this question for some time. In Korea, the Park Jeong-hui government, which was showing its true colors as a dictatorship, especially in the 1970s, fabricated the notorious incident of the General League of Democratic Students of Korea.[14] They contrived a spy incident in order to demolish the resistant forces. They arrested a number of young people fighting for the minjung on the charge of being involved in the communist party of North Korea. They mercilessly tortured, disabled, and finally executed these young people.[15] By nailing the lids of the coffins, they

---

13. This quote is based on Mark 6:34, 37 and 8:1.
14. Park Jeong-hui ordered the abduction of Kim Dae-jung in August 1973, which triggered the anti-Yushin movement. In April 1974, Park announced that the General League of Democratic Students of Korea (GLDSK), under the guidance by some communists, joined forces with different groups in order to accomplish a communist revolution. One hundred and eighty people were arrested, and many of them received a heavy sentence. Most of the imprisoned, however, were released in February 1975 due to the domestic protest and the international pressure. In 2005, the National Intelligence Service's Committee for Investigating the Truth of the Past History announced that the GLDSK incident was an incident of persecuting student activism through distorting an anti-government rally as an attempt at a communist revolution. In 2009, the judiciary found all of the convicts of the incident not guilty.
15. The way Ahn describes the incident sounds as if all of the many young people arrested had been executed. However, this is not what actually took place. Eight of the 180 arrested persons, who were related to the People's Revolutionary Party, were

prevented the families of the victims from seeing the bodies. It was said that the torture was so severe that the victims' faces were unrecognizable. While the coffins were being transported over to the cemetery, some pastors and priests ran after them, demanding that the bodies be shown. They were kicked and trampled. Unable to overcome the violence, they failed to see the bodies. The government could not dare show the mangled bodies. Also, they buried the bodies the day after the victims were sentenced to death.[16] It was an unbelievably shocking event. In addition, there were incidents in which the government attempted to frame many Koreans studying abroad in Japan as spies of North Korea and execute them. The well-known Mr. Seo Jun-sik and his brother are still in prison.[17] Pastors, students, professors, and laborers were thrown in prison.

Yet it was never just a lonely fight. Speaking of my own experience, I was tortured for ten full days in the Korean Central Intelligence Agency since the day after I was put in prison. My interrogators didn't beat me and spoke to me in a respectful manner. But they seated me on a square table without a back or armrest and flashed an electric lamp in my face. They didn't let me sleep for the ten days. At the same time, they repeated the same questions again and again. I lost all strength to fight. There is no worse mental torture than not sleeping for a single minute for ten days. I believe they gave me a relatively good treatment because I was a professor and well-known. I can't share all the stories, but one professor was killed for a reason that is still unknown to us. Of the families of the victims, some were Christians; others were not. They had nowhere else to turn to but the

---

executed; they were not all young people, their ages ranging between thirty-one and fifty-two.

16. The executions took place on April 9, 1975, only eighteen hours after the victims were sentenced to death. This barbarous act was domestically and internationally criticized as "judicial murder." The Switzerland-based International Commission of Jurists called April 9, 1975 a dark in judicial history. Only two of the corpses were handed over to the bereaved families. The others were taken away and cremated by the government without consent by the victims' families.

17. Seo Jun-sik (b. 1948) was born in Kyoto, Japan, and, after finishing high school in Japan, entered Seoul National University to study law in 1968. In 1970, while staying in Japan, he visited North Korea with his elder brother Seo Seung. This involved these two brothers in the incident of the students-abroad spy ring in 1970. They were sentenced to a seven-year term in 1972 on the charge of violating the National Security Law. Upon the completion of their term, however, they were not released because of refusing to change their ideology. They remained in prison for another ten years.

church. They went to a Catholic or Protestant church with faint hope in their hearts. They also made international appeals. Our friends in Japan helped us in various ways, and we also tried to forge a connection with conscientious people in Germany to create other channels of support. But the most important and difficult question was how to introduce Jesus to these families.

The question of what kind of Jesus to introduce was also a pressing concern for Mark. Was it Jesus the victor? Jesus the almighty? Jesus as a transcendent being as God? Jesus the resurrected? But these approaches to Jesus seemed to have little meaning to the families of the victims. For such a Jesus could not comfort them in the least. If Jesus was endowed with special powers, his suffering would mean nothing. For example, Jesus says three times, "I will be killed and rise again after three days."[18] However, even though I could say, "Jesus was killed," I could not possibly say, "He rose again after three days."

Imagine the following situation. If I were certain to come back to life after three days like Jesus, I would die with no difficulty. There cannot be any agony to such a death. If that were the case, Jesus was a mere actor, who was saying, "My God, why have you forsaken me?" (Matt 27:46). If he was sure he would come back to life after three days, why did he make such a *scene*? Wouldn't it be a dramatic act?

In light of the prospect of being resurrected after three days, being killed is not hopeless. But Jesus was in deep despair facing his own death. Therefore, I assert, "Being resurrected after three days has nothing to do with Jesus." Recalling Bonhoeffer in connection with this point, I have often said, "Jesus was tormented and finally was killed by Hitler."

There are various ways of being killed. You can be killed as a great and heroic person revered by people. Or you can be killed as a punishment for what you have done. The case of Jesus belongs to neither type. Everyone fled, and no one was proud of Jesus's death. He had nothing but despair—nothing but sheer darkness itself. Even God was absent. In this kind of situation, how can you introduce Jesus? Jesus as a hero? Jesus as a victor?

The only possibility left was Jesus who weeps with you! Nothing else was available. The only image was Jesus who takes the plunge, suffers and is tormented with you, and weeps and dies together with you. This is not a Jesus who was victorious or glorified but a Jesus who was in a hopeless

---

18. This quote is based on Mark 8:31, 9:31, and 10:34.

circumstance of suffering and being killed, a Jesus who was abandoned by not only his disciples and his people but even God. This was the Jesus Mark conveyed. This was indeed the most appropriate representation of Jesus for the site of suffering. For this reason, the suffering Jesus, the Christ of passion became the most important motif in formulating minjung theology.

I shared this conclusion during the sermon for the service with the families of the imprisoned people: "Jesus in the midst of his passion was in exactly the same situation as you find yourselves in now. From Gethsemane through the illegitimate trial up to the moment of crucifixion, only violence was rampant without God's intervention. The weak are beaten, insulted, and killed for the mere reason that they are weak." In this kind of life setting, I had no other way to preach than saying that Jesus and they find themselves in precisely the same situation. But I was not making an unrealistic connection, for it was precisely this representation of Jesus that Mark presented. If anything, this kind of Jesus greatly comforted people in the circumstances under discussion.

10.6. The Meaning of Jesus's Passion and Death

Only there did they come to sense solidarity with Jesus. Jesus was tormented in the same circumstances and conditions. Jesus was not tortured alone but together with us. They realized that our present suffering could never be separated from Jesus's suffering. To go a little further, the torment and death of Jesus is the torment and death of minjung themselves. If not, what relation could exist between Jesus and us? If the fate of Jesus had been that of an individual, merely that of a young Jewish person two thousand years ago, Jesus and I would have nothing to do with each other.

When I was in prison, the prosecutor said to me at one point of his interrogation, "I hope you realize this. Someone must be doing what I am doing. If it's not me, then it's someone else. For even an evil law is still a law." I responded, "I have nothing to do with you. You are not here as an individual. So I have no grudge against you. You are not acting of your own accord. You are questioning me as a representative, as a member of a collective body."

Could Walesa of Poland have been a single person? A single-person hero? No. He is the symbol of the Polish laborers—not an individual.

I have always thought that the Western idea of the individual is wrong. In the East we have no such ideas as individual personhood. Yesterday I told you about the word *wuri* (we), and the Bible does not understand humans as individuals. This fact has never left my mind. So I have in the end reached the conclusion that the passion of Jesus was not an individual's passion.

Then what is the passion of Jesus? The expression "the son of Man," which Jesus liked to use to refer to himself, changes meaning between first- and third-person usage. When Jesus was using it for himself as a first-person reference, it has nothing to do with the meaning of the messiah. If it had meant the messiah, the disciples, not Jesus himself, would have addressed him as the son of Man.

The son of Man is an expression that appears in Dan 7:13–14 and must be considered in connection with Dan 2:44–45. What becomes clear in so doing is that this the son of Man is identified with the collective notion of people. It is not an individual. The son of Man can be translated as "corporate" in English. It is not an individual. Both Noth and Ferdinand Hahn are of this opinion. Hahn in particular connects Dan 7:13–14 with Ps 110:1 in order to confirm that it is a collective concept. Even though they try to leave room for the notion that Jesus is a special person. The collective concept view is also supported by Schweitzer, Dodd, and Thomas Walter Manson.

Therefore, the son of Man is not an individual but a collective concept. Consulting scholarly opinions supports this conclusion. Similarly, "the suffering servant" in Isa 53—an influential text for the characterization of Jesus in the New Testament—is not an individual but collective term.

The passion of Jesus is the minjung's passion. It is the passion of all humanity. It is an event that arose out of a clash between the old age and the new age. Therefore, the fate of Jesus of Nazareth, as an individual, is less important. The event took place between the old world ruled by Satan and the advent of the kingdom of God. At this juncture is the passion of Jesus. That is my conclusion.

To connect this with what I said yesterday, the passion of Jesus in the Gospel of John faithfully reveals the entirety of a being that has *sarks*. Jesus bleeds like us when he is pierced; he hurts when beaten as we are. When he was praying at Gethsemane, he received no response from God. He was utterly at a loss. He was so miserable, deserted, and lonely that Luke changed part of the narrative to say, "An angel came down and comforted Jesus."[19] But this cannot lessen the suffering of Jesus.

In the long history of Korea's suffering, God did not descend. Korea was a place of divine absence just like the passion. We cannot expect miracles in the religious sense of the word. That kind of miracle has not taken place. This is true of Koreans and of Jesus, who we Christians worship as the son of God and messiah. This realization comforted those who were suffering in indescribable measure.

In this way, we saw in the passion of Jesus our own selves and situation in the 1970s. We became conscious of our solidarity with Jesus. We understood that it was not the case that Jesus as an individual died according to his individual fate. Instead, we believed he was tormented in our torment; he died in our death. The passion narrative of the Gospel of Mark played a decisive role in our understanding.

10.7. After John Was Arrested

Now let's look at an example where Jesus is described from this perspective. A significant passage is Mark 1:14–15: "Now after John was arrested, Jesus came to Galilee, proclaiming the good news of God, and saying, 'The time is fulfilled, and the kingdom of God has come near; repent, and believe in the good news.'"

In the past I was taught that the important verse in this passage was verse 15. There is unanimous agreement that verse 15 sums up the preaching of Jesus. So I was under the impression that only verse 15 was important. Only later on did I discover that verse 15 without verse 14 means nothing and that verse 14 is more significant. My eyes were opened when I read the Bible again in the situation we found ourselves in.

What verse 14 says is this: Jesus did not begin his public ministry at the right timing after his training. He did not, as in the case of Buddha, recognize the problem of suffering, make preparations for leaving home, and leave at the right moment. Jesus made his start when he heard that John the Baptist was arrested by Antipas, precisely when such a political event took place. This is where the Bible differs from other scriptures. It is not abstract but concrete and captures the context of the occasion.

---

19. This quote is based on Luke 22:43: "Then an angel from heaven appeared to him and gave him strength."

When some colleagues and I were sent to prison, many pastors who were our former pupils preached on this very passage. Since their former teachers had gone to prison, they realized it was their time to act. As a result, they were thrown into prison one after another, following in our footsteps. After hearing that John the Baptist was arrested by Antipas, the king of Galilee, Jesus started to act. The Christians of Korea started to act in the same situation.

Mark only writes that John was arrested for calling out Antipas for his adultery. But according to Josephus, John was spotted as a dangerous instigator of the minjung and was arrested as a political criminal. Upon hearing this news, where did Jesus go? He did not go to Jerusalem or anywhere else. He went straight "to Galilee" (Mark 1:14), the very place where the person who arrested John the Baptist was ruler. That is, Jesus went straight to the very site of the event! This was what actually happened.

In the phrase "to Galilee" (Mark 1:14) is condensed significance of truly immense proportions. Whether or not Jesus used violence is beside the point here. What is beyond doubt is that Jesus had specifically protest in mind. Instead of avoiding conflict, he went straight to the scene. As you know, Galilee at the time was the staging ground for an independence movement of the Zealots. A great number of guerillas were operating in the mountains.

Galilee was also the land of the minjung as the people of the land (*am ha'aretz*). Even though the soil was fertile, most of the people living there did not have their own land and were living in poverty. Unable to eke out a living, they went up into the mountains to join the Zealots. The move was not necessarily politically motivated but was for survival. In Korea these days, several novels deal with the same situation as the Galilean minjung (especially the Zealots) of Jesus's time and have been favorably received.

The abandoned Galilee. The Galilee that was dominated by foreign powers for six hundred years and despised by Judah. But for this very reason, Galilee had been independent and persevering in its own way. The rule by foreign powers motivated Galileans to preserve the purity of their Jewish faith. Jesus went to Galilee like this. This is precisely what verse 14 means. Ignoring a verse of such importance comes natural to the Westerners, who lack the sensitivity to *real-life circumstances*.[20] Far too often Western theologians overlook an important passage in the Gospels.

---

20. The Korean word for "real-life circumstances" is *hyeongjang*.

Allow me to give an illustration. The disciples of Jesus felt hungry while going somewhere on the Sabbath. So they plucked and ate unripe ears of wheat. Then Jesus's opponents criticized him and the disciples. In response, Jesus utters the famous words: "The Sabbath was made for humankind, and not humankind for the Sabbath" (Mark 2:27). I have always referred to this passage as "the first chapter of the human rights declaration." From the perspective of the minjung's storytelling, the entirety of this story matters, in which the disciples' hunger forced them to do what they did on the Sabbath. It is not right to attach importance to one part of a story and dismiss another part as unimportant. With a story of the minjung, the whole story counts. We must not cut a part of it away. For example, Joachim Jeremias, in his analysis of the parables, says such things as "the heart of this passage is this" and "there are two main points here." But this is mere intellectualism that offers little for the minjung. The minjung speak through the whole story. Tearing the story apart by analysis leaves nothing worthwhile. Scholars observe that such-and-such form is to be found here or sort out texts according to form. But some of the minjung stories have form while others do not. Form does not hold a special importance for them.

In verse 15, Jesus proclaims, "The kingdom of God has come near; repent." This, too, is important. "The kingdom of God" (*basileia tou theou*) literally translates into "the kingdom of deity." What did it mean to Romans that the kingdom of deity would come? Could they have thought that, being a religious language, it did not pose any problem? The phrase is translated into "the sovereignty of deity" (*Gottesherrschaft*) in German, which is a political language. What does it mean to bring "the sovereignty of deity" to the fore where "the sovereignty of Rome" dominates? Isn't there any political meaning here? Could it have challenged the existing political power? This was indeed a revolutionary declaration. Jesus is saying, "*Basileia tou theou, Gottesherrschaft* is coming soon. Repent." Then what is repentance? What is *metanoia*? It is closely related with the revival of things fundamental.

10.8. The Pinnacle of the Yahweh Faith

You are well aware of the constant tension between the kingdom of Israel and the kingdom of Judah. David seized the royal power of the kingdom of Judah by force and continually fought with the kingdom of Israel. Because the kingdom of Israel was in the plight of warring with Pleshet in those days, David was able to eventually conquer it and establish the

Israelite monarchy. David was crafty enough to appoint half of his ministers from the kingdom of Israel and the other half from the kingdom of Judah. In addition, in order to show he was partial to neither, he captured Jerusalem, which did not belong to Judah or Israel. It used to be the city of the Jebusites, and David made it his privately-owned land. He built palaces there and enshrined the ark of the Covenant. He constructed the temple there. Now Yahweh became the prisoner of the temple and since then only served as the ideology of the Davidic monarchy. This became the major occasion for the corruption of the Yahweh faith. Yahweh before David was not the God of the temple but the God who ruled the world and history.

I was surprised to see Gerhard von Rad point out in *Old Testament Theology* that the word *Hebrew* originally referred to a certain social class, not the people of Israel.[21] That is, it was the name of lower-class people scattered around the Middle and Near East at the time. Hebrews were scattered over many regions. For example, we have an Egyptian report about subduing Hebrews. The Israelites were not the only Hebrews. Of course, there were also Hebrews in the region of Canaan. It seems that there were at least thirty to thirty-one monarchies in the land of Canaan. The monarchs were exploiting all of the people in the land as their serfs. It is not certain if the exodus triggered it, but the Hebrews who were treated like slaves rose up to defeat the monarchs to form the amphictyony. This was the original embryo of ancient Israel.

Israel was formed against monarchy. Its mantra was, "No human as our king" or "No human over another human." This was how the age of the judges came to be. In this age, there was no king; instead, there was in place a system which was less military than minjung-oriented. In response to each conflict, a charismatic person (she or he could be a farmer or a shepherd) led the war efforts. When the battle was over, the soldiers returned to their original occupations. How was this possible among different ethnic groups? What helped them unite? It was mono-Yahwism, that is, a common faith in Yahweh. Western scholars maintain that mono-Yahwism was the assertion that "Yahweh is the only true God" among the gods of different religions. But this is not true. Mono-Yahwism was the faith, "A human must not possess sovereignty over other humans. Only

---

21. Gerhard von Rad, *Old Testament Theology*, trans. David Stalker, 2 vols. (London: SCM, 1975); translation of *Theologie des Alten Testaments* (Munich: Kaiser, 1961).

Yahweh as God rules over us." It was inseparably related to the resistance against the forces of absolute monarchy.

In trying to defend the basic rights of human beings and the minjung, we cannot help advocating for mono-Yahwism. This is the resistance against the present ruling class. It is not a claim of Christianity's superiority to other religions such as Buddhism. Mono-Yahwism is in unity with the declaration that no forces can rule over humans before *basileia tou theou* (the kingdom of deity).

When the disciples of Jesus were arguing over who was the greatest, Jesus said to them, "You should not oppress the people like the Gentile powers. If you want to stand above people, you must serve them."[22] It goes without saying that this was a political statement. I think that *gentile* here means "Roman." Mono-Yahwism does not permit monopoly of power or rule over other people.

Therefore, Jesus's emphasis on the advent of the kingdom of God signifies the end of human power for eternity, the advent of a new world, where humans do not rule over humans. The result is an organic community of shared destiny. He practiced this in a concrete way by standing on the side of those who were branded as sinners in his day, selecting Galilee as the stage of his work on behalf of the minjung, and marching up to Jerusalem in the end.

10.9. Up to Jerusalem

Several problems are involved in Jesus's advance to Jerusalem. According to Bultmann, Jesus didn't march to Jerusalem with a purpose: he went there by accident and was killed by accident. However, this is to treat the death of Jesus just as if it were an accidental death. I cannot help but feel angry with this view. I agree with Bornkamm, who contends that Jesus went up to Jerusalem with a clear purpose. Let me bring up specific evidence. We have a passage that suggests that Jesus marched up to Jerusalem with a certain purpose. Jesus went up to Jerusalem with his disciples. It is written that Jesus's attitude at this time was so serious that no one could

---

22. This quote is based on Jesus's remark in Mark 10:42–43: "You know that among the Gentiles those whom they recognize as their rulers lord it over them, and their great ones are tyrants over them. But it is not so among you; but whoever wishes to become great among you must be your servant."

open their mouth to say anything (Mark 10:32).[23] This is a very important material that supports the above hypothesis.

There are many different theories regarding the conflict with the Jerusalem temple. There is no way to reconstruct the actual facts. However, it is certain that Jesus's destination was the temple in Jerusalem, and that he acted on the idea that the temple must not be allowed to stay the way it was. This is beyond all doubt.

There is other evidence that Jesus marched up to Jerusalem with a clear purpose. Even before the revolt of the Maccabees, a faith community called Hasidim was in existence. They appear in the books of the Maccabees. This community rejected Jerusalem as irrevocably corrupt and became the leader of an anti-Jerusalem movement: "Jerusalem has been corrupted. So we can no longer live there." For this reason, they led an ascetic life on the outskirts of Jerusalem. They played a decisive role in the victory of the revolt of the Maccabees. After the revolt was over, the power-hungry family of the Maccabees formed the Hasmonean dynasty. There was backlash that caused a division of the Hasidim into two sects. The anti-Jerusalem tradition was inherited by the Essenes, while those who remained became the Pharisees. The Zealots were also an anti-Jerusalem sect but went one step further to participate in the Jerusalem liberation movement. They carried out the struggles for the liberation from Rome. Their aim of attack was Jerusalem: "It is inevitable to purge Jerusalem, which makes an immediate compromise with the foreign powers upon their invasion." On this one point, the anti-Jerusalem sects and the sects for Jerusalem liberation agreed. This was the climate of the age.

Jesus also wanted to liberate Jerusalem. Many surviving records say that, whereas most of Galileans were landless farmers, many rabbis and priests led a rich and luxurious life in Jerusalem. They were absentee landowners who had land in Galilee. For this reason, when the Zealots attacked Jerusalem, the very first thing they did was burn all of the deeds for land, debts, and slaves. Jerusalem was thus the enemy of the minjung! Jesus headed up to Jerusalem given these circumstances, which was no accident. It is certain that he did so for a purpose.

Regretfully, we have no other materials outside the gospels to tell us what Jesus did. Some hold that he led guerilla troops and attempted to

---

23. The verse in question reads, "They were on the road, going up to Jerusalem, and Jesus was walking ahead of them; they were amazed, and those who followed were afraid."

carry out a violent operation, but the gospel texts do not allow for this kind of imagination. Mr. Ham Seok-heon came up with this description: "He entered Jerusalem without even so much as a needle in his hand." Isn't it funny to see Jesus arriving in the city riding a small donkey with a small group of country people? Jesus was a person with a sense of humor. If someone trudged into Sapporo, Tokyo, or Seoul in this manner to do something, they would surely be subject to ridicule. But Jesus indeed entered the city in this manner. He was determined to be killed.

If Jesus had resorted to violence, wouldn't it have defeated his purpose right then? It was wise of Christians not to combine forces with the Zealots. While all of the Zealots perished, Christians did not. I believe that Jesus refused to involve himself in the vicious cycle of withstanding evil with evil. At any rate, Jesus was perceived as a Jewish political leader, arrested as a political criminal against the Roman Empire, and executed by crucifixion. No one would have imagined that the Galilean minjung, who had been such cowards, would subsequently arise and conquer the world. The circumstances surrounding this event remain a mystery because we have no reliable materials for a conclusive answer. All we have is the Jesus that Mark conveys to us.

11
The Realization of the Table Community

"I am the living bread that came down from heaven ... the bread I will give for the life of the world is my flesh." These are the words of Jesus from John 6:51.[1] These words must have created a stir among his audience. Flesh (*sarx*) is the opposite to mind or spirit. It was a despised object in the Jewish or Hellenistic society. Hellenistic society was characterized by a strong dualism, especially among the gnostics, which maintained that flesh and spirit should not be combined and that the true salvation only comes when spirit is liberated from flesh. Against this kind of thinking, the words of Jesus were shocking to his audience. Jesus emphatically states, "Those who eat my flesh and drink my blood have eternal life, and I will raise them up on the last day; for my flesh is true food and my blood is true drink" (John 6:54–55). We must be attentive to the fact that John 6:51–59 presents words such as heaven, eternity, true life, and so on without hesitation and in a natural manner. How exactly are we supposed to understand these expressions?

The general understanding is that the Gospel of John does not take much interest in the historical Jesus. It has also been judged to be distinct from the Synoptic Gospels. Not being interested in the historical Jesus means not being interested in history in general. It is no accident, therefore, that those scholars who take no interest in the historical Jesus, the kerygmatists, make the Gospel of John the criterion of their theology. It is surprising that even Käsemann deemed that the Gospel of John was caught up in a naïve Docetism as far as it constantly speaks of a celestial being rather than a human Jesus.[2] Was the author of the Gospel of

---

1. The omitted words in the middle of this quote are: "whoever eats of this bread will live forever; and."

2. Here the editor of the original Korean text gives an in-text note to say: "Docetism is the view that, as a being from the world of the spirit, Jesus was not really able to

John really not interested in historical facts? I believe he was. Certainly the Gospel of John sees Jesus and his age differently than the Synoptics do. Yet John begins with the Historical Jesus and the historical reality. Under this assumption, I will attempt to interpret the Gospel of John from the minjung's standpoint.

11.1. On Community

In order to clarify what kinds of social realities are presupposed by the Gospel of John, I am going to introduce Sorokin's three types of modes of existence: collective juxtaposition, indirect coexistence, and integral community (community of shared destiny). For collective juxtaposition, think of a trashcan where all kinds of odds and ends are thrown away. Inorganic things include glass shards, broken bowls, various objects of plastic, and so on; organic things include fish scraps, rotten fruits, and what not. But these things are put together only by accident, not out of necessity. There is no meaningful interaction. They are in the same place to be thrown out with other useless items. Here, a certain change can occur in the decomposition process. But it would be nothing more than a process of extinction. The second is indirect coexistence. As in the first case, there is no necessity for coexistence. On the desk I am sitting at, I see flowers, pencils, paper, a cup, and a Bible. This coexistence has not happened for a direct reason; it is indirectly caused by the needs I have while I am sitting here. Or consider what you have in your pocket. You could take them out or just feel them with your hand. A handkerchief, a pocketbook, a fountain pen, a lighter. These various items are in an indirect relationship with one another according to the needs of the person who has them. Therefore, these needs dictate their coexistence. So, for example, if a sick person gets well, the medicine in her or his pocket will be gone out of it; if a smoker quits smoking, a lighter will no longer be there. This kind of indirect coexistence happens frequently. Similarly, siblings who live together with their mother could move away if she passes away. The material or spiritual things of a country are contingent upon the dictator's tastes and preferences. The breakout of a war mobilizes everything, including people, into one direction. Things that don't need

---

become a human, a combination of spirit and flesh. Despite appearing to be a person in human flesh, he in truth had nothing to do with flesh."

to be together in one place are forced into indirect relationship only by the will of the one who wants to wage war. Or a disaster or great event may push people into similar fates.

Indirect coexistence loses its raison d'être as soon as the main cause or responsible agent is removed. Right now, after the fall of the long-drawn dictatorship of Ferdinand Marcos in the Philippines, we are seeing the rapid collapse of the system of coexistence. Our world today is rushing into a state where impersonal forces such as capital and power force people into indirect coexistence.

The third mode is organic community or the community of shared destiny. It is not a community where the coexistence of people is caused in a forced or indirect way by something external. It is a community where the meaning of one member's existence depends on the existence of another member. The members share their joy, pain, and suffering. Because a member is not replaceable like a machine part, the pain from his or her loss must simply be lived with. How could I be happy while you are unhappy? How could I be full or satisfied while you are hungry? Paul called the community of Christ *sōma Christou* (the body of Christ). This phrase expresses the community of shared destiny. I suggest that you read carefully the passages that include this word *sōma* in them. *Sōma*, it is not flesh (*sarx*). Neither is it an opposite concept to *pneuma* (spirit). Paul used this word to try and overcome the worldview based on a spirit-flesh dualism. The body of Christ is constituted by Christians and intended to be the church as an organic community.

11.2. The Table Community

Early Christians who were conscious of themselves as the body of Christ belonged to various sects. They knew what the most basic requirement is for becoming an organic body. Perhaps it would be better to say community formed naturally through the sharing of meals. The Bible offers a few examples of this practice. The first is the emergence of a commune in the Acts of the Apostles. The minjung of Jesus fell in despair over Jesus's death but came back to life. They came together—the wealthy and the poor came together to form a table community (Acts 4:32–37). People who had possessions sold them and donated proceeds to the community. We do not know how long this practice lasted. But the people of the community experienced the happiness of the kingdom of God in advance through turning their private material possessions into the public. But this did not last long. A community that only practiced common distribution without common production could not have lasted long. Another example is the practice of coming together on the Lord's Day, the day of the resurrection, to worship and share a meal. Some brought more than enough, while others contributed nothing at all. But sharing a meal before the one Lord corresponds to Jesus's practice while he was alive. But here something ugly happened. Class consciousness arose between the haves and the have-nots. The wealthy sat together and ate their fill, despising the poor who brought no food. Consequently, meal sharing became an occasion for the destruction of the community. Indignant at this, Paul said, "When the time comes to eat, each of you goes ahead with your own supper, and one goes hungry and another becomes drunk. Do you not have home to eat and drink in? Or do you show contempt for the church of God and humiliate those who have nothing?" (1 Cor 11:21-22). He reached the conclusion: "when you come together, it is not really to eat the Lord's supper" (1 Cor 11:20). Paul turned the Lord's supper into a sacrament (1 Cor 11:23-29). He said, "If you are hungry, eat at home" (1 Cor 11:34). As a result, the Lord's supper became a mere hypocritical event. We see hints in the Bible suggesting that the supper of love and holy communion existed together before the latter became a sacrament. The Gospel of Mark 14:17-25 is an example. The word for eating in verses 18-21 and verses 22-25 refer to two different occasions. These two passages represent two different scenes put together.

It was a grave error that the leadership of the early church turned the Lord's supper of sharing a meal into the holy communion as a sacrament. This destroyed table community by turning it into a religious ritual. Only this religious ritual for sharing Jesus's blood and flesh remained, serving as a good excuse for giving up the path that goes from *sharing* through *eating* through *being full* to *becoming family*.

Table community is a specific image of Paul's "body of Christ" or the organic community in sociology. I believe you have already noticed that I place a special emphasis on the table. I do so for the purpose of clarifying the fact that today's Christianity has lost one of the most important things. It is for the purpose of divulging the fiction hidden in the beautiful language such as "spiritual *koinōnia*" and "the community of love."

If a family is an organic community, what should make up its core? Let me rephrase the question more directly. Can you imagine a family that does not share rice boiled in the same pot? If there is such a family, it is not an organic community. The Korean language has another word for family[3] that conveys the true meaning of family: the word *shikgu* (eating mouth). Why refer to family as "eating mouths"? What other nation would understand "eating mouths" as family? For Koreans, an organic community is inseparable from eating together. This is the essence of an organic community. A community is never created through a certain idea. It is always based on experience. Perhaps the long history of poverty in Korea helped us realize this truth. Those who are well-fed do not know the joy and peace that the table community gives to those who struggle for their daily bread. Those who have never been hungry are oblivious of the significance of the fact that eating and drinking with the minjung figures prominently among Jesus's doings. Jesus ate and drank together with his disciples before his death. He envisioned the place of reunion with his disciples in the kingdom of God as one of eating together. Therefore, I wonder if Koreans with the word *shikgu* for family are not the people who can understand Jesus best. But here I want to add a caveat: it is not probable that the aristocracy of the Joseon Dynasty, who were the ruling nobility under a Confucian bureaucracy that despised labor and only interested in self-preservation, called family *shikgu*. Therefore, I suppose that this word was made by the hungry minjung.

Next, I would like to explain the meaning of the Korean word *wuri*. Although the Korean *na* means the same as the Japanese *watashi* and the English "I," the plural *wuri* is different in nuance from both the Japanese *wareware* or *watashitachi* and the English "we." *Wuri* means not the plurality of individuals but a community of shared destiny. The fence that keeps animals is *wuri* in Korean. So we have such words as *sowuri* (bull pen) and *dwaejiwuri* (pig pen). This means that those in the same *wuri* share the same destiny.[4] When Koreans introduce their husband or wife to someone else, they do not say "my husband" or "my wife" but "our husband" or "our wife" without hesitation. Similarly, they do not say "my house" or "my child" but "our house" or "our child." This means that they place the community above the individual. A person cannot be my possession but

---

3. The expression "another word" suggests that Ahn has some other word for family in mind that he does not explicitly mention. The word in question is *gajok*.

4. In this discussion Ahn implies that the first-person plural *wuri* comes from *wuri* as animal fencing. In terms of Korean linguistics, however, this is only one of the multiple theories of the etymology of *wuri* as "we."

belongs to the same *shikgu*. So the phrase *wuri shikgu* captures the essence of community.

Materialism contends that material is the basic constitutive energy of society. Marx's emphasis on material is important in drawing attention to the fallacy of Christianity of being immersed in idealism and escaping the reality. Marxism emerged after a long-drawn history of Christianity despising material or flesh. Rice (material) is something absolutely indispensible for every person. People tend to hold material or flesh in contempt, despite the tendency that the higher social status a person achieves, the more fleshly pleasures they pursue.

As I have already pointed out, it seems to me that there is a correlation between looking down on material and looking down on the minjung, the agents of production. On the contrary, material is very important to laborers. A bowl of rice, even a grain of rice, is precious to them. It is even more precious since it the work of their blood and sweat. Therefore, eating together and community consciousness are linked together and cannot be torn apart. Material is not evil. The flesh cannot be an object of contempt. There has been in Christianity a history of despising minjung who produce food through manual labor. This is the result of being brainwashed by the vanity of aristocratic tradition.

We must not wait another day to clarify the theological importance of material, namely, food, drink, and the laboring body that produces them. It is only those who eat their fill that look down on things to eat. Failure to acknowledge the value of material will lead to misunderstanding the core of the Bible.

The Lord's prayer starts with the advent of the kingdom of God. The Matthean tradition added "Your will be done on earth as it is in heaven" (Matt 6:10). Therefore, "Give us this day our daily bread" is immediately connected to "Your kingdom come."[5] This fact has been so far ignored. Being true to this prayer would have set Christianity on a different course, preventing it from critique by Marxism. How could this prayer be ignored? It was because religious leadership became aristocratic. They became well fed, ignorant of poverty, and did not understand the preciousness of material, because they took material goods out of the hands of producers for nothing. This severed them from the poor Jesus who ate and drank

---

5. In the Matthean Lord's Prayer, the two clauses are separated by "Your will be done as it is in heaven." In the Lucan version of the prayer "Your kingdom come" (Luke 11:2) is immediately followed by "Give us each day our daily bread" (11:3).

together with the minjung. The gospels pass on to us the story of Jesus resisting devil's temptation to turn stone into bread. Jesus responds, "One does not live by bread alone, but by every word that comes from the mouth of God" (Matt 4:4). But wealthy theologians in the church interpret this saying as meaning "One lives by God's words alone" and disregard the question of bread. Preaching on the body of Christ, *koinōnia*, love, and what-not from this standpoint are nothing but fiction.

The word *shikgu*, beyond the meaning of eating, has a religious background. I don't know whether Japan has the same kind of tradition, but in Korea we keep an ancestral tablet in a shrine. At every meal, the ancestors are served first before eating together with family members. What matters here is having a meal together with our ancestors. Sharing food that has been offered to the same recipient is what *shikgu* is all about. For this reason, there is an expression, "the relationship of eating rice from the same pot," that indicates a close relationship.

In addition, we have the village ritual. Each year people collect money for the cow and pigs to be slaughtered. Each household brings a generous portion of carefully and cleanly cooked rice. These offerings are spread out in a consecrated spot. An elder of the village fills the role of the priest and presides over the ritual. All of the participants eat the offerings together. This is a happy and festive occasion. For you enjoy eating meat, which you cannot taste at any other time of the year. More importantly, eating food offered to one god—together with the rich and poor alike, the upper and lower class alike—is joyful. In this event, everyone in the village experiences one another as *wuri*. The following words of Paul's seem to refer to such an experience: "Consider the people of Israel; are not those who eat the sacrifices partners in the altar?" (1 Cor 10:18). With this historical background in mind, Korean poet Kim Ji-ha wrote a short poem as follows:

> Rice is the sky.
> As you cannot have the sky to yourself
> You eat rice together with someone.
> Rice is the sky.
> As you see the stars on the sky together with someone
> You eat rice together with many others.
> When the rice goes into your mouth
> You enshrine the sky in your body.
> Rice is the sky.
> Ah, rice is
> What we eat together with all.

I experienced this truth first-hand as a young boy. Around 1910, many Koreans, after being forcibly deprived of their land and rights by Japan, moved to Jiandao in Manchuria. On March 1, 1919, our minjung rose up in movement for independence only to be defeated again by Japanese militarism. Many were forced to flee into Jiandao. My parents also fled to this place carrying me on their back and raised me there. The people who came together there were uprooted out of their homeland, namely, the people who lost *wuri*. Since they came from different regions, their dialects and customs differed. For these people, the repeated village ritual became the impetus for forging a new *wuri*.

11.3. Those Who Destroyed the Table Community

Christianity came to these villages. It received a warm welcome from our minjung. Christians preached love and equality. They gave leftover food and spare clothes to the needy. However, something unexpected took place. Wherever they went, table community broke down. The communal identity of the Korean nation as *wuri* diminished, while Christianity spread as an occupying force. Christians framed our minjung culture as superstitious and replaced it with Western culture. Although I became a member of a church, I now realize how far I drifted from the Korean people. The ancestral rituals were rejected. All of the festivals and sharing events, including the village ritual, were viewed as superstition and quarantined off from us. We forfeited *wuri* and became displaced like a lost animal. What they gave us instead was the church. The church met often, and its preaching focused everyone's attention on one being. Nevertheless, it was surprising that the *wuri* consciousness faded away with each passing day. Only later did I realize that the most important reason for this was that the church took away our *wuri* consciousness as a table community. Of course, the church also was aware of the importance of sharing meals. But it was nothing more than religious ritualism. The original spirit of meal sharing was lost. I would like to reflect on the underlying reasons for this in a couple of ways.

First, the foreign concept of Western individualism crept into Korea through Christianity. Before we knew it, we were infected by the consciousness of "you" versus "me." We praised this Western consciousness of the self or subjectivity. Meanwhile, however, *wuri* was gone, and all that was left was the individual. The initial purpose of this kind of thinking was less to respect the individual as a personality than secure vested material interests. Privacy! Privacy! The stress on private life was a convenient thing for those with power and wealth. It was an important tool for protecting their vested interests. As a result, the vested interests were made absolute, and privatization was legitimatized in the name of God. This is the archenemy that destroys the table community. The reason there is so great a number of hungry and poor people in this world is not that we lack material resources; those with vested interests claim exclusive possession on what is not supposed to be privatized. It is said that today 20 percent of the world's population occupy 80 percent of the world's wealth. Included in this 20 percent are those who perform the role of propagating Christianity but assume their vested interests to be inviolable. How can they convey the true spirit of Jesus?

The Genesis account of paradise is really a story of the human condition related to vested interests. A person cannot live alone, and at least two people should live together. Human living means continually creating a new land and a new world through labor. Human labor is the act of producing that comes from love of nature and the heaven. The joy of unforced labor is creation and participation. However, everything was allowed in this paradise except for one: eating of the fruit of one particular tree. What could have been this fruit? Some say it was divine wisdom, and others say sexuality. Whatever it was, it was essentially something public that no one could privatize. What is God? God is the public. The earth, the sky, and the sea are all the public. Therefore, all of the food produced through collective labor is of the public, too. The public is what you are not supposed to privatize. And the process in which this public, namely, the fruit that should not be eaten of, is relentlessly monopolized is the sinful degeneration of human history. Privatizing the public is precisely corruption and sin. But with the passing of each day, the realm of the private is expanding through international law, military might, and economic power. Privatization is the greatest enemy that destroys the organic community and makes table community impossible.

The second reason is the mode of thinking that dichotomizes everything: sky and earth, body and soul, spirit and material, sacred and secular, and so on. This is another strategy that protects those in power. Fleeing to the soul in order to avoid the responsibility for material, fleeing to material when the spiritual solution is not available, leaving a problem of the earth up to the heaven when they do not like to solve it on their own, and so forth—these were the sly methods by which they monopolized the interpretation. And this has made Christianity a religion skillful in dualistic thinking. And theirs were the kind of claims that were very bendable according to the interests of the religious aristocracy.

Luther's doctrine of the two kingdoms distinguishes between politics and religion, or state and church. It was the outcome of a compromise between the haves and the have-nots. However, he made this distinction like a revelation from heaven—what a sin it is! This vile fallacy was passed on to the Korean church by Christian missionaries who came to Korea in the last years of the Joseon Dynasty. They argued for the separation of religion and politics even before Korea was fully occupied by Japan and continued to uphold this position during the colonial years. This was responsible for the Korean church betraying the minjung of Korea despite being a church of the minjung. The truth cannot be monopolized. Material cannot be monopolized. Power cannot be monopolized. For they are the public. It is God who protects the public, and only when it is protected does the problem of sharing meals find a solution.

11.4. Eat My Flesh

Let's come back to the biblical text. Certainly "Eat my flesh and drink my blood" is a radical expression. That is why we read that some of those who heard these words left Jesus because they couldn't accept them. But Jesus's mention of his blood and flesh is already to be found in the Synoptic Gospels. The night before his arrest, that is, before giving himself as a meal to be shared by people, on the occasion where he was sharing bread and wine at the table with the disciples, he referred to these as his flesh and blood. Paul also conveys the words Jesus uses on this occasion. But compared to the narrative in the Gospel of John, there is an important difference. In the Synoptics, the scene is described during the Last Supper on the night before the Passover. But that is not the case in the Gospel of John. Why? The implication, I believe, is resistance against the ritual of the institutional church. The Gospel of John tells us that on the last night Jesus washed the feet of the disciples instead of having the holy communion. By contrast, his words at the Last Supper in the Synoptics are moved to the site of everyday life with the minjung (John 6). I think that this signifies a challenge to confining the act of sharing to a certain time and place, which is essential to the formation of an organic community of shared destiny. To religious people who believe they fulfill their duty of sharing by partaking of the sacrament, the Gospel of John presented a Jesus who offers not only rice (material) but himself. This was a strong exhortation made by John in the name of Jesus for the Christians of that time, who had already been ossified religiously.

Love is authentic when it incarnates itself in material. The God that does not materialize is a fiction. In this sense, the great declaration of John, "The Word became flesh and lived among us. He was full of grace and truth,"[6] presents a serious challenge to all metaphysical religions and the two-thousand-year history of theology. It suggests that truth and grace should be realized in the incarnation itself. This reality is expressed in sharing meals and thereby forming a new community.

Paul knew this, too. He said, "The cup of blessing that we bless, is it not a sharing in the blood of Christ? The bread that we break, is it not a sharing in the body of Christ? Because there is one bread, we who are many are one body, for we all partake of the one bread" (1 Cor 10:16–17). But how was Paul indifferent to forming a body as an organic community that produces and eats food together? He overlooked this task, and it was turned over to his successors for its fulfillment. No. It was already realized with Jesus and should continue to incarnate itself today.

Mr. Ham Seok-heon of Korea wrote *The History of Korea as Seen from the Biblical Perspective*[7] in the 1930s during Japanese occupation of Korea. After liberation in 1945, he revised the book with commentary on the meaning of the Korean War. He argued that suffering was prominent in the history of Korea and compared Korea to an old prostitute abandoned in the streets. Korea has been violated by China, Japan, and many other countries. Mr. Ham asks for the reason for this sad history. He declares that the Korean history of suffering has not resulted from the country's own sins but has been carrying the sins of the world. Why did the conflict between East and West break out in this poor country? Why does our land have to be the cemetery of United Nations? Why does all of the world's rottenness have to flow into this land? Likening Korea with the suffering servant in Isa 53, Mr. Ham boldly asserts that this suffering has been the act of bearing the sins of the world. Furthermore, he asks which nation will bear the sins of today's world. America? Japan? Or some country in Europe? No, they would be too arrogant to accept such a position. Only Korea, he preaches, is destined to be a sewer where the sins of the world

---

6. This quote is based on John 1:14: "And the Word became flesh and lived among us, and we have seen his glory, the glory as of a father's only son, full of grace and truth."

7. This is the original title of *The History of Korea Seen in Terms of Its Meaning* mentioned in ch. 1, n. 24.

flow. Since the 1970s I have read this book again and was reminded of the words of John the Baptist about Jesus, "Here is the lamb of God who takes away the sin of the world!" (John 1:29) At the same time, I thought of Jeon Tae-il, a Christian, age twenty-two, who poured oil on his body and burned himself to death on November 13, 1970. According to his diary, his monthly salary was 1,500 won, while the minimum daily expenses for food were 120 won. This means that working twelve hours a day could not even pay for his food. He got up early in the morning to shine shoes and sold gum in the evening to eke out a living. He had no time for studying, which was one of his great desires. It would be natural for him to feel resentment towards the world and live in a state of depression. Yet, he forgot himself and put every ounce of his energy to helping his fellow laborers. He took secret surveys from the laborers to gather information about their circumstances. And he tried to convey his message to business owners and concerned officials in the Labor Administration to no avail. So finally he turned to the pastors of large churches for help, and again did not receive any help. He discovered he had no power or possessions. All he had was his body with blood coursing through it. At last he decided to present himself to God as a living sacrifice. By burning himself, he cried out to the world as a stone would. His death alerted us to pay attention to the miserable realities of the laborers and made us discover the minjung. The deeds of Jeon Tae-il were an act of sharing not just his food but his own body with others. Therefore, I heard the cry of Jesus through him, "Eat my flesh. Drink my blood." Similar events of this nature continue to take place in Korea.

12
The Event of Minjung's Resurrection

12.1. What Kind of Resurrection?

Yesterday one of you asked a question about resurrection. So this evening I am going to talk about resurrection as promised. I often get an opportunity to give a lecture and have received many questions of the same sort. The question that particularly baffles me is "Do you believe in resurrection?"

I was under Bultmann's influence for a long time. I read all of his works closely and agreed with him on many points. Furthermore, as a member of Alter Marbourg Society, practically a Bultmann society, I spent a week with him every year. Let me share with you an episode about resurrection. A bold and dedicated pastor paid a visit to Bultmann's home. Upon entering his study, he said, "Let us pray," and prayed for the blessing on both Bultmann and his scholarship. After the prayer, when he was sitting face to face with Bultmann, he asked with a solemn face, "Professor Bultmann, do you believe in the resurrection?" To this Bultmann said neither yes nor no, but stayed silent for a moment with a pipe in his mouth. Then he asked, "What kind of resurrection?" At this question, the pastor got angry and said, "Resurrection is simply resurrection, and how can you say, 'What kind of resurrection?' I don't need to listen to you any more. I take back my prayer of blessing." And he rushed out.

The question "What kind of resurrection?" means two things. The first meaning is what kind of answer could satisfy the questioner. For different questioners have different understandings of resurrection. The second meaning is which resurrection tradition in the Bible the questioner has in mind, since there is more than one testimony of the resurrection in the Bible.

Why don't we begin by addressing the second meaning? The first thing to note is that every one of the gospels makes an immediate connection between the resurrection and the empty tomb. I will come back to this point later on. The next thing that deserves our attention is the kerygma of the resurrection transmitted in 1 Cor 15:3 and 1 Thess 4:13. The passage in Corinthians emphasizes the historicity of Jesus's resurrection. There is no agreement on this issue. For example, Barth, who is well-respected in Japan, holds that the passage does not suggest historical resurrection. Bultmann, who is skeptical, argues that the confession refers to a historical resurrection. I myself stand with Bultmann. But what this view means is that the passage in question attempted to prove the factuality of Jesus's resurrection—not that its descriptions of who witnessed the resurrected Jesus were historical. This assumption, however, brings with it the following problems. First, the text makes no mention of the empty tomb. In addition, it never gives the specific locations where the eyewitnesses met with the resurrected Jesus. Some people argue that 1 Cor 15:4, "and that he was buried, and that he was raised on the third day," presupposes the existence of the empty tomb, but this sounds unreasonable.

As you know, what the passage of 1 Cor 15:3–7 says was, as Paul himself says at the head of verse 3, what had been passed on to him. It was the confession of the earliest Christian groups and was formed before Paul. But he added a personal experience in verse 8, "Last of all, as to one untimely born, he appeared also to me," to give himself the same weight as other witnesses, and thereby changed the meaning of the resurrection. This move of Paul has a strong connection with the claim to the apostolic authority. The disciples of Jesus based their authority on them having been the first witnesses to his resurrection. The traditions limit the location of the epiphany of the resurrection to two places: Galilee and Jerusalem. Luke distinguishes between the resurrection and the ascension, postulating a period of Jesus's post-resurrection activities on earth. Comparing the resurrection as Luke understood it to Paul's experience, which happened at least one or two years after Jesus's ascension, gives us a different understanding of the resurrection. That is, the resurrection Paul speaks of is not the kind of resurrection through which a dead person arises and walks around on earth. It is the kind that can occur to anyone, anywhere, and anytime existentially. Nonetheless, Paul emphasizes the resurrection of Christ as the essential cornerstone of his faith: "If Christ has not been raised, your faith is futile and you are still in your sins" (1 Cor 15:17). He is convinced that the resurrection of Christ guarantees the resurrection of Christians (1 Cor 15:20). Despite such firmness of Paul's faith of resurrection, it is difficult to know about what kind of resurrection he speaks. As

I mentioned earlier, he does not speak of the empty tomb. What's more, he asserts, "Flesh and blood cannot inherit the kingdom of God, nor does the perishable inherit the imperishable" (1 Cor 15:50). It may be safe to say that this statement denies the resurrection of flesh (*sarx*). So is he merely talking about the resurrection of spirit (*pneuma*)? No, he is not. Paul uses bizarre expressions: "the resurrected body" and "the spiritual body." The latter makes no sense in a dualistic paradigm. Spirit is only spirit, and body is only body—what is a spiritual body? We can easily recognize here that Paul is using the word "body" (*sōma*) in a special sense. The body Paul is speaking of is not the flesh. Neither is it the spirit. Jesus resurrected in body. At the same time, people are resurrected in body. What does this mean? Certainly, Paul is trying to overcome the dualistic understanding of human and to introduce a holistic person. He also says that the fleshly body changes into a spiritual body. From these remarks, I can see what he wants to reject, but I still cannot grasp what kind of resurrection he is discussing.

Usually we do not differentiate body and flesh. Therefore, when the Bible speaks of the resurrection of the body, we generally understand it as dead flesh coming back to life. I personally object to this view of resurrection. If this were the case, life after resurrection would be an extension of life before death. A dead child is resurrected as a child, a woman as a woman, an old person as an old person. The implication is that an ugly person would live eternally ugly and a beautiful person as eternally beautiful—how wrong this representation is! Here, we need to make it clear that the resurrection of body is not the resurrection of flesh. At the same time, we can understand that Paul, in speaking of the resurrection of body, does not define resurrection as becoming a ghostly being. But Paul only corrects the mistaken representation of resurrection held by people of his time. However, the precise nature of resurrection is unclear due to the limits of language.

As a matter of fact, we see the same kind of limitation in the Gospel of John. When Thomas stubbornly doubted the resurrection, Jesus let him touch the nail marks in his hands and the spear mark in his side (John 20:24). This tradition speaks of a fleshly resurrection. At the same time, however, we read that Jesus entered like a ghost through the locked door into the room where the disciples were trembling with fear (John 20:19). These narratives only confuse those who are interested in knowing what the resurrection means. Even though everyone shared the conviction that Jesus was resurrected, they found it impossible to describe its exact nature.

12.2. The Resurrection as an Event

Let's go back to the gospels. As I pointed out, all four gospels are in agreement regarding the empty tomb, but they differ concerning the location and manner of Jesus's resurrected epiphany. Luke transmits Jesus's epiphany as an event that only happened in Jerusalem. On the contrary, Matthew only transmits the Galilean epiphany. John conveys both epiphanies in Galilee and Jerusalem, but their contents differ from Matthew and Luke. For this reason, it is difficult to identify which account to prioritize. How does Mark, the supposed source material of Matthew and Luke, narrate the resurrection? Mark 16 concludes with verse 8. To the women who went to the tomb for the dead Jesus, a young man sitting next to the tomb says, "Do not be alarmed; you are looking for Jesus of Nazareth, who was crucified. He has been raised; he is not here. Look, there is the place they laid him. But go, tell his disciples and Peter that he is going ahead of you to Galilee; there you will see him, just as he told you" (Mark 16:6–7). In Mark there is no scene of Jesus's epiphany. Why is this so? Is it the case that the Markan tradition did not believe in the epiphany of the resurrected Jesus? We cannot be sure because, already in Mark 14:28, Jesus promises to meet the disciples again in Galilee after his resurrection. Matthew expands this material with the epiphany in Galilee. Some people conjecture that the text after Mark 16:8 was lost. But I don't think so. I believe that it is exactly in this way of narration that we have to read the Mark's view of the resurrection. Mark ended the narrative abruptly to suggest that we not put an end to the resurrection event at a particular point in time. I will return to this issue later.

Luke only transmits the epiphany in Jerusalem. Why did Mark believe that Galilee was the place to meet Jesus again? The answer is really simple. Galilee was the site of Jesus's public life and the place where he lived together with the minjung. It is the place where a number of minjung placed their hope in him and anticipated the advent of the new heaven and the new earth. This story came to a halt when Jesus went to Jerusalem and was executed. Therefore, Galilee was also the site of the minjung's disappointment. According to the Markan tradition, Jesus shared his Last Supper with the Galilean minjung near Jerusalem shortly before his death: "Truly I tell you, I will never again drink of the fruit of the vine until that day when I drink it new in the kingdom of God" (Mark 14:25). This saying expresses the hope of the Galilean minjung. Looking at the scenes of the epiphany to the minjung makes me wonder how they could become for them the reality of the advent of the new kingdom. It was certain that the Galilean minjung were in despair and experienced great transformation. This event cannot be explained based on the subject-object frame of reference. That is to say, we cannot imagine that the disappointed disciples changed into new persons after seeing the resurrected Jesus. Rather, the event of the resurrection of the dead Jesus and the disciples' rally took place not in two separate events but in one and the same event—this is an explanation that is more realistic. In trying to convey this kind of event, a silence that leaves the content of the event up to the imagination of the readers would serve the purpose much better than a fairy-tale-like story about the epiphany. In short, an event of a great transformation happened to the minjung of Galilee. The event of resurrection took place in Galilee. This was an enormous event of great transformation from despair to hope, from cowardice to courage, and from the consciousness of alienation to that of being the subject of history. This event and the event of Jesus's resurrection cannot be separated from each other. In the death of Jesus they experienced their own death; in his pains they experienced their own pains. They became convinced that his death was not an accident but a necessity. This belief and the conviction in the resurrection are never two separate things.

Let's look at how Luke records this fact in the famous story of Pentecost in Acts 2. The weak and cowardly Galilean minjung, who fled from the place where Jesus was arrested and executed, were transformed. They charged into Jerusalem when the executors of Jesus were still in full possession of power and Jesus's blood had not yet dried up in the soil. It was a time when a great many Jews gathered in Jerusalem for the feast that celebrated their liberation. Jerusalem was already a place of privilege, where such people as the Galilean minjung were unwelcome. A group of the Galilean minjung, who had no education, status, or qualification stood valiantly before the crowd and delivered a grand speech. They entered the city not to avenge themselves with weapons but to testify that God resurrected Jesus, who the Jews had killed. This narrative is all the more credible since Luke does not pay much attention to Galilee. The crowd, amazed by their testimony, murmured, "Are not all these who are speaking Galileans? And how is it that we hear, each of us, in our own native language?" (Acts 2:7–8) The minjung from Galilee! This was a pejorative designation. They pinned their hopes on Jesus but were driven to fear and disappointment and scattered away. But they now showed up again as the subject of a new history. Now they testify to the resurrected Jesus. Thanks to them, the crowd who gathered there must have experienced the resurrection event.

Approximately 150 Galileans, women included, were gathered in Jerusalem. People from Sapporo wouldn't be able to muster this kind of courage in Tokyo, would they? This would have been impossible for them, who had betrayed their teacher by fleeing from Jerusalem, without an extraordinary experience that transcended their linguistic capacity. Isn't it possible that these Galilean minjung were the alter ego of the resurrected Jesus? Could we meet with the resurrected Jesus apart from them, at some other location? The resurrection of Jesus was an event that took place simultaneously with the rise of the Galilean minjung.

12.3. The Resurrection Event as Present

A key characteristic of the minjung is the ability to transcend themselves. A group of people that transcend their own talents, personalities, helplessness, despair, and possibilities—these are the true minjung.

If Jesus reveals himself in the event of self-transcendence, wouldn't it be the case that the event of Jesus's resurrection continues taking place in history? The event of self-transcendence takes place even now, especially in minjung. This kind of phenomenon escapes a social-scientific analysis. A social-scientific analysis makes an objective judgment that such-and-such cause leads to such-and-such effect. To experience the events at the site of the minjung's life today as the resurrection event is possible only when they are seen in light of Jesus's resurrection. For this reason, theologians become witnesses to the resurrection event taking place here and now. I am here to testify that resurrection events of this kind are occurring continually in Korea now. Right now over one thousand students are in prison in Korea. Back in 1974, the Park government imprisoned many young students as communists for the incident of the General League of Democratic Students of Korea. But the number of the imprisoned students is much greater now. The alleged leaders of the incident at that time were mostly Christians. In those days, prayer meetings for the imprisoned were carried on at the Hall of Christians on Thursdays and Fridays. Initially, the prayer meeting only took place on Thursdays. But after some colleagues and I were jailed for the incident of the Democratic Declaration for Saving the Country[1] on March 1, 1976, Friday meetings were added because our

---

1. While about seven hundred people were saying mass for those in jail as political criminals at the Myeongdong Catholic Cathedral on March 1, 1976, some politicians, Catholic priests, Protestant ministers, and college professors made a statement

proceedings took place on Saturdays. (A ludicrous development is that the current [Jeon Du-hwan] government has banned Friday meetings based on the judgment that our Friday meetings made the Park government fall. Now only the Thursday meetings continue.) At one meeting, a mother whose two sons were sent to prison for the incident of the General League of Democratic Students of Korea prayed. I won't forget how touching her prayer was to me. I would like to share a part of it with you:

> Father God, since our beloved sons were put in prison, spring passed, and summer passed. And now into the chilly autumn, we mothers are in tears overwhelmed with sadness a few days before the Chuseok holiday.[2] I sometimes wandered in the high mountains weeping before you and crying out to you unable to bear this feeling of frustration. Now please do not delay any longer. Please take pity on us and accept our prayers. Father God, please look into the heart of our sons. They paid no mind of their own comfort and happiness. They loved their neighbors. They served the children of the Yeonheedong[3] poor people by teaching night school. They gave comfort to young impoverished boys who worked menial jobs by testifying to the Word of God. They cared for orphans.
>
> Father God, please be merciful to them. If they have committed wrong, we earnestly wish that you help them repent and ask for forgiveness so that the day we long for would come soon.
>
> Please take pity on Hwang In-seong's mother. In her countryside town her family was misunderstood as communists, and out of despair she attempted suicide. So please comfort them. Please take pity on Kim

---

called the Democratic Declaration for Saving the Country. This declaration emphasized raising the democratic capabilities of Korea, critical reflection on the economy-first approach to developing national power, and understanding the unification of the people as the supreme task of the Korean people. Included in this statement was the request that Park Jeong-hui step down. The signatories to this declaration included such figures as Yun Bo-seon (the second president of Korea), Kim Dae-jung, Ham Seok-heon, Ahn Byung-mu, and Seo Nam-dong. The government arrested eleven of the twenty people concerned and claimed that those concerned plotted an overthrow of the current government. The eighteen people tried were given sentences ranging from probation to five years in jail.

2. Chuseok is one of the two most significant traditional holidays in Korea, the other being Lunar New Year's Day. Chuseok falls on August 15 in the lunar calendar and celebrates the first harvest and honors the ancestors. Chuseok and Lunar New Year's Day are two most important occasions of family reunion.

3. Yeonheedong is an area in the central Seoul that is located a little to the west of the royal palaces of Joseon Dynasty.

> Gyeong-nam's mother. She hires herself out as a day laborer to send private supplies to his son in prison, so please give her a helping hand. Kim Yeong-jun's mother passed away without seeing her son again. Her son fasted for five days crying tears. Please comfort the bereaved family. Besides these ones, many other mothers are also suffering. Please intercede for them. We mothers have had many sleepless nights. When it blows hard or rains, we cannot sleep thinking about our sons. When we run into their friend on the street, we are unable to speak for the lump in our throat. Every time we see the food at a mealtime, how could we not think of our sons? Father God, we truly repent before you. Please take pity on this nation and this country. Forgive me thinking in the past only about feeding and clothing my own children well. Forgive me not realizing the true meaning of the suffering of the cross and only wishing that my children would be successful in the world. Forgive me the sin of having been reluctant to be a neighbor to the many poor neighbors around me. Also, forgive some mothers the sin of looking away from the sufferings of the unfortunate widows and orphans in this country while living in luxury. Now we have realized thanks to our beloved sons what you want from us the mothers. It is that we should love the children of others as our own.

The mother's prayer continues. What is noteworthy is that an ordinary mother transcended her own pain and considered the pain of others. I experienced in this moment a concrete example of self-transcendence.

Ten years later the president of the Student Association of Korea (something very different from the Student Association of Japan) was arrested and put in prison. This student was a member of the church I was involved in, and he was not a communist. His mother prayed at the same prayer meeting the following:

> Lord, our sons and daughters ... cried out with a good intention because they were unable to tolerate injustice, unable to just sit and watch the pains of poor neighbors and relatives. They are making great sacrifices and shouting in one voice in order not to pass on to the later generations all of the wrong history of rotting in a comfortable life, not to be a shameful generation. Our children are striving to live the valuable bottom-stratum life of this age and history. Please do not let the hearts of these children, who are feeling the pains of this history, be misunderstood. Please do not let the bitterest *han*, sorrows, lofty will, and love of these children come to nothing. Please do not let the *han*-filled sites of our nation's history be stained. Please listen to the truthful voices of our sons and daughters and give them inexhaustible strength and courage so

that we give to you the glory of the future of this country. We pray for Your direction and care when we work towards this goal. Help our sons and daughters be honorable workers to lead this country up to a bright and glorious tomorrow.

The first mother's pain of having her son imprisoned ten years ago enabled her to see the truth that her neighbors' pain was the same as her own. But the prayer of another mother, now ten years later, shows a further growth because it presents her children as a sacrificial offering to God for the development of a new history of the nation. She asks not for the release of the sons and daughters; rather, she prays for the nation as a whole by praying for strength to fight against injustice and for the realization of an authentic history in Korea after God's will.

On November 13, 1970, a twenty-two-year-old laborer named Jeon Tae-il poured oil on his body and burned himself to death in order to wake up the society indifferent to the laborers' question. This was certainly an act of self-transcendence. Ten years after that, in 1980, Kim Jong-tae committed suicide in the same manner. These kinds of martyrdoms took place in increasingly shorter intervals: ten years later, four years later, one year later, and four months later. I often tearfully pleaded against committing suicide at churches or pastors' gatherings to prevent other instances from occurring. The history of Christianity has been a series of martyrdoms. Jesus was the first example. Jesus died. But he came back to life. The powerless minjung, through walking on the path Jesus had gone on, proved his coming back to life. The history of early Christianity was a succession of martyrdoms. The history of deaths and resurrections made up Christianity. Today's church, however, is quietly withering away as a realm where people are secure and comfortable. Outside of the church, a history of martyrdom continues. Be alert and listen carefully. Where is the Christ event of resurrection taking place? Is it in the church or outside of the church?

I will bear witness to another incident. I brought with me a record of self-sacrifice that occurred in September 1985. It is one of the many suicides by fire that have recently happened in Korea.

There were student rallies at many universities, and the police laid siege to these universities. At one school, a student named Song Gwang-yeong[4] shouted to the other students as follows:

---

4. See 92 n. 20.

> Now is the time to save the country by giving up our own self. We have no violent means for resistance; nor are we in any position to kill. The only way available is to pray by offering ourselves to God.

After saying these words, he burned himself. He was immediately transported to hospital but died in the end. Upon hearing this news, thousands of students and democratic figures rushed to the hospital to pay homage to this martyr. But the police were blocking the entrance of the building letting nobody in. When Mr. Song's mother was entering the hospital to take over his body, Rev. Mun Ik-hwan,[5] my colleague, was able to go in with the mother to see her son's body. Rev. Mun recorded his conversation with the mother in the form of poetry. Outside the hospital at that time, about three thousand students stood in opposition to the police. They were singing the song, "Oh, Freedom," with torches in their hands. Let me share Rev. Mun's poem with you here:

> Your mother stopped crying.
> She is no longer writhing, either.
> She is sitting quietly hugging her young grandson in her bosom.
> And mumbles:
>
> Strange, whenever I close my eyes
> I see Gwang-yeong running here and there
> Aren't they all my sons
> I see hot flames bursting up here and there.
> Aren't those cries all Gwang-yeong
> Aren't the sighs, sorrows, pains, echoes of the mountains before and behind, heat shimmer
> All Gwang-yeong

---

5. Mun Ik-hwan (1918–1994) was a Presbyterian minister, theologian, poet who worked hard for the democracy and reunification of Korea in the 1970s and 1980s. He was born and grew up in Jiandao and, as Ahn Byung-Mu and Yun Dong-ju, went to Eunjin Middle School. He was the elder brother of Mun Dong-hwan, who Ahn mentions in part 1, chapter 1, as his schoolmate (see n. 12). After studying at Princeton Theological Seminary, he taught Hebrew Bible at Hanshin University and Yonsei University and contributed to the translation of Hebrew Bible into Korean. In 1989, he violated the positive law of South Korea by going to North Korea to meet Kim Il-seong. His political activities led to six imprisonments for a total of about ten years. He was nominated for Nobel Peace Prize in 1992.

12. The Event of Minjung's Resurrection

Oh, Freedom!
Oh, Freedom!

What is that song by the way
That is Gwang-yeong, too
Perhaps, perhaps

(That's right. Gwang-yeong is the nation
The *han*-filled Military Demarcation Line
The bloody tears pouring down on the Military Demarcation Line
The wind fluttering caught in the barbed-wire fence
The flag that is crying hanging onto your clothes as wind
The flag of democracy)

I am too ignorant to know what democracy is

(You know Gwang-yeong's heart, though)

I do know the heart of my own child, who came out of myself

(Then it's good
Gwang-yeong's heart is democracy)

Gwang-yeong's heart fluttering on my skirt
If that's democracy
Long live democracy.
Gwang-yeong, my son, Gwang-yeong.

Why on earth are they so afraid of my son Gwang-yeong, who is dead
While he cannot even speak now.
He set fire on his own body and cannot even run
Why set fire
Why are they having this fit
Why are they surrounding us in layers and not allowing condolence calls
Why are they pulling out Rev. Mun, Mr. Gye, and Rev. Lee
They say a thief knows his own guilt before anyone else and that must be true
They look like a rabbit startled by its own flatulence

(They are afraid of Gwang-yeong's unyielding heart, aren't they?)

True that must be it

Though Gwang-yeong's body has gone cold, how would his heart go cold
In no way at all
When his mother's heart is aflame like this how would that heart go cold
The motherland and democracy you are talking about are all a lie, a lie
Freedom, truth, justice, these are all rubbish.

(You're right Mother in saying so
If that heart goes cold everything is rubbish as you say
Absolutely totally right)

My son was a stranger to telling a lie since childhood
He called a stone a stone called a tree a tree
He said he would not live like his elder brother
So he set a quick fire on his own body like this and died

(I see Mother
The truth of him who lives through dying is so terrifying)

Those who got fat with lies
How should they not feel terrified of the mirror-like heart of my son Gwang-yeong

(Before his truth all the lies of the world cannot have a hiding)

If that's the case, how good would it be
Even though my son didn't graduate from college
Didn't even get married but would rot underground
If this world would become sensible just enough to smell the stench of its own feces
Gwang-yeong wouldn't mind setting fire on his own body one hundred times over

A simple mother, who was neither a Christian nor educated, fell in such a deep grief upon seeing his son dead. But at one point she perceived her son singing "Oh, Freedom! Oh, Freedom!" as thousands of people in thousands of voices. I now give you the testimony to the fact that the resurrection event of Jesus is occurring in this mother, who does not even know the name of Christ. Certainly he is not dead. The many students standing in confrontation with the police out there are his alter egos. He is alive now. His mother does not expect much. She says that if his son's death could influence many comrades, then he would have done it a hundred times over: "Long live my son, long live my son who will never die."

Toward the end of his study on the lives of Jesus, Schweitzer says to this effect: "A young man about thirty years of age, nothing in his hand, attempted to stop the giant wheel of history with his small body in order to change the direction of world history. But the wheel rolled on relentlessly and killed him brutally. But a surprising thing took place. The dead body, which was stuck on the wheel, grew ever larger until it finally stopped the wheel and even reversed its direction."[6] This is how Schweitzer attempts to describe the victorious event of Jesus's death. And in Korea now, the number of people who throw themselves upon the wheel of this evil history increases at an accelerating rate: ten years later at first, then four years later, then one year later, and then four months later. Not just watching these events occurring outside of the church, but testifying that the resurrection event of Jesus continues in this minjung event—this is the mission of minjung theologians. I believe that the church, pastors, theologians, and all Christians are responsible for testifying at the very site where they occur. Events of this kind are taking place not only in Korea, but everywhere in the world. I assert that preaching or evangelism that fail to take into account these resurrection events mean nothing at all.

---

6. This passage seems to be Ahn's rendering of the following passage by Albert Schweitzer, *The Quest of the Historical Jesus*, trans. William Montgomery (Mineola, NY: Dover, 2012), 368–69: "There is silence all around. The Baptist appears, and cries: 'Repent, for the Kingdom of Heaven is at hand.' Soon after that comes Jesus, and in the knowledge that He is the coming Son of Man lays hold of the wheel of the world to set it moving on that last revolution which is to bring all ordinary history to a close. It refuses to turn, and He throws Himself upon it. Then it does turn; and crushes Him. Instead of bringing in the eschatological conditions, He has destroyed them. The wheel rolls onward, and the mangled body of the one immeasurably great Man, who was strong enough to think of Himself as the spiritual ruler of mankind and to bend history to His purpose, is hanging upon it still. That is His victory and His reign."

Ancient Sources Index

Old Testament

Psalm
  110:1 — 237

Isaiah
  53 — 70, 237, 255
  61:1–2 — 59, 194

Daniel
  2:44–45 — 237
  7:13–14 — 237

Hosea
  6:6 — 112 n. 11

New Testament

Matthew
  4:4 — 251
  5:44 — 155
  5:48 — 108
  6:9 — 73
  7:12 — 155
  9:13 — 225 n. 5
  11:4–5 — 194
  11:28 — 140, 160
  12:28 — 95
  13:58 — 230
  16:17–18 — 212
  16:18 — 125
  18:13–20 — 130
  18:15–17 — 214
  18:17 — 125
  18:19 — 130
  19:28 — xvii
  23:6–8 — 140
  25 — 63, 79–81, 92
  26:52 — 75
  27:46 — 235

Mark
  1:14 — 61, 179, 239
  1:15 — 59, 61, 117, 139, 183, 194
  1:30 — 229
  1:35 — 207
  1:36–38 — 207 n. 7
  2:17 — 225 n. 5
  2:23–28 — 22
  2:27 — 62, 240
  3:13 — 207
  3:31 — 212
  3:33 — 212
  4:11 — 208
  4:13 — 208
  4:19 — 157
  4:35 — 208
  6:7 — 208
  6:10 — 250
  6:12–13 — 132
  6:30–44 — 127
  6:34 — 80, 128, 233 n. 13
  7:33 — 228
  8:1–10 — 128
  8:17–18 — 209
  8:23 — 228
  8:27 — 130, 210
  8:27–30 — 130

Mark (cont.)		John	
8:31	235 n. 18	1:13	150
8:33	210, 212	1:14	187, 188, 255 n. 6
9:19	209 n. 9	1:29	23, 99, 256
9:31	235 n. 18	2:19	188
10:13	210	3:3	188 n. 8
10:15	210	3:10	188 n. 8
10:25	210	3:22	124
10:28	211 n. 10	4:2	124
10:31	211 n. 11	4:20–21	188 n. 7
10:32	211, 243	4:23	188 n. 7
10:34	235 n. 18	6	254
10:42–43	211 n. 12, 242 n. 22	6:35	190 n. 10
11	211	6:48–51	190 n. 10
12:33	112	6:51	245
12:35	223	6:51–59	245
12:35–37	43, 223	6:54–55	245
12:37	223 n. 1	9:6	228 n. 9
14:3	212	13:3–15	140
14:9	212	20:19	259
14:17–25	248	20:24	259
14:25	185 n. 2, 260		
14:28	224, 260	Acts	
15:40–41	187 n. 6	1:4	128
16:6–7	260	1:6	7
16:7	127, 224	2	128
16:8	216, 260	2:7	128
		2:7–8	216
Luke		2:38	128
3:23	230	4:32–37	247
4	131	24:5	112
4:18	172		
4:18–19	194	Romans	
5:32	140	1:19	153
4:19	157, 194	1:24	157
6:20	97 n. 21, 186 n. 3	2:12	153
9:58	230	4:12	129
11:2	181, 184, 250 n. 5	4:16	129
20:25	156	5:10	153
22:29–30	xvii	7:6	152
22:43	238 n. 19	7:7–8	150
23:55	187 n. 6	7:12	152
24:47	171	11:25	113
		12:1	91, 159

1 Corinthians		2 Peter	55
2:2	215 n. 15		
3:16	129	1 John	
10:16–17	255	1:8	154
10:18	251		
11:20	248	2–3 John	55
11:21–22	248		
11:23–39	248	Revelation	
11:34	248	21:3–4	191
14:5	173 n. 1		
14:19	173		
15:3	203		

Confucius

15:3–7	203	*Analects*	
15:5	204	3.12.1–2	106 n. 5
15:17	258	7.20.1	106 n. 4
15:20	258	11.8.1	106 n. 7
15:50	259	11.11.1	106 n. 3
		14.35	106 n. 8
2 Corinthians		20.3.1	106 n. 6
5:16	205		

Galatians	
1:8–9	232
3:28	239
3:29	129
5:24	150

Philippians	
1:12	63
2:6–11	204

1 Thessalonians 4:13	258

Titus	55

Philemon	55

Hebrews	
10:32–34	63
11:36–37	63
13	79, 81
13:12–13	26, 63
13:13	80, 136

Subject Index

amphictyony, 42, 44–45, 60, 109, 142, 241
apophthegma, 22, 46
apocalyptic literature, 70–71, 84, 138, 177, 180, 194
atonement, 66–69, 74, 94, 97
Augustine, 150, 164
Barth, Karl, xii, 14, 20, 104, 121, 153, 258
basic communities, 27, 133, 144, 176
Belo, Fernando, 47
Bornkamm, Günther, xiv, 14, 20, 40, 50, 119, 185, 203, 208, 242
Brakelmann, Günter, 49–50
Braun, Herbert, xii, 40–41, 58, 68, 119
Buddhism, 15, 36, 40, 48, 66, 105–7, 116, 119, 141, 174 n. 2, 179 n. 1, 215, 238, 242
Bultmann, Rudolf, xi, xiii-xv, 14–16, 20–24, 39–41, 43, 46, 48, 52, 57–58, 65–66, 69, 73, 79, 104–5, 118, 120–22, 153, 169, 171, 199, 202–3, 208, 210, 220, 224, 242, 257–58
Buri, Fritz, 52
Busan, 12, 38
Calvin, John, 130, 143
capitalism, 5, 31–32, 193
Catholicism, 6, 36 n. 2, 37–38, 134, 136–37, 141, 165, 187, 189, 220, 235, 262 n. 1
Christ, 3, 15 n. 22, 19, 23–24, 26–27, 39–40, 43–45, 51, 64–69, 71–75, 78–85, 90–92, 94–97, 99–100, 114–117, 119, 122, 125, 129–130, 133, 139, 150, 153, 164–166, 169, 172, 174, 192, 202–5, 210, 215 n. 15, 226, 236, 247–48, 251, 255, 258, 265, 268. See also *Jesus*

Christ (cont.)
  as event, 26, 45, 69, 79–80, 84, 92, 94–85, 114, 169–70, 265
  cosmic, 96–97
  hymn, 203–204
  kerygmatic, 65, 202, 205
  minjung, 65, 79, 81, 84, 96–97
Christology, 37, 40, 51, 62, 65–70, 73, 79, 81, 83, 96–97, 114, 119, 122, 129, 153. See also *Christ*
Chuseok, 263
communism, 31–32, 98
Confucianism, 3, 40, 48, 66, 105–6, 116
Confucius, 3, 15, 75, 106, 182
cross, 6, 15, 19, 25, 62–63, 66–68, 71, 75, 80, 99, 120–21, 136, 165, 203–5, 213, 215–17, 219–21, 230, 232, 264
Dandelion Society, 148, 158
Daoism, 48 n. 10, 66, 106–7, 174 n. 2
Docetism, 14, 205, 245
Dodd, C. H., 126, 205, 237
Dongducheon, 147–48
Donghak Peasant Revolution, 4 n. 5, 19–20
Dostoevsky, Fyodor, 83, 90, 118–21, 206
East Berlin Affair, 17
East Sea, 9, 11 n. 16, 157 n. 6
ecclesiology, 40, 119, 123, 125, 130, 135–37, 143
ekklēsia, 27, 124–26, 130, 214
Enlightenment, 49, 143
eschaton, 77, 114–15, 120, 126, 138, 170, 173, 189
Eucharist, 83, 124, 128, 190
existential, xiii, 14, 119

form criticism, 22–23, 45–47, 199, 213
Full Gospel Church, 88, 92–95, 173
Galilee, xvi, 10, 18, 43–44, 61, 127–28, 134, 142, 179–88, 208, 212, 224–25, 231, 238–39, 242–43, 258, 260–61
Germany, xiii, xv, xix, 13–16, 17 n. 27, 25, 27, 39, 49, 94, 119, 218 n. 17, 221, 235
Gottwald, Norman, 41, 44, 109
Gnilka, Joachim, 224, 231
Gwangju, 92 n. 20, 160, 224
Ham Seok-heon, 16, 48 n. 10, 49, 91, 159, 244, 255, 263 n. 1
han, 10 n. 14, 16, 18, 96, 134–136, 146, 160, 180, 225–227, 264, 267
Han Gyeong-jik, 38 n. 5
Han River, 146
Hanshin University, ix, 31 n. 33, 51, 266 n. 5
Hegel, xiv, 21, 63, 104
Heidegger, Martin, 102, 118
Hellenism, 65, 110, 112–13, 129, 143, 167, 169, 215, 219, 224, 245
hermeneutics, xvi, 22–23
    Bultmannian, 14, 16
    identity, xii
    liberationist, xvii
    minjung, xi, xiii, xiv, xvii, 23, 37, 134
    sociological, 14, 46
    third world, 53
    Western, 35, 45, 49, 53, 62
historical criticism, 36, 45–49, 51, 55–56. *See also* hermeneutics
Holy Spirit, 37, 95–96, 122, 128
    as personality, 18
    as spirit of Christ, 79–80
    as minjung liberation, 163–176
imperialism, 5
    Japanese, 4
    Roman, xvii
Japan, 4 n. 5, 8 n. 11, 52, 157 n. 6, 209, 214 n. 14, 220, 225, 228, 234–35, 249, 251, 258, 264
    Ahn's visit, xiii, xix, 20
    anti-Japanese sentiment, 16 n. 24, 36 n. 3

Japan (*cont.*)
    churches, 227
    militarism, 252
    occupation of Korea, xvii, 4–5, 7–8, 10–11, 13, 15, 38 n. 5, 178, 252, 254–55
    pro-Japanese sentiment, 8, 214
    scholarship, 47, 118, 189, 202
    theology, 20–21
Jeju Island, 224, 225 n. 4
Jeon Tae-il, xiii, 78, 83, 90, 92, 199–200, 256, 265
Jeonju, 12
Jesus, xi, xix, 7, 12, 22, 30, 39, 47, 49, 58, 102–3, 110, 112–13, 134–44, 153. *See also* Christ
    as event, 19–20, 26, 46, 54–55, 61–63, 199
    as liberator from *han*, 225–227
    historical, xiii, xiv–xv, xv n. 1, 13–16,
    in relation to Christ of faith, 40
    in relation to *ekklēsia*, 124–35, 212–15. *See also ekklēsia*.
    in relation to God, 114–22
    in relation to Holy Spirit, 169–72, 175–76
    in relation to kerygmatic Christ, 202–6
    in relation to kingdom of God, 177–81, 183–87, 192–95
    in relation to prophetic tradition, 42–45, 60
    in relation to table community, 247, 249, 250–55
    resurrected, 258–62, 265, 268–69
    in John, 187–90, 245–46
    in Mark, 206–12, 223–25, 233, 238–42
    Korean understandings, 35
    minjung, xvii, 18, 23–24, 27, 51, 65–75, 77–84, 89–91, 94–100, 215–21, 227–30, 233, 235–38
    teachings on sin, 154–55, 158, 160
Joachim of Flora, 164
Joseon Dynasty, 36, 146 n. 3, 179 n. 1, 249, 254, 263

Subject Index 277

Judaism, 39, 67–68, 71, 84, 112, 128–30, 135, 142–43, 151–52, 155, 171, 181, 188, 214, 231
Kant, Immanuel, xiv, 21
Kenzo, Tagawa, 47
kerygma, xv, 23, 71, 130, 202–4, 206–7, 212, 214–16, 258
Kierkegaard, Søren, 14, 104, 226
Kim Il-seong, 4, 6,
Kim Jae-jun, 8 , 31 n. 33, 38
Kim Yong-taek, 83–84, 87 n. 16, 89–90, 97–98
Korea, ix, xi, xiii, xvi-xvii, xix, 4, 7, 14–17, 20–22, 24–27, 29–30, 199, 201, 206, 214, 219, 251
   Buri visit, 52
   churches, 37–38, 133, 137, 173–76, 200, 227, 239
   context of minjung theology, 31–32, 56–57, 116, 118, 220, 224–25, 255–56, 269
   first American missionaries, 36
   history of oppression, 238, 249, 255, 264–65
   liberation from Japanese colonial rule, 10
   Moltmann visit, 50
   North, 4, 8, 11 n. 16, 12 n. 19, 17 n. 27, 31, 225 n. 4, 233–34, 266 n. 5,
   religious plurality, 66
   Park Jeong-hui government, 233–34, 262–63
   South, xiii, xvi n. 6, 12 n. 19, 17 n. 27, 31, 83 n. 9, 87 n. 17, 98 n. 22, 225 n. 4, 266 n. 5
   westernization, 252, 254
Korea Theological Study Institute, vii, xix, 31, 48, 111 n. 10
Korean Independence Army, 4
Korean War, 8, 11, 12 n. 19, 87 n. 17, 255
Kang Won-ryong, 8
Käsemann, Ernst, xiv, 40, 119, 203, 245
Kim Jae-jun, 8, 31 n. 33, 38
Kim Ji-ha, 200, 201 n. 3, 251
kingdom of God, xvi, 40, 43, 59, 61–62,

kingdom of God (*cont.*)
   66, 72, 74, 77, 79, 95, 97, 117, 125–27, 131–32, 135, 138–40, 144, 154, 170, 175, 208, 210, 232, 237–38, 240, 242, 247, 249–50, 259–60
   as kingdom of minjung, 177–87, 190–93
   as minjung liberation, 193–95
laborer, 19, 25, 27, 58, 78, 88, 90, 98 n. 22, 111, 134, 136 n. 2, 151, 166, 191, 230, 264, 234, 236, 250, 256, 265
   as starting point for minjung theology, 199–200, 219, 221
Lee Yong-do, 174
liberation xii, 59, 93, 139–140
   as biblical event, 59–60, 64, 70, 109–11, 115, 142, 182, 185–86, 194, 243, 261
   black theology, xii, 49–50, 53
   from *han*, 225
   from sin, 151, 154
   Latin American theology, xii, 49, 53
   minjung theology, 53, 98–100, 123
   of all humanity, 95–96, 161
   of Korea, 8 n. 11, 10–11, 16 n. 24, 17 n. 25, 31, 38 n. 5, 255
   third world theology, 53
   through Holy Spirit, 170, 172–74, 176
Luther, Martin, 50–51, 55–56, 130, 143, 165, 174, 254
materialist criticism, 47, 93
Marković, Mihailo, 72, 81
Marx, Karl, xiii, 47, 102, 150, 155, 158, 250
marxism, xiii, 58, 72, 81, 250
March First Movement, 36–37, 136, 172
minjung
   aims of, 31–32, 83
   Christology, 65, 79, 81, 83, 96–97, 252
   church, 27, 123, 133–36
   community, 140, 142
   consciousness, xviii, xii, 25, 76
   context of, 54–56
   definition, xiii, xvii, 220–21, 236
   differences with Rev. Suh Nam-dong, 51–52, 54, 56–57, 116

minjung (cont.)
    ecclesiology, 123–27, 130–31, 133, 140, 143
    event, xv, xvii, xix, 19, 26, 39, 54–57, 61–62, 83–84, 91–92, 96–97, 99, 115–17, 119–21, 136, 138, 170, 172, 192, 221, 269
    facts, 39, 83, 121
    Galilean, 43–44, 171, 180–81, 187, 239, 244, 260–62
    in relation to biblical interpretation, xiv, 35, 39, 41–44, 48, 53–54, 68, 134
    in relation to *han*, 227
    in relation to postcolonial hermeneutics, xvii
    in relation to reunification, xvii, 28–29, 31–32
    Jesus, xv, xvii, 23–27, 65, 223
    liberation, 29, 44, 75–76, 92, 98–100, 121–22, 172, 163, 193
    minjung-like, 16, 28
    origins of, 10, 16, 18–20, 22–23, 199–200
    Palestinian, 178, 180
    postminjung, xvi
    studies, ix, 56–57, 83
    theology, ix, xi-xiii, xv n. 2, xvi n. 5, xix, 3, 16, 18–20, 22, 31–32, 35, 57–64, 65, 98, 156, 208, 217–20
    tradition, 54, 57, 71, 134, 139
missio Dei, 119, 122, 135, 144
Moltmann, Jürgen, 19, 24, 49–50, 97–99, 99 n. 23, 223
Mun Dong-hwan, 8, 266 n. 5
Mun Ik-hwan, 266
Müntzer, Thomas, 130, 163, 165–66, 174
Nietzsche, Friedrich, 101–3, 206
nonviolence, 16 n. 24, 29–30, 180
Noth, Martin, 142, 237
ochlos, xiv, xvi-xvii, 18, 27, 54, 62, 188, 211–12, 217–18
Park Jeong-hui, 8 n. 12, 10 n. 13, 15 n. 23, 17, 85, 160, 200, 201 n. 2, 233, 263 n. 1
Park No-hae, 98

pneumatology, 40, 163–64, 166–71, 205, 247, 259
Plato, 21
postcolonialism, xvi-xvii, xvi
poverty, 11, 78 n. 5, 88, 90, 93–94, 97–98, 146, 148, 175, 239, 249
Phipps, William E., 229 n. 10
Pixley, George, 41, 42. 8, 192, 193 n. 11
Protestantism, 38, 82, 136–37
Rad, Gerhard von, 241
redaction criticism, 45–47, 61, 199
Reformation, 117, 130, 143, 163, 165–66
resurrection, xiv, xv, 43, 62, 66, 68, 77, 103, 120, 125, 127–28, 136, 143, 170, 189, 203, 207, 211, 216, 221, 232, 248, 257–62, 265, 268–69
reunification, xiii, xvii, 28, 31–32, 84, 200 n. 2, 263 n. 1, 266 n. 5,
Roman Empire, xvi, 44, 70, 129–30, 143, 171, 179, 215, 230, 245
Sánchez, David, xvii
sammin, 28
Sasaku, Arai, 20, 118
Sasanggye, 15, 17 n. 25, 200 n. 2
Schleiermacher, Friedrich, xiv,
Schweitzer, Albert, 177, 210, 237, 269
Segundo, Juan Luis, 57–58
self-immolation, xiii, 265
Seo Jun-sik, 234
Seo Nam-dong, 21 n. 30, 263 n. 1
Seoul, vii, 11, 12 n. 17, 12 n. 19, 16–17, 78 n. 6, 85, 87, 88 n. 18, 91, 98 n. 22, 145, 146 n. 3, 147 n. 4, 149, 157 n. 6, 158, 160 n. 7, 199–200, 225, 234 n. 17, 244, 263 n. 3
shamanism, 95–96, 135, 226
socialism, 6, 98 n. 22, 164, 174 n. 2
sola fide, 117, 143
sola scriptura, 35, 50
Son of man, xv, 50, 73, 230, 237, 269 n. 6
Song Chang-geun, 38
Song Gwang-yeong, 92
Song Ki-deuk, 51
Spengler, Oswald, 103
Sugirtharajah, R. S., vii, xv n. 1

Suh Nam-dong, ix, 21, 25, 51, 54–56, 92, 94, 116, 135–36, 160, 219, 225
Synoptic Gospels, 14, 16, 37, 124, 132, 177, 189–90, 223, 228–29, 245, 254
Taibo, Li, 74
Tertullian, 163
Theißen, Gerd, 47, 72
Third world, 3, 32, 53, 66, 77, 221
Tödt, Heinz Eduard, 30, 49–50
Tolstoy, Leo, 48 n. 10, 120
Trinitarianism, 79, 122, 163, 166–67
Yahweh, 30, 41 n. 8, 42–43, 60, 107–10, 113–14, 142, 151, 182, 240–42
Yao and Shun, Emperors, 75, 182
Yeonheedong, 263
Yi Gi-yeong, 48
Yim Kkeok-jeong, 179
Yu Yeong-mo, 48
Yun Dong-ju, 8 n. 11, 266 n. 5
Yushin system, 10, 17 n. 25
Western theology, 22–23, 45, 47, 51, 53–54, 61, 66–67, 103, 105, 121, 123, 177–78
Wiesel, Elie, 82
Wrede, William, 73
wuri, 237, 249–252
Zealots, 72, 78, 81, 179, 183–85, 193, 239, 243–44